THE WHITE POSSESSIVE

Indigenous Americas

Robert Warrior, Series Editor

THE WHITE POSSESSIVE

Property, Power, and Indigenous
Sovereignty

AILEEN MORETON-ROBINSON

Indigenous Americas

University of Minnesota Press
Minneapolis
London

See pages 223–24 for information on previous publications.

Published by the University of Minnesota Press
111 Third Avenue South, Suite 290
Minneapolis, MN 55401-2520
http://www.upress.umn.edu

Library of Congress Cataloging-in-Publication Data
Moreton-Robinson, Aileen.
    The white possessive : property, power, and indigenous sovereignty /
Aileen Moreton-Robinson. (Indigenous Americas)
    Includes bibliographical references and index.
    ISBN 978-0-8166-9214-9 (hc) — ISBN 978-0-8166-9216-3 (pb)
    1. Aboriginal Australians—Ethnic identity. 2. Aboriginal Australians—Land tenure.
3. Whites—Race identity—Australia. 4. Property—Social aspects—Australia.
5. Self-determination, National—Australia. 6. Race awareness—Australia.
7. Australia—Race relations. 8. National characteristics, Australian. I. Title.
    DU124.E74M67 2015
    333.30994—dc23

                                                        2014028050

Printed in the United States of America on acid-free paper

The University of Minnesota is an equal-opportunity educator and employer.

23 22 21 20   10 9 8 7 6

For those who have passed this life
my mum Joan Moreton, Uncle Dennis,
Aunty Shirley, Sister Glenis,
and my son Cameron.

Your dignity and love always made a difference.

CONTENTS

ACKNOWLEDGMENTS

As an Aboriginal girl growing up on Minjerribah (Stradbroke Island), the size of the world was hard to imagine, though glimpses of its magnitude were available in the collection of *National Geographic* magazines in the school library. The world now seems a great deal smaller, and I have been very fortunate to have met and worked with many wonderful people. I want to thank Deborah Madsen at the University of Geneva, who first encouraged me to consider publishing a collection of my work. Thanks especially to Robert Warrior at the University of Illinois for the kindness and generosity he extended to me in supporting my endeavors to make the book become a reality. His intellectual warrior-ship inspires and influences those of us fortunate enough to know him as a friend and a brother. I also would like to extend thanks to the following scholars for your friendship and collegiality: Sara Ahmed, Chris Andersen, Larissa Behrendt, Vince Diaz, Pat Dudgeon, Bronwyn Fredericks, Mishauana Goeman, David Theo Goldberg, Cheryl Harris, Daniel Heath-Justice, Brendan Hokowhitu, LeAnne Howe, Trish Lukas, Alissa Macoun, John Maynard, Mark McMillan, Toula Nicolacopoulos, Fiona Nicoll, Jacki Thompson Rand, Daryle Rigney, Lester Irabinna Rigney, Audra Simpson, David Singh, Kim Tall-Bear, Jacki Troy, and George Vassilacopoulos. All of you, in one way or another, continue to shape and stretch my thinking in productive ways.

My appreciation and thanks extends to my staff at the Queensland University of Technology for your hard work and support, which made it easier to complete this book.

I am especially grateful to Jason Weidemann at the University of Minnesota Press for his magnanimous support and the reviewers for their generous and helpful comments.

I acknowledge my extended family, who are too numerous to mention, and honor the ancestors and elders of *Quandamooka*. To Paul and Angela Leitch, thank you for giving bucketloads of love and friendship to weather many a storm. I cannot thank enough the most important people who, every day, make my living and working possible. My love and thanks to my partner Ian, my children Rhiannon and Adam, and my grandchildren Mamindah, Grace, Lucy, and Charlie—I am truly blessed.

INTRODUCTION

White Possession and Indigenous Sovereignty
Matters

The problem with white people is they think and behave like they
own everything.

—Dennis Benjamin Moreton (personal communication,
April 10, 2005)

IT SEEMS APT TO BEGIN WITH A QUOTE from my recently departed
Gami (uncle) because he was a humble, kind, and wise man. Gami's
words succinctly encapsulate what I am striving to reveal in this book.
While writing this introduction, race as a socially constructed phenomenon is busy doing its work within Australia, measuring Aboriginality
by the shade of skin color. It is as though race travels back and forth
in time to show us its indeterminacy, seductively enticing us to commit
ourselves to its truths. We know not its origins, as a form of exclusion,
though there is some consensus that the manifestation of race, conceptualized as having biological form, emerged in the seventeenth century,
occurring simultaneously with the rise of liberal democracy. Indigenous
peoples did not produce this history, but the conditions under which
we live shape our experiences of how well race and state operate in
tandem to condition each other.[1] It takes a great deal of work to maintain Canada, the United States, Hawai'i, New Zealand, and Australia
as white possessions. The regulatory mechanisms of these nation-states
are extremely busy reaffirming and reproducing this possessiveness
through a process of perpetual Indigenous dispossession, ranging from
the refusal of Indigenous sovereignty to overregulated piecemeal concessions. However, as this book will reveal, it is not the only way the
possessive logics of patriarchal white sovereignty are operationalized,

deployed, and affirmed. I use the concept "possessive logics" to denote a mode of rationalization, rather than a set of positions that produce a more or less inevitable answer, that is underpinned by an excessive desire to invest in reproducing and reaffirming the nation-state's ownership, control, and domination. As such, white possessive logics are operationalized within discourses to circulate sets of meanings about ownership of the nation, as part of commonsense knowledge, decision making, and socially produced conventions.

Subjects embody white possessive logics. A leading Australian conservative journalist, Andrew Bolt, was found guilty in 2011 of breaching the Racial Discrimination Act 1975 on two counts, accusing "fair-skinned" Aboriginal people of only claiming their Aboriginal identity in order to gain access to social and economic benefits. The presiding judge, Justice Bromberg, found that Bolt's articles were not written in good faith, contained factual errors, and were offensive.[2] Across the Pacific, in the United States, the case of Baby Veronica continues to play out in the media after the Supreme Court ruled that her Cherokee father's parental rights, under the Indian Child Welfare Act (ICWA), should not be privileged over those of the white adoptive parents.[3] We could ask what it is that links these two seemingly unrelated cases across an expanse of ocean. Perhaps the answer lies in what is common to both. As racial signifiers the "Aborigine" and the "Cherokee" are presupposed as being "known," and they can be used by the courts to assess the identity and parental attributes of those whose bodies are deemed to be marked by this racial knowledge. The courts operationalize a patriarchal white possessive logic through the way in which they rationalize the nonexistence of race while simultaneously deploying it through their racial signifiers "Aboriginal" and "Cherokee."

Race indelibly marks the law's possessiveness. At the turn of the twentieth century, the founding white fathers of Australia's federation feared that nonwhite races would want to invade the country. They were concerned with white racial usurpation and dispossession and took action to ensure that Australia would be a nation controlled by and for whites. Their possessive logics were embedded in the law through the passage of the Immigration Restriction Act 1901, which the new federal government implemented in the form of the White Australia Policy. Australia was not the only nation-state to use immigration legislation as a means to regulate and keep out nonwhite populations.

The United States produced the Naturalization Act of 1790, which was designed explicitly for whites only, while Canada's and New Zealand's nineteenth-century Immigration Acts strongly preferred the migration of British citizens to their shores. The development of these different pieces of immigration legislation, though at different times in history, illustrates that there are inextricable connections between white possessive logics, race, and the founding of nation-states. As will become evident in this book, it is one of the ways that the logics of white possession and the disavowal of Indigenous sovereignty are materially and discursively linked.

Race matters in the lives of all peoples; for some people it confers unearned privileges, and for others it is the mark of inferiority. Daily newspapers, radio, television, and social media usually portray Indigenous peoples as a deficit model of humanity. We are overrepresented as always lacking, dysfunctional, alcoholic, violent, needy, and lazy, whether we are living in Illinois, Auckland, Honolulu, Toronto, or Brisbane. For Indigenous people, white possession is not unmarked, unnamed, or invisible; it is hypervisible. In our quotidian encounters, whether it is on the streets of Otago or Sydney, in the tourist shops in Vancouver or Waipahu, or sitting in a restaurant in New York, we experience ontologically the effects of white possession. These cities signify with every building and every street that this land is now possessed by others; signs of white possession are embedded everywhere in the landscape. The omnipresence of Indigenous sovereignties exists here too, but it is disavowed through the materiality of these significations, which are perceived as evidence of ownership by those who have taken possession. This is territory that has been marked by and through violence and race. Racism is thus inextricably tied to the theft and appropriation of Indigenous lands in the first world. In fact, its existence in the United States, Canada, Australia, Hawai'i, and New Zealand was dependent on this happening. The dehumanizing impulses of colonization are successfully acted upon because racisms in these countries are predicated on the logic of possession. Yet, from our respective standpoints, Indigenous studies scholarship has rarely interrogated the mutual constitution of the possessiveness of patriarchal white sovereignty and racialization. Perhaps to a large degree this is an outcome of the development of Indigenous studies shaped by the rights discourse that emerged in the late 1960s and early 1970s.

Indigenous Studies as Cultural Difference

Debates by Indigenous scholars over what constitutes the field of Indigenous studies began in the early 1970s and were primarily informed by the global Indigenous political movement for self-determination and sovereignty. Crow Creek Sioux scholar and elder Elizabeth Cook-Lynn argues that in the United States a concerted address about what should constitute Native American studies was made by Indian scholars at Princeton University in March 1970.[4] Discussions were centered on the defense of Indigenous lands and nationhood, as well as Indigenous knowledges and rights. After this initial gathering, further symposiums were held and the disciplinary principles of Native American studies were developed. Native American studies would focus on the endogenous study of Indigenous cultures and history with Indigenous belief systems constituting its bases so that it differentiated itself from the traditional disciplines that pursued exogenous studies of Native American communities. Two key concepts would be epistemic drivers in developing the discipline: Indigenousness and Sovereignty. Indigenousness would encompass culture, place, and philosophy and Sovereignty would include history and law.

Across the Pacific Ocean, and writing a year earlier, Māori scholar Mason Durie gave an overview of the development of Māori studies in New Zealand universities. He noted that the field was uncomfortably constituted by "being an area of study in its own right, an academic discipline, and a potential component of every other area of study."[5] While acknowledging that Māori studies has been "enriched by the several disciplines of law, science, linguistics, anthropology, philosophy, history, education and sociology," Durie argued that Māori philosophies, worldviews, language, and methods formed the basis of Māori studies within the academy.[6] It is a Māori-centered approach to producing knowledge that is neither exclusively traditional nor Western in orientation. He noted that "a greater emphasis on whanau (family models) group learning, and peer support as well as the observation of some customary practices . . . tend to distinguish Māori studies" as it is taught by Māori scholars. This Indigenous focus on an endogenous approach to history, language, politics, culture, literature, and traditions is also reflected in the development of Native studies in Canada, Kanaka Maoli studies in Hawai'i, and, to a lesser degree, Aboriginal and Torres Strait Islander studies in Australia.

The Indigenous endogenous approach to Indigenous studies discursively centers the Indigenous world as the object of study. The corpus of knowledge that Indigenous scholars have produced over the past four decades has been primarily concerned with expressing and theorizing the specificities of our cultural differences in multiple forms in order to stake our claim in the production of knowledge about us. This early scholarship is extremely important, but it has developed alongside, not through, a rigorous engagement with the traditional disciplines that have shaped Indigenous scholarship. In making this point, I am not condemning Indigenous scholarship to a state of existential oblivion, nor am I denying that ethnographic refusal exists in the production of this knowledge.[7] What I am arguing is that an unintended consequence of the Indigenous endogenous approach to knowledge production is the reification of cultural difference. We compel "culture" to function discursively as a category of analysis in the process of differentiation, while the exogenous disciplinary knowledges that have been produced about us operationalize "race" as the marker of our difference, even when defining Indigenous "cultures."

Moving Indigenous Studies beyond Cultural Difference: Whiteness and Race

In recent years new Indigenous scholarship has emerged within Indigenous studies to challenge the epistemic fixation with our cultural differences. In Métis scholar Chris Andersen's critique of Native American Duane Champagne's articulation of Indigenous studies as a discipline marked by cultural difference, he argues that it is our density rather than our difference from Western disciplines that should be integral to Indigenous studies.[8] Andersen explains that our density is constituted through our lived subject positions within modernity. Thus we exist within and outside the Orientalist discourses producing Indigenous cultural difference. The complexity of our density consists of more than the knowledge that has been produced about us. For example, being Indigenous includes the complexity of the life we live in webs of kinship as mothers, daughters, teachers, healers, performers, and professors. Andersen acknowledges that an important part of our analyses should continue to be the focus on Indigenous communities, but he explains that the "temporal and epistemological complexity of our relationships with 'whitestream' society means that Indigenous studies must counter hegemonic representations of Indigeneity, which marginalize or altogether ignore our density." This will require an interdisciplinary approach to Indigenous studies, one that requires an engagement with the epistemic complexity of our communities. A similar point is made by Torres Strait Islander scholar Martin Nakata, who argues that what is required is scholarship that engages with the traditional disciplines in order to demonstrate how this knowledge is limited in its ability to understand us.[9] Nakata opines that at this point in our history we need more Indigenous scholars to undertake this kind of intellectual labor to move beyond Indigenous endogenous objectification.

Andersen explicates that when we restrict the scope of our analyses to "the continuity of land, community, self-government and culture," Indigenous studies is misreading the conditions of its possibility. That is, Indigenous studies for Andersen "must focus on Indigenous communities as a critique of colonial society." He calls into question Champagne's rejection of concepts such as ethnicity, race, and nation, arguing that this negation naively fails to grasp that these are concepts through which we understand ourselves. Andersen argues that Champagne's focus on cultural difference precludes any sustained analysis of "our knowledge about whiteness . . . which requires expertise in the very 'Western' disciplinary concepts he dismisses." Hence Andersen proposes that the critique of whiteness must also be a central element in any Indigenous studies discipline. Concepts such as nation, race, and ethnicity (and, I would add, gender) form part of our density, and as Indigenous peoples we operationalize them in our daily struggles.

Andersen's argument for an epistemic shift in Indigenous studies from difference to density resonates in the work of Andrea Smith, though from a different theoretical and methodological orientation. Smith argues that queer theory offers Native studies the most enabling strategy out of the ethnographic entrapment from which it suffers. Smith explains that in our quest to demonstrate our humanity we subscribe to colonial logics that require us to be objects waiting to be found.[10] Drawing on the work of Denise Ferreira da Silva, Smith further argues that nativeness is the other of a Western subject that is already racialized, a subject that requires an affectable racialized other as the measure of its difference. Smith maintains that queer theory's "more thorough resistance to regimes of the normal" and its method of subjectless critique "disallows any positing of a proper subject of or object for the field, which has no fixed political referent," and centers a "wide field of normalization as the site of social violence."[11] Smith explicates that embracing a subjectless critique enables Native studies to challenge the "normalizing logics of academia" beyond the articulation of an Indigenous inclusive politics. By operationalizing subjectless critique, Native studies can move beyond identity concerns to develop and expand its mode of inquiry to a range of intellectual projects that "structure inquiry around the logics of race, colonialism, capitalism, gender and sexuality."[12] I concur with Smith's proposal to use a different mode of critique, one that opens up the field of Indigenous studies to become a site of knowledge production that is exogenous in approach, and one that requires configurations of normalizing power to be studied. However, I remain unconvinced that there can ever be a subjectless critique, because queer theory discursively constructs normalization as both object and subject of inquiry. That is, normalization becomes object and subject through queer theory's discursive negation of it within analysis.

Smith advocates that Native studies should expand its intellectual repertoire of inquiry to "race, colonialism, capitalism, gender and sexuality" as a way out of our ethnographic entrapment. She further argues that Indigenous scholars work to explain our cultural differences in order to counter how we are "known" by outsiders; in doing so, we believe that if we can bring understanding to white subjects about our cultures, then things will improve. Smith's insightful analysis leads me to ask the following questions: Has the intellectual investment in defining our cultural differences resulted in the valuing of our knowledges? Has the academy become a more enlightened place in which to work, and, more important, in what ways have our communities benefited? These are somewhat rhetorical questions, but they are posed for us to consider how we as Indigenous peoples have been sociohistorically constructed through first world Western knowledge systems that are ontologically and epistemologically grounded in differentiation. Patriarchal white nation-states and universities insist on producing cultural difference in order to manage the existence and claims of Indigenous people. In this way the production of knowledge about cultural specificity is complicit with state requirements for manageable forms of difference that are racially configured through whiteness.

Andersen's, Smith's, and Nakata's work signals an epistemological shift away from designating Indigenous people as the objects of study to analyzing both the conditions of our existence and the disciplinary knowledges that shape and produce Indigeneity. They call for operationalizing our respective standpoints as Indigenous scholars in order that we may strategically develop and define our intellectual projects, theories, and methodologies. Andersen and Smith both identify that "whiteness" is an important category of analysis; other Indigenous scholars such as Circe Sturm, Kim TallBear, and Brendan Hokowhitu demonstrate that race matters in our lives, but their scholarship is more the exception than the rule.[13] Additionally, Tiya Miles's work on Cherokee slaveholding complicates how race and whiteness operate in tandem through a socially constructed racial hierarchy.[14]

My claim to the apparent race blindness of Indigenous studies is further supported by the dearth of papers presented on race and racism at the annual Native American and Indigenous Studies Association (NAISA) conference. An audit of NAISA's programs from 2009 to 2011 reveals that race is addressed in around fifteen papers per year out of an average of seven hundred papers. The relative paucity of intellectual interest in operationalizing race and whiteness as categories of analysis indicates that "culture" continues to be the epistemological a priori of our analyses, so confirming Andersen's concern with our preoccupation with difference. In doing so, we have foreclosed the possibility of theorizing how racialization works to produce Indigeneity through whiteness.

Making the Indigenous Visible in Whiteness Studies

In the way that I have read and understood the African American scholarship on whiteness, I have noted that it is theorized conceptually as a form of power, as supremacy, as hegemony, as ideology, as epistemology and ontology. Rarely, however, are the theoretical focuses drawn to the social constructions of white identity. As Knadler notes, "In contrast to whites who have traditionally located racism in 'colour consciousness and find its absence in colour blindness' peoples of colour have emphasized more how racism involves 'institutionalized systems of power' and racialised practices that are part of everyday experience."[15] This literature, with its focus on structural forces and conditions that shape racist praxis in everyday life, is valuable because it provides numerous ways to operationalize race as a category of analysis. However, when we complicate this theorizing by bringing into the mix Indigenous sovereignty and the United States's former status as a colony, a different picture of analysis emerges. The existence of white supremacy as hegemony, ideology, epistemology, and ontology requires the possession of Indigenous lands as its proprietary anchor within capitalist economies such as the United States. This point is rarely addressed in the African American whiteness studies literature, despite its focus on structural conditions and institutionalized forms of power. One of the few African American scholars to connect the formation of whiteness to the appropriation of Indigenous lands is Cheryl Harris in her seminal work on how whiteness is a form of property in law.[16] She argues that whiteness operates proprietarily both tangibly and intangibly. White propriety rights were cemented in law through the appropriation of Native American lands and the subsequent enslavement of Africans. Harris's theoretical framework opens the door for an Indigenous reading of how white property rights are connected to the internal territoriality of patriarchal white sovereignty in the form of the nation-state. As a form of property, whiteness accumulates capital and social appreciation as white people are recognized within the law primarily as property-owning subjects. As such, they are heavily invested in the nation being a white possession. Several of the chapters in this book illustrate how white possession and power in its discursive and material forms operate in tandem through identity, institutions, and practices in everyday life.

The invisibility of Indigeneity within the early whiteness studies literature produced by white scholars is also clearly evident. The work of Theodore Allen, David Roediger, George Lipsitz, Ruth Frankenberg, and Karen Brodkin on the acquisition and formation of white identity is discursively grounded in migration, slavery, and the logic of capital.[17] Yet when their work is read through an Indigenous lens, the logic of white possession is apparent; for it is clear that white identity has cultural and social purchase, and as a possession it enhances one's life chances as configured through the logic of capital. Some of the most recent whiteness studies literature does engage with Native Americans, arguing that white supremacy operates through a racial logic of dispossession and that within the racial hierarchy that was imposed, Native Americans could be whitened.[18]

Despite this new work, the constitutive absence within the American literature on whiteness is how the presumption of patriarchal white sovereignty enables the historically contingent formation of white identity through dispossession, slavery, and migration. That is, the conceptualizing of whiteness disavows colonization where the first racialized colonial encounters and warfare are tied to the appropriation of Native American lands, as demonstrated, for instance, in Jean O'Brien's ethnohistory of New England.[19] The focus on how people achieve white identity and white race privilege precludes analyses of the roots of racialized knowledge production, processes of racialization, and the formation of racial states.[20] As I have argued elsewhere in relation to Indigenous peoples, "The specificities of our cultural densities have not been the dominant way we are known by those who took our lands. Instead, it has been the race lens by which most of their looking and knowing has been and continues to be done."[21]

This book is a collection of my work over the past decade, though it is informed by a lifetime of experiencing and witnessing racism in its many forms. To this end, I have tried to find answers to two questions: How did Aboriginal people come to be known as racialized subjects, and is this "knowing" implicated in a structure of white subjectivity that is tied ontologically to the possession of Aboriginal lands and Aboriginal people? While these questions arise out of the Australian context, they can also be asked where Indigenous peoples have been colonized by the British, or their descendants, as in the United States, Canada, Hawai'i, and New Zealand. White possession is the common denominator we all share, even though its specificities and manifestations vary. We are no longer the sole possessors of our ancestral lands taken by conquest, cessation, or as *terra nullius* (land belonging to no one). These lands are appropriated in the name of the Crown, signifying the rule of the king and the masculine capacity to possess property and to bear arms. Furthermore, these masculine attributes are embodied in nation-states, as the representation of patriarchal white sovereignty, and displayed in bodily form as the police, the army, and the judiciary. Though the concept of possession in modernity is usually associated with tangible and intangible property within the law, it is much more, and its roots predate capitalism. For centuries humans have produced things and named things.

An aim of this book is to reveal how racialization is the process by which whiteness operates possessively to define and construct itself as the pinnacle of its own racial hierarchy. The thread that weaves the chapters together is the intersubstantive relations between white possession and Aboriginal sovereignty. In particular, I will focus on demonstrating how white possession disavows Aboriginal sovereignty through racist techniques, conventions, laws, and knowledges, each shaping and affecting the lives of Aboriginal people. Thus the conceptual framework that structures each chapter concerns the inextricable link between white possession and Aboriginal sovereignty and its articulation through the possessive logics of patriarchal white sovereignty. Each chapter has been written independently of the other, but together they form a thematic body of work, which I have divided into three parts: "Owning Property," "Becoming Propertyless," and "Being Property."

Part One: Owning Property

In chapter 1, "I Still Call Australia Home: Indigenous Belonging and Place in a Postcolonizing Society," I examine the ways in which national belonging for Indigenous and white Australians is configured differently. I argue that Indigenous ontological relations to land are incommensurate with those developed through capitalism, and they continue to unsettle white Australia's sense of belonging, which is inextricably tied to white possession and power configured through the logic of capital and profound individual attachment. In chapter 2, "The House That Jack Built: Britishness and White Possession," I explain how the core values of Australian national identity continue to have their roots in Britishness and colonization. I argue that Australian national identity is built on the disavowal of Indigenous sovereignty because the nation is socially and culturally constructed as a white possession. In chapter 3, "Bodies That Matter on the Beach," I discuss how the beach functions as a site of Indigenous dispossession and white possession. I argue that as a border the beach is a site of ontological, epistemological, and axiological violence that erases Indigenous sovereignty through the performative acts of possession that ontologically and socially anchor white male bodies as surfers, lifesavers, soldiers, and "concerned citizens" as the embodiment of the nation. Shifting to the United States in chapter 4, I analyze how white possession functions within whiteness studies literature. In "Writing Off Treaties: Possession in the U.S. Critical Whiteness Literature," I illustrate how blackness functions as a white epistemological tool servicing the social construction of whiteness in its multiple and possessive forms, displacing Indigenous sovereignties and rendering them invisible through a civil rights discourse. This chapter highlights an epistemological and ontological a priori within whiteness studies literature: the unequivocal acceptance that the United States is a white possession.

Part Two: Becoming Propertyless

In chapter 5, "Nullifying Native Title: A Possessive Investment in Whiteness," I argue that patriarchal whiteness, as a form of property and an organizing principle shaping social relations and economic development, denies Indigenous people opportunities to generate wealth. I demonstrate this by showing how through legal discourse the Australian government affirmed and prioritized its possessive investment in sovereignty through circumscribing native title rights and privileging the interests of pastoralists and mining companies. In chapter 6, "The High Court and the *Yorta Yorta* Decision," I argue that the possessive logic is a mode of rationalization based on an excessive desire to invest in the reproduction and maintenance of the Australian nation-state's sovereignty, control, and domination. I argue that this racialized possessive logic is deployed to circulate meanings in commonsense knowledge, social conventions, and decision-making bodies about white possession of the nation and is omnipresent, invisible, and unnamed within legal discourse. In chapter 7, "Leesa's Story: White Possession in the Workplace," I demonstrate how white possession functions subjectively through the ascription of racial inferiority, exclusion, and collusion within the work environment by examining the affidavits presented in a racial discrimination case involving an Aboriginal nurse and her white coworkers at a major metropolitan hospital. I argue that these daily intersubjective relations are the mechanisms by which Indigenous people experience white possession as racist acts. In chapter 8, The Legacy of Cook's Choice," I focus on the origins of white possession by analyzing Captain James Cook's reasoning not to follow instructions to make a treaty with the natives, instead declaring that the land was uninhabited. I argue that white possession as configured through the logic of capital functions sociodiscursively to inform and shape subjectivity and the law. Cook, as the embodiment of patriarchal white sovereignty, willed away the sovereignty of Indigenous peoples by placing them in and of nature as propertyless subjects to claim the land as *terra nullius*.

Part Three: Being Property

Chapter 9 draws on Foucault's sovereignty, race, and biopower thesis to propose a new research agenda for Critical Indigenous studies. In "Toward a New Research Agenda: Foucault, Whiteness, and Sovereignty,"

I demonstrate that we need to investigate how white possession functions through a discourse of rights within the disciplines of law, political science, history, and anthropology. Critical analysis of the role of these disciplines and regulatory mechanisms in reinforcing the prerogatives of white possession should provide a significant new perspective on the politics of sovereignty in Australia. In chapter 10, "Writing Off Sovereignty: The Discourse of Security and Patriarchal White Sovereignty," I argue that patriarchal white sovereignty, as a regime of power, operates ideologically, materially, and discursively to reproduce and maintain its investment in the nation as a white possession through a discourse of security. The central elements of this discourse are economic, military, and cultural protection, which are assumed as justified responses because of the threat posed to the nation's security by Indigenous people and asylum seekers. White colonial paranoia is inextricably tied to an anxiety about being dispossessed by racial others. In chapter 11, "Imagining the Good Indigenous Citizen: Race War and the Pathology of White Sovereignty," I examine the federal government's military and police intervention into the lives and communities of Aboriginal people in the Northern Territory on the fictional basis of the rampant sexual abuse of children. I argue that patriarchal white sovereignty operationalized a discourse of pathology to legitimize its subjugation and disciplining of Indigenous subjects while acting pathologically within a race war whereby Indigenous counterclaims challenge its possession. In chapter 12, "Virtuous Racial States: White Sovereignty and the UN Declaration on the Rights of Indigenous Peoples," I examine the logic of the declaration's initial rejection and subsequent endorsement by Canada, Australia, New Zealand, and the United States. I argue that the declaration created an ontological disturbance within the patriarchal white sovereignties of these nation-states, and in response they used moral force to disavow Indigenous rights claims. In this way white virtue functioned discursively to dispossess Indigenous peoples from the grounds of moral rectitude, thus enabling racism to be practiced with the best of intentions.

Conclusion

Read together, these chapters reveal that from the sixteenth century onward race and gender divided humans into three categories: owning property, becoming propertyless, and being property. These three categories of proprietaryness are born of the episteme of Western culture, which has made manifest the existence of order functioning through the logic of possession. Consider the conceptual schemata constituted by and of racialized discourse: "Classification, order, value and hierarchy; differentiation and identity, discrimination and identification; exclusion, domination, subjection, and subjugation as well as entitlement and restriction."[22] Knowledge and power are produced in and through these concepts in relation to possession. You cannot dominate without seeking to possess the dominated. You cannot exclude unless you assume you already own. Classification therefore ascribes value and identification, which manifest in racial markers like blood quantum and skin color. Thus white possession is a discursive predisposition servicing the conditions, practices, implications, and racialized discourses that are embedded within and central to white first world patriarchal nation-states.

As I close this introduction, it is my hope that this book makes a contribution to Critical Indigenous studies by invigorating debate and discussion about race and whiteness. In particular, I hope it ignites and inspires scholarship about Indigenous sovereignty, race, and racisms in the first world because of the mortifying impact that the logics of white possession have on Indigenous sovereignty.

I. Owning Property

1 I STILL CALL AUSTRALIA HOME

Indigenous Belonging and Place in a
Postcolonizing Society

> Our story is in the land . . . it is written in those sacred places. My
> children will look after those places, that's the law. Dreaming
> place . . . you can't change it no matter who you are. No matter
> you rich man, no matter you King. You can't change it. . . . Rock
> stays, earth stays. I die and put my bones in cave or earth. Soon
> my bones become earth . . . all the same. My spirit has gone back
> to my country . . . my mother.
>
> —Big Bill Neidjie, *Kakadu Man*

MIGRANCY AND DISPOSSESSION indelibly mark configurations of
belonging, home, and place in the postcolonizing nation-state.[1] In the
Australian context, the sense of belonging, home, and place enjoyed by
the non-Indigenous subject—colonizer/migrant—is based on the dispossession of the original owners of the land and the denial of our rights
under international customary law. It is a sense of belonging derived
from ownership as understood within the logic of capital, and it mobilizes the legend of the pioneer, "the battler," in its self-legitimization.
Against this stands the Indigenous sense of belonging, home, and place
in its incommensurable difference. It is these differences in conceptions
and experiences of belonging that I address in this chapter. I do this
through a reconsideration of the discourses on British migrancy and a
critique of the ways that migrancy is mobilized in postcolonial theory.
I will focus on white British migrancy because of its role in colonization
and the dominant and privileged location of white people and institutions, which remain at the center of Australian society. I then discuss
some of the ways in which Indigenous people configure home, place,
and belonging and the social, political, and legal impositions that define

us, the original owners, as not belonging, but as homeless and out of place. I argue that Indigenous belonging challenges the assumption that Australia is postcolonial because our relation to land, what I conceptualize as an ontological belonging, is omnipresent, and continues to unsettle non-Indigenous belonging based on illegal dispossession.

British Migrancy and the Sentiment of Belonging

The words of Bill Neidjie and Peter Allen carry the marks of these differences in relations of belonging. Bill Neidjie is of the Bunitj clan, Gagudju language group, a traditional owner of Kakadu National Park in the Northern Territory, a World Heritage Site. The late Peter Allen was a white Australian entertainer and songwriter who mostly lived outside Australia. His song "I Still Call Australia Home" is used by Australia's international airline to promote travel. The song has wide appeal among many non-Indigenous white Australians because it captures the experience of "awayness" and "belonging." It points to the current of movement and migrancy that runs through conceptions of belonging among non-Indigenous white Australians and that is at the heart of Australian colonial history. This sense of belonging is often expressed as a profound feeling of attachment. It is derived from ownership and achievement and is inextricably tied to a racialized social status that confers certain privileges: a social status that is enhanced by a version of Australian history that privileges the exploits of white Australians by representing them as the people who made this country what it is today.

The British Empire established itself through colonization and the concomitant waves of migrants from British shores to colonized ones. This was not a passive enterprise but was bound inextricably with the dispossession of the original owners of the land. Under international customary law, colonies were established usually under the doctrines of conquest or cession. Possession of Australia was taken on a different basis. The first wave of invading white British immigrants landed on our shores in 1788. They claimed the land under the legal fiction of *terra nullius*—land belonging to no one—and systematically dispossessed, murdered, raped, and incarcerated the original owners on cattle stations, missions, and reserves. In all these contexts, the lives of Indigenous people were controlled by white people sanctioned by the same system of law that enabled dispossession. Indigenous people were denied their customary proprietary rights under international law and their rights as subjects of the crown. Indigenous people only attained citizenship in the late 1960s and continue to be the most socioeconomically impoverished group in Australian society. The non-Indigenous sense of belonging is inextricably tied to this original theft: through the fiction of *terra nullius*, the migrant has been able to claim the right to live in our land. This right is one of the fundamental benefits that white British migrants derived from dispossession.

This fiction is constitutive of discourses on British migrancy. Recent studies of British migrants who came to Australia in the 1880s show that their sense of belonging was to Britain and their relationship to Australia was as a resource for the empire. The migrants' vision was to establish a new colony for Britain. They were its "pioneers," with all the associations that term has with notions of the new and previously unexplored, the unknown. They saw themselves as the first to take control of and manage the land; according to these discourses, it was the hard work and determination of these early migrants that developed the nation.[2] Through their achievement, usually understood as being individual in nature, singular, and independent, they brought us "civilization" and "gave" us democracy and the market economy.

The British migrants represented the newly emerging national identity. Belonging to this new nation, therefore, was racialized and inextricably tied to the accumulation of capital and the social worth, authority, and ownership that this conferred. The Indigenous were excluded from this condition of belonging. The right to determine who was allowed into the country and therefore who could belong was exercised by a white British constituency at the heart of the nation. They legally ensured their social reproduction through the Immigration Restriction Act 1901 and the white Australia policy, which until the 1950s gave preference to white British, Canadian, American, and New Zealand migrants.[3] The white body was the norm and measure for identifying who could belong. The white Australia policy, despite being revoked in 1973, continued in practice for many years as Cavan Hogue, a former Australian ambassador to the Philippines in the 1970s, notes:

> Mixed race applicants could be approved if they were 75 percent European in appearance. We had some guidance on what to look for but measurement was difficult. You had to measure their noses, check the skin colour, gaze into their eyes and try to calculate the percentage of European appearance. . . . In 1981 I went to work for Ian MacPhee (minister) and John Menadue (secretary)

in Immigration. They wanted someone with Asian experience to help cope with the refugee influx and also to participate in a review of policies and practices. We found many leftovers of White Australia. . . . For example, staffing patterns still reflected the good old days so processing was quicker and easier in the "traditional" countries. We had some anomalies such as the British Boys Scheme where the taxpayer paid to send to Australia people who wouldn't make it if they applied in the normal way.[4]

The need to socially reproduce whiteness saw the continued migration of British after World War II, and the pioneer legend continued well into the mid-twentieth century. It is evident in the accounts of postwar British migrants and their representations of themselves as "battlers," people who struggled to overcome adversity, worked hard, and achieved a better life in the new society.[5] Their achievements were perceived as positive contributions to and investments in the nation and reinforced their social status. Their "right to be here" attached particular capacities, opportunities, and privileges to them, including a sense of ownership and authority, by virtue of their legal and social status as white immigrants. This notion of rights and the sense of belonging it engendered were reinforced institutionally and socially.

Australia is less white than it used to be because of the global shift to decolonization and economic necessity. Multiculturalism was adopted as the charter for the nation in the 1970s by the Commonwealth government. In his book *Belonging: Australians, Place, and Aboriginal Ownership*, Peter Read analyzes a cross section of migrant Australians of different ethnicities about their sense of belonging, in particular with reference to Indigenous ownership and the history of dispossession. Many of the nonwhite migrants' responses echoed a familiar theme. They felt that they belonged to Australia because they had chosen to live here and had contributed to the nation through their hard work. However, many believed that other Australians questioned their right to belong. They can belong, but they cannot possess. Nonwhite migrants' sense of belonging is tied to the fiction of *terra nullius* and the logic of capital because their legal right to belong is sanctioned by the law that enabled dispossession. However, whiteness is the invisible measure of who can hold possession. The majority of the voices in this book were troubled by the history of dispossession and Indigenous ownership, but this did not erase their sense of belonging. Read himself feels similarly, and in his book he tries to apprehend his own sense of belonging and its groundings. As a white Anglo middle-class male who considers himself "native-born," he writes that for him, his "profound attachments derive from many sources: from literature, awe, fear and fascination, respect for spirituality. They derive from listening rather than speaking, sharing rather than competing, the self flowing into and part of the whole, a sadness at the violation of what we first encountered. And belonging derives partly from law."[6] Read later goes on to say:

> I have no right to claim on behalf of non-Aboriginal Australia that all the non-Indigenous are now part of Australia's deep past, nor do I wish to. Belonging ultimately is personal. There are as many routes to belonging as there are non-Aboriginal Australians to find them. My sense of the native-born has come—is coming. It comes through listening but with discernment; through thinking but not asserting; through good times with my Aboriginal friends but not through wanting to be the same as them; through understanding our history but being enriched by the sites of past evil as well as good. It comes from believing that belonging means sharing and that sharing demands equal partnership.[7]

For Read and others, belonging is experienced as a profound attachment, one figured as personal. In Read's account, personal sentiment is privileged. This is problematic for a number of reasons, notably for its denial of the racialized structural power relations that have produced the legal conditions in which this sentiment is possible, enabled, and inscribed. In the context of Australian postcolonizing relations, these power relations are themselves based on the denial of original dispossession.[8] It is the foundation of the nation and its structures. Likewise it is the denial of original (and continuing) dispossession that forms the foundation for Read's belief that his personal sense of belonging is based on an equal partnership with Indigenous people. There can be no equal partnership while there is illegal dispossession.

Who calls Australia home is inextricably connected to who has possession, and possession is jealously guarded by white Australians. Australia's migration patterns are less white than they used to be in part out of economic necessity, including the perceived imperative that Australia's influence in the Asia-Pacific region has increased. However, the dominant institutions such as law and government, and their epistemologies, remain anglicized. The current Australian government, under the leadership of Prime Minister John Howard, conducted its recent election campaign along racial lines. The campaign played on the widely held fears among white Australians that the country is under threat of invasion from "queue jumpers" and terrorists among the refugees from Iran, Iraq, and Afghanistan. Since arriving in Australia, they have been placed in detention centers, under conditions many have argued are in breach of international law. In this move, the government asserted white sovereignty. It asserted its right to choose who enters Australia—that is, who will be granted the status of migrant and who will be deemed an "illegal" trespasser—and to choose along racial lines. This occurred despite its avowed policies of "multiculturalism" and the ostensible breakdown of hegemonic whiteness.

Postcolonial Theory and the Metaphor of Migrancy

Postcolonial theorists provide us with useful concepts such as diaspora and hybridity to explain the experience of migration by coercion and choice.[9] In particular, these theorists explore the ways in which, under conditions of diaspora, multiple and hybrid identities and cultures emerge. According to them, in this hybridity lie possibilities for counterhegemonic discourses. Diasporas are seen to produce conditions in which the cultural traditions of an imagined homeland are infused with structures of subordination and oppression in the new country, producing hybridity. Experiences of dislocation disrupt the migrant's sense of belonging to a particular place and provide the conditions for multiple identities.

In the process of theorizing the postcolonial, the narrative of colonization is significantly restaged. As Stuart Hall writes, it has come to signify "the whole process of expansion, exploration, conquest, colonization and imperial hegemonization which constituted the 'outer face,' the constitutive outside, of European and then Western Capitalist modernity after 1492."[10] Postcolonial theory examines the effects of colonization and reconfigures the colonizer/colonized axis in different ways. The utility of postcolonialism lies in its ability to reveal the operations of counterhegemonic discourses as produced by the dispersed, or diasporic, subject. However, for many it does so through a metaphor of migrancy that privileges the positionalities, multiplicities, and specificities of migration. In doing so, it can say very little about the effects, or the positionalities, multiplicities, and specificities, of Indigenous subjects. As Huggan eloquently surmises:

> What is noticeable in much of this work, which might be loosely bracketed under the fashionable heading of "travelling theory," is the metaphorisation of migration as a composite figure for a series of metaphysical, as well as

physical, displacements. The metaphor of migration serves a variety of different purposes: to illustrate the increasing fragmentation of subjecthood and subjectivity under (post)modernity; to reflect on the semantic instability underlying all constructions of (personal/cultural/national) identity; to insist on the homology between experiences of dislocation and the destabilisation of essentialist ideologies and "fixed" paradigms and patterns of thought. Migration has become a useful code-word for the different kinds of conceptual slippage that are characteristic of postmodern/poststructuralist approaches toward linguistic and cultural systems; in addition, migration functions as a catalysing metaphor of the exploration of cultural change and the apprehension of new, mobile cultural subjects in the nominally postnational era. . . . Migration and other patterns of human movement in the modern era tend to carry an imperial legacy that is often mystified in the voguish academic categories of nomadism, migrancy and displacement.[11]

In the work of Homi Bhabha and Iain Chambers, for example,[12] what is often overlooked is the particular situatedness of different migrants in relation to power and the legal context in which their hybridity has been and is manufactured. Social constructions of home, place, and belonging depend not just on ethnicity and ties to an imagined homeland. They are conditional upon a legal and social status as well as the economic and political relations in the new country and its imperial legacy. Social constructions often emphasized the emergence of hybridity in the new country. This forecloses considerations of, for instance, the specificities of Irish, Scottish, and English migrants' situatedness because it refuses the hybridity that has already resulted from the Irish and Scottish diasporas in England. That is, all British migrants are not positioned the same in relation to British imperialism because of their ethnicity, but in the Australian context whiteness confers certain privileges to those whose skin color represents sameness. Irish, English, and Scottish postwar migrants to Australia are differently positioned in relation to British imperialism than, say, Italian, Greek, and Vietnamese migrants, and thus have different conceptions of home, place, and belonging. The elision of certain kinds of migration denies the way in which whiteness as a possession will mark migrants' differing implications in a colonizing relationship between themselves and Indigenous people.

This possessiveness is also evident where postcolonial critics have recognized the ambivalent relationship of Australia to its colonial past through the terms "settler" and "settler culture." Some analyses tend to equate the empirical and substantive with the semantic and the metaphorical, which has the effect of reducing racialized power relations to the symbolic through the figurative possibility of language. In *Uncanny Australia: Sacredness and Identity in a Postcolonial Nation*, Ken Gelder and Jane Jacobs argue that Australia is postcolonial because the Indigenous population has now been inserted into the national imaginary through the symbolic rendering of "the sacred."[13] They argue that this is an outcome of land rights struggles and the recognition of sacred sites. What they fail to acknowledge is that the majority of Indigenous people in Australia do not have land rights, nor do they have legal ownership of their sacred sites. This representation of postcolonial Australia offers the symbolic appropriation of the sacred as a way that white Australia can seek to achieve the unattainable imperative of becoming Indigenous in order to erase its unbelonging. A sentiment of belonging is enhanced through white possession of the "Indigenous sacred" as well as Indigenous lands. This is a problematic view of postcolonialism, for it rests on the premise that the Indigenous population and white Australia have equal access to symbolic and material power.[14]

Against this and other representations of Australia as postcolonial, I argue that it is not postcolonial in the same way as India, Malaysia, or Algeria can be said to be. These nations do not have a dominant white setter population. In Australia the colonials did not go home, and "postcolonial" remains based on whiteness.[15] This must be theorized in a way that allows for incommensurable difference between the situatedness of the Indigenous people in a colonizing settler society such as Australia and those who have come here. Indigenous and non-Indigenous peoples are situated in relation to (post)colonization in radically different ways—ways that cannot be made into sameness. There may well be spaces in Australia that could be described as postcolonial, but these are not spaces inhabited by Indigenous people. It may be more useful, therefore, to conceptualize the current condition not as postcolonial but as postcolonizing with the associations of ongoing process, which that implies. Through my use of the term "postcolonizing," I seek to distinguish between the specificities of Indigenous/white settler societies such as Australia and those countries such as India and Algeria where the different specificities of historical experience are theorized within postcolonial studies. For the majority of the population in Australia, belonging, home, and place are inextricably linked to dispossession because "the resonance of migrancy is compounded . . . by the twinning of the always having arrived with the wilful forgetting of the nature of that arrival—of colonial conquest and racism—such that a sense of belonging and being at home was always reliant on a tension between awareness of arrival and skating over the nature of that arrival and its consequences."[16]

In postcolonizing settler societies, Indigenous people cannot forget the nature of migrancy, and we position all non-Indigenous people as migrants and diasporic. Our ontological relationship to land, the ways that country is constitutive of us, and therefore the inalienable nature of our relation to land, marks a radical, indeed incommensurable, difference between us and the non-Indigenous. This ontological relation to land constitutes a subject position that we do not share, that cannot be shared, with the postcolonial subject, whose sense of belonging in this place is tied to migrancy. Indigenous people may have been incorporated in and seduced by the cultural forms of the colonizer, but this has not diminished the ontological relationship to land. Rather, it has produced a doubleness whereby Indigenous subjects can "perform" whiteness while being Indigenous. In this sense, we are not "other" or "non-other," as Frantz Fanon describes the colonized subject in the Algerian context. There is always a subject position that can be thought of as fixed in its inalienable relation to land. This subject position cannot be erased by colonizing processes, which seek to position the Indigenous as object, inferior, other, and its origins are not tied to migration. It is an incommensurate subject position evident in the work of Indigenous scholars such Gunn Allen, Huggins, and Monture-Angus but undertheorized within postcolonial theory.[17]

Indigenous Belonging

Australia was a multicultural society long before migrants arrived. It is estimated that more than five hundred language groups held title to land before colonization. Indigenous people owned, lived on, were taught to know, and belonged to particular tracts of "country," which is the term used to refer to one's territory/land of origin or a person connected to the same piece of land. Indigenous people's sense of belonging is derived from an ontological relationship to country derived from the Dreaming, which provides the precedents for what is believed to have occurred in the beginning in the original form of social living created by ancestral beings.[18] During the dreaming, ancestral beings created the land and life, and they are tied to particular tracks of country. Knowledge and beliefs tied to the Dreaming inform the present and future. Within this system of beliefs, there is scope for interpretation and change by individuals through dreams and their lived experiences.

The ancestral beings created animals, plants, humans, and the physiographic features of the country associated with them. They also established the Aboriginal ways of life: a moral code for its social institutions and patterns of activity. Ancestral beings provided the rules for what can and cannot be done through both good and bad behavior. Ancestral beings are immortal. They are creatures of the Dreaming who moved across the country leaving behind possessions, which designate specific sites of significance. They met others of their kind; they created and left the world of humans through being metamorphosed as stone or some other form, disappearing into the territory of another group or into the sky, ground, or water. In doing so, they leave behind tangible evidence of their presence on earth.

Ancestral beings also changed form and gender and in many cases are associated with elements or natural species. For example, an ancestral being who is in one form an owl is in the mundane world associated with all owls today, thus the spirit character of the ancestral being continues today. Because the ancestral spirits gave birth to humans, they share a common life force, which emphasizes the unity of humans with the earth rather than their separation. The ontological relationship occurs through the intersubstantiation of ancestral beings, humans, and land; it is a form of embodiment. As the descendants and reincarnation of these ancestral beings, Indigenous people derive their sense of belonging to country through and from them. Thus, for example, Warlpiri, Kaurna, and Quandamooka people belong to Warlpiri, Kaurna, and Quandamooka countries. Colonization did not destroy this ontological relationship to country.

It may be argued that to suggest an ontological relationship to describe Indigenous belonging is essentialist or is a form of strategic essentialism because I am imputing an essence to belonging. From an Indigenous epistemology, what is essentialist is the premise upon which such criticism depends: the Western definition of the self as not unitary or fixed. This is a form of strategic essentialism that can silence and dismiss non-Western constructions, which do not define the self in the same way. The politics of such silencing is enabled by the power of Western knowledge and its ability to be the definitive measure of what it means to be human and what does and what does not constitute knowledge. Questioning the integrity and legitimacy of Indigenous ways of knowing and being has more to do with who has the power to be a knower and whether their knowledge is commensurate with the West's "rational" belief system. The anti-essentialist critique is commendable, but it is premised on a contradiction embedded within the Western construction of essentialism; it is applied as a universal despite its epistemological recognition of difference.

Home and Place

The premise of colonization that Australia belonged to no one informed the relationship between Indigenous people and the nation-state from its very inception, and it continues to do so. Legislation and state policies served to exclude Indigenous people from participation as citizens through their removal to reserves, missions, and cattle stations, where they lived their everyday lives under regimes of surveillance. Many people were removed from their traditional countries but carried with them knowledges of those countries, while others were not removed. Some reserves and missions were set up on other people's traditional country where the incarcerated traditional owners retained close links and ties to that country. Similarly, cattle stations usually had traditional owners of that country attached to them, and hunting and gathering subsidized their de facto indentured labor. Other Indigenous people were stolen from their families and placed in institutions or adopted by white families. In effect, colonization produced multiple contexts that shaped the construction of Indigenous subjectivities that were and are positioned within discursive formations of history relative to a particular space, country, and time. These subjectivities are tied to our ontological relationship to the land and serve to ground our political as well as our cultural identities.

We are not migrants in the sense that we have moved from one nation-state to another, but the policies of removal transferred different indigenous peoples from their specific country to another's. This dislocation in effect means that Indigenous people can be out of place in another's country, but through cultural protocols and the commonality of our ontological relationship to country we can be in place but away from our home country. This is a different experience of migrancy to that of the postcolonial subject. It is not a hybridity derived from a third space, a kind of menagerie of fluid diasporic subjects. Instead, there is an incommensurate doubleness superimposed by marginality and centering. Marginality is the result of colonization and the proximity to whiteness, while centering is achieved through the continuity of ontology and cultural protocols between and among Indigenous people. This suggests that Indigenous subjectivity represents a dialectical unity between humans and the earth consisting of subject positions whose integration requires a degree of mimetic performativity.

The effects of removal and dislocation have resulted in different constructions of subjectivity that link people to place in multiple ways. In the last two decades, Indigenous women have written their life histories. All these women were removed from their families and country of origin. Indigenous women's life histories are based on the collective memories of intergenerational relationships between predominantly Indigenous women, extended families, and communities. These relationships are underpinned by connections with one's country and the spirit world. In all the life histories, Indigenous people are related either by descent, country, place, or shared experiences.

Social relationships are important in all cultural domains, but their nature differs, and the moral universe, which informs these relationships in Indigenous cultural domains, is outside the experience of migrants. Relationality is one dimension of this moral universe that is spiritually interconnected. Indigenous women perceive the world as organic and populated by spirits, which connect places and people. In *My Place*, Sally Morgan's grandmother and mother hear the corroboree in the swamp when Sally's father is ill and understand this as the spirit's recognition of the father's mental turmoil.[19] After the father's death, the corroboree is no longer heard. When Daisy Corunna dies, it is the call of the bird that tells Sally about the end of her grandmother's life. In *Wandering Girl*, Glenyse Ward learns from the older girls of the spiritual beings, the mumaries, in the caves near Wandering mission. The older girls tell her that if she and the other children are naughty the mumaries will come and take them away.[20] And in *When the Pelican Laughed*, Alice Nannup returns to make peace with her country by performing a water-based ritual to appease the snake that lives in the waterhole at Mallina.[21] In *Don't Take Your Love to Town*, Ruby Langford receives a sign of bad news when late at night there are three knocks at her door but no one is in sight.[22] The next morning Ruby's friend Harold Leslie is told that his father has died.

These experiences illustrate the way in which the spiritual nature of the world is incorporated into one's connection to place, home, and country. The spiritual world is immediately experienced because it is synonymous with the physiography of the land. In the life histories the reality of spirituality is a physical fact because it is experienced as part of one's life. Indigenous women perceive themselves as being an extension of the earth, which is alive and unpredictable. Hence their understandings of themselves, their place and country, also reflect this view. In their life histories, Indigenous women perceive their experiences and others' experiences as extensions of themselves. This is a construction of subjectivity that extends beyond the immediate family. As Barry Morris points out: "The interconnectedness of self to others is related to those with whom one is familiar: those with whom one is related, one grows up with or, more specifically, those with whom one engages in relations of mutuality . . . where notions of generalized reciprocity shape and inform daily interactions."[23] The life histories of Indigenous women show a moral ordering of sociality that emphasizes mutual support and concern for those with whom they are interconnected. Their ontological relationship to home and place facilitates this connectedness and belonging. While this ontology is omnipresent, it is rarely visible, often elusive, and most often unrecognizable for many non-Indigenous people in their intersubjective relations with Indigenous people.

Homelessness

This ontological relationship to land is one that the nation-state has sought to diminish through its social, legal, and cultural practices. The nation-state's land rights regime is still premised on the legal fiction of *terra nullius*. After a sustained effort over a number of years by Koiki Mabo and others, the existence of Indigenous proprietary rights in land was recognized by the High Court of Australia in *Mabo and Ors v. Queensland (No. 2)* (1992). However, Professor Kent McNeil argues that the rule of extinguishment the High Court used in the *Mabo* decision is inconsistent with the broad rule of common law. The High Court's interpretation that at common law, native title can be extinguished by the nation-state if it is inconsistent with its sovereign power transgresses the common-law rule that the Crown cannot derogate from the vested interests of its subjects.[24] This rule is encapsulated in the Privy Council decision in *Attorney General of the Isle of Man v. Mylchreest*.[25] McNeil argues that "it doesn't matter whether those rights were derived from Crown grant or adverse possession or customary law. That is a fundamental limitation on the executive power."[26] Effectively what the High Court did in *Mabo* was invent a rule of extinguishment that did not exist under common law, to allow for inconsistent grants to extinguish native title prior to the Racial Discrimination Act 1975. That is, it invented a rule of extinguishment that allowed the Crown to retrospectively derogate from the vested rights of its Indigenous subjects. In doing so, the High Court judges made a decision based on politics and economics rather than the rule of the law. The decision affirms the nation-state's sovereignty by creating in law a hybrid of settlement that diminishes but does not erase *terra nullius*.

Pursuant to the *Mabo* decision and the subsequent Native Title Act 1993, we Indigenous people have in effect become trespassers in our own land until we prove our native title. Tragically and ironically, even though we were dispossessed of our lands by white people, the burden of proof for repossession of our lands is now placed on us, and we must demonstrate proof in accordance with the white legal structure in courts controlled predominantly by white men.[27] As the written word is generally regarded as more reliable by courts, all claimants must be able to substantiate their oral histories with documents written by white people, such as explorers, public servants, historians, lawyers, anthropologists, and police. These documents often distort and misrepresent events because the courts are racially and culturally biased. Preparing a native title claim often results in the generation of conflicting reports that lawyers usually seek to resolve by introducing the words or texts of yet another white expert. Confirmation of the Indigenous belonging to country is dependent on the interpretation of white people.

The legal regime of the nation-state places Indigenous people in a state of homelessness because our ontological relationship to the land, which is the way we hold title, is incommensurable with its own exclusive claims of sovereignty. The legal regime has reproduced the doctrine of *terra nullius* in order to give place and a sense of belonging to itself and its citizens. According to this regime, it is Indigenous people who belong nowhere unless they can prove their title according to the criteria established by the state. Those who are unable to demonstrate ritual, ceremonial, and the exercising of continuous rights in land do not belong anywhere other than to be positioned within a discourse of citizenship that seeks to erase dispossession through privileging white sameness over Indigenous difference.

Conclusion

Our ontological relationship to land is a condition of our embodied subjectivity. The Indigenous body signifies our title to land, and our death reintegrates our body with that of our mother, the earth. However, the state's legal regime privileges other practices and signs over our bodies because underpinning this legal regime is the Western ontology in which the body is theorized as being separate from the earth and it has no bearing on the way subjectivities, identities, and bodies are constituted. In Australia, Indigenous subjectivity operates through a doubling of marginality and centering, which produces an incommensurate subject that negotiates and manages disruption, dislocation, and proximity to whiteness. This process does not erase Indigenous ontology; rather, it suggests that Indigenous subjectivity is processual because it represents a dialectical unity between humans and the earth. It is a state of embodiment that continues to unsettle white Australia.

The subsequent legal regimes we all live under are outcomes of postcolonizing conditions. Indigenous people's circumstances are tied to non-Indigenous migration, and our dislocation is the result of our land being acquired for the new immigrants. We share this common experience as Indigenous people just as all migrants share the benefits of our dispossession. In most postcolonial theory, the postcolonial is positioned in relation to the dominant culture in the country of arrival and the one they left. In this sense postcolonialism, or as Ahmed argues, postcoloniality, exists in Australia, but it too is shaped by white possession.[28] What requires further theorizing is how the white and nonwhite postcolonial subject is positioned in relation to the original owners not through migrancy but by possession in countries such as Australia.

As I have argued, Indigenous people's sense of home and place are configured differently from that of migrants. There is no other homeland that provides a point of origin or a place for multiple identities. Instead, our rendering of place, home, and country through our ontological relation to country is the basis of our ownership. It informs a counterhegemonic discourse to that of citizenship and migrancy. Jacobs and Gelder's assertion that Australia is postcolonial because of the symbolic incorporation of the sacred into the national imagery belies the kind of discourses whereby we are symbolically and legally placed outside such an imaginary.

Under Australia's white anglicized legal regime, Indigenous people are homeless and out of place because the hybrid of settlement, which now exists in common law, continues the legal fiction of *terra nullius* by positioning us as trespassers. Who belongs, and the degree of that belonging, is inextricably tied to white possession. The right to be here and the sense of belonging it creates are reinforced institutionally and socially; personal profound sentiment is enabled by structural conditions. The colonizer/colonized axis continues to be configured within this postcolonizing society through power relations that are premised on our dispossession and resisted through our ontological relationship to land. Indigenous people's position within the nation-state is not one where colonizing power relations have been discontinued. Instead, these power relations are at the very heart of the white national imaginary and belonging; they are postcolonizing.

2 THE HOUSE THAT JACK BUILT

Britishness and White Possession

The formation of specifically white subject positions has in fact been [the] key, at times as cause and at times as effect, to the socio-political processes inherent in taking land and making nations.

> —Ruth Frankenberg, *Displacing Whiteness: Essays in Social and Cultural Criticism*

"I do not believe that the real life of this nation is to be found either in the great luxury hotels and the petty gossip of so called fashionable suburbs, or in the officialdom of organised masses. It is to be found in the homes of people who are nameless and unadvertised and who, whatever their individual religious conviction or dogma, see in their children their greatest contribution to the immortality of their race." Those words are in substance as true today as they were then.

> —John Howard quoting Robert Menzies, *The Australian*, September 3, 1997

The Prime Minister is touring the battlefields of France where his father and grandfather fought, carrying with him one of their wartime diaries. Is such wallowing in the past healthy? Sounds like black armband travel to me.

> —Melissa Lucashenko, *The Australian*, April 29, 2000

THE BRITISH IMPERIAL PROJECT was predicated on taking possession of other peoples' lands and resources for the benefit of Empire. Britain took possession in a number of ways. In Canada, the United States, and New Zealand, it was through negotiated settlements and treaties with Indigenous peoples that lands became appropriated by the Crown. The right to take possession was embedded in British and

international common law and rationalized through a discourse of civilization that supported war, physical occupation, and the will and desire
to possess. Underpinning property rights, possession entails values,
beliefs, norms, and social conventions as well as legal protection as it
operates ideologically, discursively, and materially. Property rights are
derived from the Crown, which in the form of the nation-state holds
possession. Possession and nationhood are thus constituted symbioti-
cally. This leads me to ask whether the form of Britishness and national
identity that developed in Australia is "free of, uninformed, and un-
shaped by" Indigenous sovereignty.[1] In this chapter, I explore how the
core values of Australian national identity are located within the house
that Jack built, a nation that in its denial of Indigenous sovereignty is
perceived to be a white possession.

The Perceived Loss of Dominance

Despite the dominance of whiteness culturally, politically, and economically, since Australia's bicentenary there has been a concerted effort
to write about and reiterate the relationship between Britishness and
Australian national identity through a discourse of loss and recuperation. The emergence of this literature coincided with Australia's bicentenary, evoking a new sense of nationalism, which celebrated and
promoted the idea of a unified nation, born in part as a response to
more than a decade of multiculturalism. Prime Minister Paul Keating's
policies (1991–96) in particular were thought to undermine the idea
that the nation was a unified white possession. The push to see Australia as part of Asia did not sit well with members of a growing conservative electorate who perceived themselves as a country with more in
common with Britain, Europe, and America than our neighbors to the
north. A discourse of loss emerged tied to the ideas that there were too
many non-British migrants, mainly Asian, entering Australia and the
granting of native title to Indigenous people after the *Mabo* decision.
Both the fear of Asian "invasion" and of "dispossession" by Indigenous
people were orchestrated to recenter white possession of the nation.
The conservative reaction to the Keating government resulted in the
election of John Howard and the emergence of Pauline Hanson, representing the One Nation Party, onto the political scene. Both Howard
and Hanson espoused a return to "core values" of the mainstream and
the reduction of fiscal and policy support for multiculturalism and

Indigenous affairs. The office of multiculturalism was closed and Howard appointed the National Multicultural Advisory Council (NMAC) in 1997 to provide policy direction and strategies for implementation over the next ten years. The NMAC's report "Australian Multiculturalism for a New Century: Towards Inclusiveness," was launched on May 5, 1999. In response, the government presented its multicultural policy in parliament in December of the same year, "highlighting the need for Australian multicultural policy to be a unifying force and relevant to all Australians."[2] The Aboriginal and Torres Strait Islander Commission's budget was decreased and its policy direction changed from one of rights-based advocacy to practical reconciliation. The Native Title legislation was amended to reduce the degree and amount of rights enshrined in the original act. By selectively demonizing migrants, Indigenous people, and later, refugees, Howard effectively recuperated national identity and white possession, which he constructed as threatened by the "political correctness" of the Hawke-Keating government (1983–96).

Another way that Howard strategically deployed the discourse of loss and recuperation was by reifying the digger (as Australian soldiers were referred to in World War I), whose embodiment in Edward "Weary" Dunlop, a white heterosexual male, represents the core national values of mateship, egalitarianism, and a fair go.[3] Such an embodiment implicitly precludes nonwhite migrants and Indigenous people from holding such core values. As Ghassan Hage argues, "It means making the ludicrous claim that other people in the world are less committed to them or actually committed to opposing values."[4] Howard's assertion of such nationally held core values paradoxically excludes the power relations that support and nurture white dominance while simultaneously exalting its seemingly invisible existence. The core values that diggers displayed on the battlefields are never linked to their colonial origins and the part they played in claiming the nation as a white possession.

Like Howard, Keating also deployed the digger in nationalist rhetoric, but he did so in a different way. As Fiona Nicoll argues in her book *From Diggers to Drag Queens*, Keating's eulogy to the unknown soldier "presented . . . a figure capable of drawing the diverse threads comprising contemporary Australian society together in tolerance."[5] In his attempt to reorient Australia's core values toward a postcolonial future, Keating walked the Kokoda Trail in the ex-colony of Papua New Guinea, relocating the digger in the Pacific and away from Europe; thus he was also signifying Australia's role as a colonizing nation. Though Keating was willing to acknowledge past injustices (and presented an Australian national identity that did not privilege Britishness), he did not alter the perception that the nation is a white possession.[6]

Prime Minister Howard has visited the majority of overseas Australian war memorials, where his attendance and conveyance of respect were televised to the nation. In particular, his visit to French battlefields while carrying a diary belonging to a member of his family signified to the nation that he too had been touched by war. Promoting his family's wartime contribution lent legitimacy to his authority as a national leader and vicariously linked him to the digger tradition. Howard's strategy of exploiting the digger connects World War I to Timor and then to Iraq to substantiate Australia's involvement in war; it is no coincidence that all our soldiers are now referred to as diggers. Howard was at Anzac Cove, Gallipoli, when ANZAC (Australia and New Zealand's Army Corps), under the command of the British, arrived in Muthanna Province in southern Iraq in April 2005.[7] The icon of the digger defending all that his country represents, in the guise of protecting other people's land and sovereignty, reaffirms in the national imaginary that Australia is a white possession. Similarly, the link between the digger and his British roots was apparent when Prince Charles presided over the Gallipoli ceremonies that year.

Hage argues that this apparent sense of loss and affirmation of white Australian heritage was tied to the perception that there was an assault on Australo-Britishness and its importance to the way in which people perceive their sense of belonging. He argues that white Australia's sense of loss was directly connected to what he terms "governmental belonging," which involves "the *possession* of a right over the nation . . . the belief that one's *possession* of national capital provides one with the right to contribute (even if only by having a legitimate opinion with regards to the internal and external politics of the nation) to its management such as it remains one's home."[8]

The right to possess is inextricably tied to perceiving the nation as a white possession. As Hage illustrates during the years when multiculturalism was policy driven, a white middle class exerted its governmental belonging to give voice to its aspirations and ideals on being cosmo-multicultural, which "presupposes a cultured and sublimated approach to otherness devoid of too materialist functionality."[9] That is, the "cosmo-multiculturalist" could be distant from the material reality of multiculturalism but appreciate and enjoy the aesthetic interaction. Extending Hage's argument, the cosmo-multiculturalist could support the granting of native title because the law and government limited the material reality for Indigenous people and Indigenous sovereignty rights were not granted. White possession was understood as not being threatened by these concessions. The discourse of loss and recuperation was in response to a split and crisis within whiteness, producing a sense of declension and melancholy that gave impetus to recentering white possession.

That such a sense of loss of governmental belonging is underpinned by the belief that the nation is a white possession is evident in the recent High Court decision in *Yorta Yorta*.[10] The decision consolidated the court's legal and political resistance to native title by creating judicial and legal impediments that were presented as though they were race blind. Yet the origin and assertion of property law in Australia continues to be based on racial domination and white possession. The denial of the Yorta Yorta's native title was based on a regime of statutory interpretation that usurped the common-law property rights of Indigenous people. By the fact of occupation under Australian common law, the Yorta Yorta proved their native title. In effect, the High Court's decision assumed that "only white possession and occupation of land was validated and therefore privileged as a basis for property rights."[11] The High Court refuses the continuity of Indigenous sovereignty as the precondition and genesis of all concomitant rights, interests, entitlements, responsibilities, obligations, customs, and law. In doing so, the court imputed reified white social standards to the Yorta Yorta, which "not only denied their right to historical change but also the reality of their paradoxical continued existence" in white Australia.[12] The perception that the nation is a white possession was visible in this decision.

The Return to Britishness

Since assuming power in 1996, Prime Minister Howard gave numerous speeches outlining the Australian core values of "fairness," "tolerance," "equality," "mateship," "down-to-earth common-sense," "decency," and "a commitment to democracy."[13] These values in one form or another are echoed in the literature on Britishness and Australian national identity. There is consensus that they are the core white values of the nation.

For Howard and writers such as Miriam Dixson, these values "hold" the nation, and they need to be reaffirmed and their social capital enhanced.

A common thread woven through the literature is that Australian national identity has been shaped by British values shared by convicts, explorers, and pioneers, the nation's founding ancestors. Their ethnic origins are acknowledged as being English, Irish, Scottish, and Welsh, but collectively they constitute the British. It is often argued that the form of Britishness that developed in Australia was homogenous due to the lack of overt class barriers, the shared experience of immigration or transportation, and the struggle to survive in a harsh and difficult landscape. This distinctly Australian and homogeneous form of Britishness is racialized as being Anglo-Saxon (English), Anglo-Celtic (English and Irish), or the British patriotic race (English, Irish, Scottish, and Welsh). Deploying these racial categories in this way suggests that there were a number of different races operating in Australia, which in effect conflates ethnicity with race and masks the homogeneity of whiteness that developed through the spread of Empire.[14] So while whiteness masked the ethnic heterogeneity of British immigrants in the service of the egalitarian myth up to the latter years of the twentieth century, today the egalitarian myth that Australia is a "tolerant society" is deployed to mask the persistently privileged position of whiteness and its possession of the nation that simultaneously disavows Indigenous sovereignty.

Representations of Britishness take a number of forms in historical narratives written since the late 1990s. In their respective articles in the journal *Australian Historical Studies* in April 2001, Neville Meaney and Stuart Ward illustrate that Australia had a British inheritance consisting of economic, cultural, and political affiliation with Britain until the late 1960s. Australians share with the British kinship and familial ties, and this is why they supported Britain in the two world wars, why they continued to trade with the motherland even when it was not in their best interests, and why they thought Britain's protection would continue. It was only after Britain decided to invest its trading future in Europe that Australia sought trade and security in the arms of the United States.[15] Meaney and Ward both fail to acknowledge that Australia's British inheritance resulted from the spoils of colonialism and British law, which provided the context for the assumption of white possession of the nation and the denial of Indigenous sovereignty. The separation of Australia's institutional affiliations with Britain may have been born of necessity in the 1960s, but that did not result in the same affiliations being established with Asia; instead they were forged with another imperialist white nation.

According to Tara Brabazon in *Tracking the Jack*, threads of British culture have been woven into the fabric of the Australian nation.[16] Australia's British inheritance was manifested in our form of government, education, legal, and industrial systems and is signified through the incorporation of the Union Jack in both the flags of New Zealand and Australia. Brabazon's excellent book traces the various forms Britishness took in its colonies and acknowledges the role of colonization in shaping their content. However, she does not extend the implications to engage with white possession and Indigenous sovereignty. In "Scatterlings of Empire," a special edition of the *Journal of Australian Studies*, Amanda Nettelbeck illustrates how British migrants who came to Australia in the 1880s envisaged their task as being the establishment of a new colony for Britain.[17] She presents them as "pioneers," who through hard work and determination contributed to the development of the nation and made it their own. (A similar portrayal was represented in the series *The Colony* on SBS television.) What is clear in Nettelbeck's work, though not argued, is how these attributes instilled a sense of possession that was connected to, but separated from, Indigenous dispossession.

In his essay "Made in England: Australia's British Inheritance," David Malouf argues that essentially the values Australians inherited from Britain involve "[a] low church puritanism and fear of the body and its pleasures, British drunkenness; British pragmatism and distrust of theory; British philistinism and dislike of anything showy, theatrical, arty or 'too serious'; British good sense and the British sense of humour."[18] According to Malouf, these attributes are tied to a habit of mind that is essentially Anglo-Saxon: "One that prefers to argue from example and practice rather than principle; that is happy, in a pragmatic way, to be in doubt as to why something works so long as it does work; is flexible, experimental, adaptive, and scornful of all those traps it sees in habit and rule."[19]

Malouf simultaneously disaggregates Anglo-Saxons into being British but does not explain why this conceptual shift is made. A racialized category (Anglo-Saxon) is a nationalist category (British). So Malouf understands that there is a relationship between race and nation, but he does not extend his analysis to engage in how Australia's inherited values were racialized (that is, whitened) in the process of becoming a nation. Instead he argues that a racialized habit of mind informed these values, one that is tolerant and finds expression in the form of English that Australians use. Malouf argues further that Australian English is derived from late Enlightenment English and as such it is "purged of all those forms of violent expression that had led men to violent action."[20] It is moderate language grounded in reason, negotiation, and compromise that created a form of social interaction in Australia, which tempered extremism and kept "the worst sorts of violence at bay." It is the language of Australian literature, courts, and the education system. What Malouf does not acknowledge is that this language is also tied epistemologically to a possessive investment in whiteness. Binary oppositions and metaphors had by the eighteenth century represented blackness within the structure of the English language as a symbol of negation and lack. Indigenous people were categorized as nomads as opposed to owners of land, uncivilized as opposed to being civilized, relegated to nature as opposed to culture. In Australian history books the violence continued in written expression by denying Indigenous sovereignty through portrayals of peaceful settlement, not invasion and war. Yet Australian nationalism is now heavily invested in the tradition and memories of war and the defending and taking of possession, albeit in other countries.[21]

Miriam Dixson, in *The Imaginary Australian: Anglo-Celts and Identity—1788 to the Present,* argues that Australia's British inheritance manifested in a core Anglo-Celtic culture primarily derived from the English and Irish free immigrants and convicts. This core culture was "shaped to a disproportionate extent not just by the politics but by the entire folkways of founding generations."[22] She notes that it was the ideas and practices associated with authority, work, freedom, liberty, individualism, community, equality, and gender that formed this core identity. She argues that whether the narrative is about bush pioneers, battlers and farmers, or the "noble" proletariats, they share common values. They involve "decency, a dedicated practicability and sense of finitude and a commitment to fairness which, as in all cultures where it appears, is a commitment within limits."[23] Dixson's preoccupation with core Anglo-Celtic values that "hold" and affirm the nation has the effect of reducing Indigenous dispossession to a mere blemish on the historical record. For Dixson whiteness does not appear to be one of the limits to making commitments that are fair and equitable through its possession of the nation.

Dixson and Malouf, among others, espouse that it was the founding ancestors' conquering of the landscape that shaped these values, for they had to battle flood, fire, disease, famine, and drought in contributing to the spread of Empire. There is also agreement among scholars of Britishness that the Australian nation in the later part of the twentieth century was changed by the introduction of multiculturalism. Some perceive this as a positive thing, though they give little explanation as to why this is so. Others perceive it in terms of loss associated with the core values of the nation, but the specificities of what has been lost is not addressed—leaving the sense that white people feel this way because there are too many racialized "others" here who are taking over. Regardless of whether multiculturalism is perceived as a threat or a promise, however, the nation must first be believed to be a white possession.

The discourse of loss and recuperation implicitly underpins studies of Britishness in contemporary Australia derived from the testimonials of British migrants who arrived after the 1940s. These studies identify similar values to those contained in historical narratives. Perseverance, struggle, self-reliance, and adaptability are encapsulated in the icon of the battler and echoed in the respective work of A. James Hammerton, Catherine Coleborne, and Alastair Thomson. Hammerton and Coleborne reveal that British migrants have a "sense of being 'left out'" of the migration experience of multicultural Australia. Alastair Thomson concurs that "though the British continued to be the most numerically significant migrant group, the British migrant experience was not central" to Australia's migration story.[24] They agree that the apparent cultural and political similarity of British migrants to the mainstream has worked against their inclusiveness in the story of migration. Hammerton and Coleborne argue that while the testimonies disclosed that there were two competing narratives—one of "misery and failure," the other of "vindicated struggle and success"—the dominant tale is one of "successful struggle." Similarly, Thomson's work illustrates how British migrants were successful in coming to terms with "a new physical and cultural environment."[25]

Jon Stratton argues that British migrants' sense of being overlooked in the migration story is directly linked to feelings of loss and a perceived decline in their ideological status as nonmigrants and thus more authentically Australian.[26] These feelings are connected to the Hawke-Keating government's attempt to shift "the thinking about Australia itself from the idea that it is some sort of offshoot of British society in the southern Pacific to seeing Australia as being, and always having been, engaged in, and to some extent moulded by, the South Asian region."[27] Stratton argues that British migrants' response to being overlooked is tied to the new self-ethnicization that is expressed in the form of associations, festivals, and pubs.

Sara Wills and Kate Darian-Smith take issue with Stratton, arguing that these performative and symbolic displays of Britishness are not so much a form of empowerment through ethnicization, "rather they can be seen as the attempted remobilisation by an uneasy but socially empowered group of a heightened public presence for their conception of history, culture and nationhood. . . . In this process, British ethnicity is positioned as 'other'—although certainly not as 'alien'—to the mainstream."[28]

Susanne Schech and Jane Haggis's study of British migrants in South Australia extends the findings of Wills and Darian-Smith. They agree that British migrants do not perceive themselves as "foreign or strange," but they argue that they perceive migrants and Indigenous people as continuing foreigners or strangers who do not belong to the nation. It is British migrants' whiteness that enables a sense of being part of the core of the nation. Schech and Haggis further argue:

> The British migrant's expectation of fitting in was predicated on their knowledge of Australia as an extension of British whiteness. The presence of family members already in Australia tended to reinforce the idea of Australia as a member of the white Commonwealth family. Despite the long journey, moving to Australia felt to many like moving next door. None of our respondents who were adults at the time of migration recall fear or trepidation commonly associated with migration to an unknown place, even though few had detailed information on Australian life and environment. They just knew it was a place they could go.[29]

The discourse of loss and recuperation is expressed in contemporary British migrants' narratives as an exclusion from the migration story, a change in their dominant ideological status as nonmigrants, and a remobilization around their ethnicity as a recuperative strategy to claim a unique space within Australia's migration history. Simultaneously they understand that they are part of the core or mainstream because of their race. However, the mobilization around British ethnicity signifies a split within Australian whiteness because British migrants' inclusion in the narrative of Australian migration history works to separate them from the history of Indigenous dispossession. This is in spite of the fact that their migration is one of the benefits they accrue from that history. They feel included in the nation because prepossession has been claimed on their behalf, hence their implicit understanding that the nation is a white possession.

Whiteness and Indigenous Dispossession: Beyond Britain

Anne Curthoys argues that "Australian popular historical mythology stresses struggle, courage and survival, amidst pain, tragedy and loss." It is "a history of suffering, sacrifice and defiance in defeat" that unfolds as narratives of victimization.[30] Similarly, the literature on colonial Britishness expressed through the bush battler, the pioneer, the explorer, and the convict place these founding ancestors as struggling against the landscape. Thus the landscape stands in as the oppressor in these narratives of victimization and a displacement occurs; the violence committed against Indigenous people is disavowed. It is the landscape that must be conquered, claimed, and named, not Indigenous people, who at the level of the subconscious are perceived to be part of the landscape and thus not human. By creating the landscape as oppressor, the values and virtues of achieving white possession can be valorized and Indigenous dispossession can be erased; the mythology of peaceful settlement is perpetuated and sustained. As Ken Inglis illustrates in his book *Sacred Places*, despite the landscape holding memories of colonial land wars, conflicts between black and white are seldom commemorated.[31] The values and virtues associated with overcoming an oppressive landscape are not easily recuperated when there is evidence of white inhumanity. As they became part of Australian national identity, these values and virtues are underpinned by the denial of violent invasion. Therefore the shaping of national identity cannot be detached from white possession of the nation and the denial of Indigenous sovereignty wars. This is why in the "history wars" the virtue of white possession and the denial of Indigenous sovereignty are inextricably woven in these debates about the nation's history.

As I have argued elsewhere, during the years of frontier wars and subsequent occupation it was the intersection between race and property that played a definitive role in constructing and affirming white domination and economic success at the cost of Indigenous racial and economic oppression.[32] The incarceration, removal, and extermination of Indigenous people were validated by regimes of common law based on the assumption that *terra nullius* gave rise to white sovereignty. "Only white possession and occupation of land was validated and therefore privileged as a basis for property rights" and national identity.[33] The white nation cannot exist as such without land and clearly defined borders; it is the legally defined and asserted territorial sovereignty that provides the context for national identifications. In this way *terra nullius* indelibly marks configurations of national identity. This is evident in Australian films ranging from *The Sentimental Bloke* to *Walkabout, Picnic at Hanging Rock, The Last Wave, Crocodile Dundee, The Man from Snowy River, Mad Max 2, Priscilla*, and *The Castle*, where myths of national belonging and identity are clearly tied to land disconnected from the continuity of Indigenous sovereignty. Representations of Indigenous people in these films are through ghostly images or nomadic props appearing and then disappearing within the landscape. Although *The Castle* purported to offer something else, it lampooned the *Mabo* decision in the common-law proceedings to reinscribe white possession. Refracted in this fantasy of film are representations of whiteness taking center stage in the narrative of adversity through virtue, intelligence, resilience, loss, and hard work, effectively disavowing Indigenous sovereignty.

The assumption that the nation is a white possession is evident in the relationship between whiteness, property, and the law, which manifested itself in the latter part of the nineteenth century in the form of comprehensive discriminatory legislation tied to national citizenship.[34] Colonial and subsequent governments legitimated the appropriation of Indigenous lands, racialized incarceration, and enslavement and limited naturalized citizenship to white immigrants.[35] While blackness was congruent with Indigenous subjugation and subordination, whiteness was perceived as being synonymous with freedom and citizenship. The right to determine who was allowed into the country and therefore who could belong was exercised by a white male British constituency at the heart of the nation. It was whiteness, not Anglo-Celtic or Anglo-Saxoness, that served to unify the nation. The social reproduction of whiteness was legalized through the Immigration Restriction Act 1901 and the white Australia policy, which until the 1940s gave preference to white British, Canadian, American, or New Zealand migrants.[36] "According whiteness actual legal status converted an aspect of identity into an external object of property, moving whiteness from privileged identity to a vested interest."[37] By 1949, The Australian definition of "white" was expanded to include a variety of Eastern and Central European refugee groups. Stratton argues that the Australian usage of white covered all the people in Europe who "were technically thought of as white. . . . The geographical definition of European had come . . . to equate with the racial classification of white."[38] The integration of various Europeans into a white Australian identity, coalesced around Anglo norms, was enabled by a worldview that defined Indigenous people until the 1960s as noncitizens. The white Australia policy, despite being revoked in 1973, continued in immigration practice for many years. "The courts played an active role in enforcing this right to exclude. . . . In that sense the courts protected whiteness as they did any other form of property."[39]

Conclusion

Contemporary and historical narratives of Britishness and Australian national identity reveal that the values required to establish the nation as a white possession are those that were also required to dispossess Indigenous people of their lands. That these values can be linked across generations of those who trace their ancestry through Britishness is evidence of the perseverance of a white national identity and its possessiveness. Through the law, politics, and culture, the nation has been created as a white possession. "White [Australians] are encouraged to invest in whiteness, to remain true to an identity that provides them with resources, power and opportunity" and to adhere to narratives that valorize their past and their present.[40] Not all white Australians benefit from whiteness in the same way, and some resist profiteering, but Australian national identity is predicated on retaining the benefits of colonial theft, on the one hand, while exalting a sense of tolerance and fair play, on the other. Britishness has metamorphosed into Australian national identity and culture, but Indigenous sovereignty continues through the presence of Indigenous people and their land, haunting the house that Jack built, shaking its foundations and rattling the picket fence.

3 BODIES THAT MATTER ON THE BEACH

Voices from the beach can be hard to hear. They can be snatched
from the lips by the wind or drowned in the white noise of the
waves. But there are beaches, too, on which voices are hard to
hear because of the silence.

—Greg Denning, *Beach Crossings: Voyaging across Times,
Cultures, and Self*

BEACHES REMAIN IMPORTANT PLACES within Indigenous coastal
peoples' territories, though the silence about our ownership is deafen-
ing. The coastline of the Australian continent was frequented for centuries by mariners and traders from Asia with whom some Indigenous
groups established trade and familial relations.[1] The first verified contact by Dutch explorer Willem Janszoon was in March 1606; he char-
tered the west coast of Cape York Peninsula in northern Queensland.
Over the next two centuries the charting of the Australian coastline was
primarily undertaken by British explorers. Since 1788, the coastline of
this continent has been colonized by British colonists and their descendants, who built the majority of Australia's capital cities near the sea.
In 2010, it is where the largest proportion of the Australian population
resides on the most prized real estate in the country. Living near the
sea ensures that the beach continues to be a place of multiple encounters for residents and visitors. The beach marks the border between
land and sea, between one nation and another, a place that stands as
the common ground upon which collective national ownership, memory, and identity are on public display; a place of pleasure, leisure, and
pride. Michael Taussig argues that the beach is a site of fantasy production, a playground where transgressions and pleasure occur. It is

"the ultimate fantasy where nature and carnival blend as prehistory in the dialectical image of modernity."[2]

As an island continent, beaches are the visible terra manifestation of Australian borders, which operate simultaneously to include and exclude. In the twenty-first century, these borders may seem to be more permeable because of economic and cultural processes of globalization, but territorial sovereignty reigns supreme in Australia and Europe, evidenced by border patrols that serve to exclude those who are uninvited. Within Australia we are constantly reminded of the central role of possession in civilizing "others" and the association between war and borders, which is reinscribed through our treatment of asylum seekers who travel by boat attempting to land on our beaches. Australian federal governments have built mandatory detention centers fenced with razor wire and patrolled by guards to accommodate the "illegal boat people" who have been successful in landing on our beaches after escaping from war-torn countries such as Iraq and Afghanistan. In taking possession of their bodies and imprisoning them, the nation-state exercises its sovereignty in violation of several human rights conventions that it has signed. This performative sovereign act of violence and disavowal has historical roots. Despite international law, the British invasion, in the form and arrival of the first naval boat people, produced invisible borders left in the wake of colonization that continues to deny Indigenous people our sovereign rights. Many authors have argued that within Australian popular culture the beach is a key site where racialized and gendered transgressions, fantasies, and desires are played out, but none have elucidated that these cultural practices reiteratively signify that the nation is a white possession.[3]

In this chapter I examine how white possession functions ontologically and performatively within Australian beach culture through the white male body. I draw on Judith Butler's idea of performativity in that a culturally determined and historically contingent act, which is internally discontinuous, is only real to the extent that it is repeated.[4] Raced and gendered norms of subjectivity are iterated in different ways through performative repetition in specific historical and cultural contexts. National racial and sexual subjects are in this sense both doings and things done, but where I differ from Butler is that I argue that they are existentially and ontologically tied to patriarchal white sovereignty. Patriarchal white sovereignty is a regime of power that derives from the illegal act of possession and is most acutely manifested in the

form of the Crown and the judiciary, but it is also evident in everyday
cultural practices and spaces. As a means of controlling differently
racialized populations enclosed within the borders of a given society,
white subjects are disciplined, though to different degrees, to invest in
the nation as their possession. As a regime of power, patriarchal white
sovereignty capillaries the performative reiteration of white possession
through white male bodies. In this way performativity functions as a
disciplinary technique that enables the white male subject to be imbued
with a sense of belonging and ownership produced by a possessive logic
that presupposes cultural familiarity and commonality applied to social
action. In this context I will examine how the beach is appropriated as
a white possession through the performative reiteration of the white
male body. I then discuss how Indigenous artist Vernon Ah Kee con-
tests this performativity in his installation entitled *Cant Chant*.

Performing the Colonial Subject

Colonization is the historical process through which the performativity
of the white male body and its relationship to the environment has been
realized and defined, particularly in former British colonies such as Australia, New Zealand, Canada, and the United States.[5] In staking possession to Indigenous lands, white male bodies were taking control and
ownership of the environments they encountered by mapping land and
naming places, which is an integral part of the colonizing process. One
of the first possessive performances by the white male body occurred
on the beach when Captain James Cook landed at a place he named
Botany Bay on April 28, 1770. For some time his boat had been under
surveillance by the Kamegal clan of Cooks River and Botany areas and
the Gwegal clan at Kundull (Kurnell). At first the Kamegal and Gwegal clans thought the large boat was a big bird entering the bay, but as
the boat approached they could see that the people onboard were
similar but different to themselves.[6] When Cook and his men landed
on the beach at Kundull, they were trespassing on Gwegal land and
hence were challenged by two Gwegal warriors who threw spears at
them while shouting out in their language Warra Warra Wai, meaning
"go away." Cook's crew retaliated by firing muskets and wounding
one of the Gwegal warriors. The warriors retreated, leaving their spears
and shields behind on the ground. This encounter was never interpreted
as an act of Indigenous sovereignty by Cook as he made his way up

the eastern coast of Australia. Instead, he rescripted us as living in a state of nature with no knowledge of, or possession of, proprietary rights.[7]

Cook took possession of the Gwegal warriors' weapons and transported them back to Britain, where they are now on display in a museum housing the property of people from different countries accumulated through purchase, plunder, and theft. After eight days in Botany Bay, Cook and his crew sailed north up the coastline of Australia. Cook made good use of his telescope, surveying the Indigenous people on the beach as he sailed past their lands, noting in his diaries that we ranged in color from chocolate to soot. After several months of sailing northward, he eventually took possession of the entire eastern coast from the 38 degree latitude in the name of King George III after landing on the beach of an island he named "Possession," situated off the tip of Cape York Peninsula. The assumption of sovereignty was ceremoniously marked by firing guns and raising the British flag as the male crew bore witness. The performative act of possession enabled by patriarchal white sovereignty is constituted by violence and transgression, voyeurism, pleasure, and pride. These originary performative acts by the white male body would eventually become an integral part of Australian beach culture.

Some eight years after Cook, eleven British naval ships arrived in Botany Bay. Governor Phillip, as the embodiment of colonial power, planted a British flag in the sand, staking a possessive claim to lands that belonged to the Eora and Gadigal nations. The invasion had begun and the lives of the people from the Kamegal and Gwegal clans were never the same as violence and smallpox took its toll. Over the next century, through containment, disease, and death, Indigenous people were displaced by colonists. In the white colonial imagination, we had become abject subjects; our lives and our bodies were physically erased from the beach.[8] Over the next century the only subjects who determined which bodies mattered on the beach were almost exclusively white males, embodying the possessive prerogative of patriarchal white sovereignty as a colonial norm.[9]

Despite the apparent promise of open access and use, public spaces are predicated upon an assumption of objectivity and rationality, which values but no longer explicitly marks or names whiteness or maleness. The beach, as a public space, continues to be controlled by white men, the embodiment of universal humanness and national identity. In the nineteenth century, the beach and its natural features were mostly of interest to white male visitors who were influenced by European romanticism. The beauty of the beach appealed to observers, along with "its sublime features: those characteristics which stimulated an intensity of emotion and sensation [valuing] poetic mystery above intellectual clarity."[10] Perceived as such, the beach enabled the performance of a gendered white ontological experience where nature fed the soul and culture nurtured white men's sensibilities. The beach was also an intersubjective place where a man could socialize with family and friends or watch other beachgoers and indulge in the British custom of promenading along the shore. The beach was and remains a heteronormative white masculine space entailing performances of sexuality, wealth, voyeurism, class, and possession. However, these different attributes of white male performativity underwent a transformation with the introduction of surf bathing. In the nineteenth century, surf bathing was performed exclusively by white males, but it was not a predominant part of beach culture because the Police Act 1838 restricted swimming to the early hours of the morning and preferably on nonpopular beaches. The public display of the white male body was perceived to offend moral sensibilities current at the time. It was not until the early twentieth century that surf bathing became a part of modern beach culture, due in part to the shifting codes of Victorian morality and increased control of the sea and the surf.[11] Eugenics also played a part in the shift. "Whereas picnicking and promenading defined masculinity in terms of an emphasis on the respectability and moral authority of colonialism, surf bathing and lifesaving defined masculinity in terms of a strong, fit, well muscled and racially pure white body."[12] This representation of the white male body was in contrast to the perception of policymakers at the turn of the century, who facilitated the displacement of the Indigenous body from the beaches and lands onto reserves and missions. The Indigenous body was represented as being terminal. The common phrase at the time to describe the containment and removal was as a benevolent act of "smoothing the dying pillow."[13]

Beach Lifesavers: Performing White Masculinity

By 1907, white middle-class men had formed the Surf Life Saving Association of Australia in response to the public representation of their surf bathing as being an "affront to decency."[14] They soon gained public approval by rationalizing their objectives as humanitarian and arguing that surf bathing was a disciplined organized sport involving military drills. Unlike lifeguards, who were paid for their services, surf lifesavers were volunteers who undertook training to protect people on the beach and were responsible for the safety and rescue of swimmers, surfers, and other water-sports participants. Regimentation, rigor, and dedication to the service of the nation produced fit and disciplined white male bodies. The media reported favorably on the suntanned white male bodies, representing them as the epitome of Australian manhood. Suntanning enhanced the aesthetic modalities of the white male body appropriating and domesticating the hypersexuality signified by black skin. Tanning simultaneously renders the presence of color as a temporary alteration that works to affirm the dominance of white masculinity and its ownership of the beach. The brownness of the white male body becomes "a detachable signifier, inessential to the subject, and hence acceptable" because it is not permanent.[15] As a detached signifier, it does not disrupt the "somatic luxury of white [male] subjects to roam and return to the tabula rasa of ideal whiteness where it is conveniently restored to its apex of privileges" as the embodiment of nation.[16] The surf lifesaver's discipline, strength, bravery, mateship, loyalty, and rigor embodied the attributes of white national identity, which were later ascribed to the body of the digger at ANZAC. The term "digger" is an appellation applied to Australian and New Zealand soldiers because of their trench-digging activities during the Gallipoli campaign, which required strong and fit bodies to undertake the hard work. The transference of the attributes of the surf lifesaver to the digger was not a coincidence. Many surf lifesavers volunteered for both world wars, and in some cases lifesaving clubs were closed because of the declining numbers of young men.[17]

The suntanned and hypermasculinized white body of the digger became inextricably tied to the birth of Australian nationalism within the white imaginary in the late twentieth century. This national identification with the performativity of invasion and taking possession of other peoples' lands embraces and legitimizes a tradition of patriarchal white sovereign violence embodied in the white male body on the beach in Australia and abroad. More than fifty thousand Australian soldiers volunteered to go to war in Europe to defend the sovereignty of the British Empire, an empire that was founded on the invasion and theft of Indigenous peoples lands. The first convoy of predominantly white male volunteers left Western Australia in November 1914, arriving on the beach at Gallipoli on April 25. Staking a possessive claim to the beach, Lieutenant General Sir William Birdwood, on April 29, 1915, decided to name the area ANZAC Cove in honor of the Australian and New Zealand Army Corps who served at Gallipoli. Despite this possessive claim, the Turkish government did not agree to officially name the site ANZAC Cove for another seventy years, due in part as a gesture of goodwill and respect tied to the Australian government's funding package to maintain the site. At that fateful site, the Turkish army decimated the Australian and New Zealand armies and thousands of soldiers lost their lives. Though Gallipoli was a spectacular strategic blunder, Fiona Nicoll, in her excellent book *From Diggers to Drag Queens: Reconfiguring National Identity*,[18] explores how the body of the white male soldier was constructed as a metonym for the ANZAC spirit, which has increasingly divested the digger of its origins in values of militarism and racial supremacy. The digger's white male body signified egalitarianism, discipline, irreverence, bravery, endurance, and constitutional opposition to authority. As Nicoll argues, the diggers' hypermasculinized and idealized body in cultural representations was in contrast to the actual traumatized and disfigured white male bodies returning home.

Following the carnage of the Great War, the lifesaver was used as a signifier of national identity to endow the broken body of the digger with new life and new masculine virility. During the interwar period and up to the 1950s, media represented the white male body of the surf lifesaver as the embodiment of the ANZAC spirit and the nation. In 1923, the president of the Surf Life Saving Association stated in the *Daily Guardian* that "we shall rear a race of men finer than the Anzacs, whom the whole world admire[s]."[19] And in 1941, the commentary in a newsreel item shot at a Bondi Beach carnival stated that "mighty deeds spawn men of might. This is the crucible from which fighting material emerges volunteer lifesavers, volunteer fighters. The amateur surf clubs have an enlistment record second to none."[20] The embodied signification of the white surf lifesavers as nation is also demonstrated by their inclusion and performance in national events such as the opening of the Harbour Bridge in Sydney in 1932, the Australian sesquicentenary in 1938, Queen Elizabeth's visit in 1954, and the Melbourne Olympics in 1956. During the 1940s, photographer Max Dupain captured Australian beach culture in his representations of white male bodies in photographs that include the infamous *Sunbaker* (1937), *Surf Race Start* (1940), and *Surfs Up* (1940). Dupain's portraits of white male bodies performing in the service of the nation represented the beach as a white possession, a space of leisure, pleasure, and pride.

In the 1930s, surf lifesaving clubs were conferred with a legal proprietary right to the beaches by local councils, which officially gave them the power to control, police, and rescue beachgoers. Despite the official sanction of surf lifesavers' ownership of the beach, their proprietorship was challenged after World War II through the emergence of a new white masculinity in the form of the surfer. In public discourse, surfing was represented as a form of hedonistic leisure, evoking anxiety about the moral decay of young men and women. Surfing produced a competitive, individualized white form of masculinity that attracted more women onto the beach. This hedonistic form of leisure was in contrast to the volunteer surf lifesavers who patrolled the beach and saved lives in the service of the nation. In the 1960s, surf lifesaving clubs attempted to restrict surfers' use of the beach by imposing taxes and restricting the use of surfboards to certain areas. Surfers responded by establishing "administrative associations to regulate, codify and legitimize what they now defined as a sport" in order to stake a possessive claim to the beach.[21] During the 1960s and 1970s, tension existed and violence occurred between these two forms of embodied white masculinity on the beach, usually over territory and sexual access to women as well as prowess in the water. Verbal abuse on the beach was common: surfers taunted lifesavers by calling them "seals" because of their regimented training, "dickheads" because their caps looked like the heads of condoms, and "budgie smugglers" because their swimming attire exhibited the outline of small male genitalia, particularly on cold days. Surf lifesavers responded to surfers by calling them "seaweed" because of their long, bleached, matted hair and their supposed inability to master the waves. These white heterosexual territorial wars abated to some degree when surfing was recognized nationally as a professional sport through organized professional tournaments that were covered by media and sponsored by corporations. Similarly, surf lifesaving became recognized as a professional sport predominantly through the "Iron Man" tournaments sponsored by corporations. The sexualized white male body of the suntanned surfer and the lifesaver was commodified to sell everything from Coca Cola to fashion and spawned a new genre of documentary surfing films and televised sport.

White male participation in surfing had begun in the 1930s, but but it did not begin to dominate the surfing scene until the 1960s. Booth argues that after the World War II mass consumer capitalism created the conditions by which leisure as a social practice became tied to individual lifestyles.[22] Surfing was and continues to be a native Hawaiian cultural practice introduced to the West by Duke Kahanamoku. Native Hawaiians' form of surfing was to flow with the waves, adhering to an ideal of soul surfing, which was part of their culture for more than fifteen hundred years.[23] Surfing was not considered to be a competitive practice, and when white Australian and South African surfers decided to invade the Native Hawaiian surfing beach of the North Shore of Oahu in the late 1970s, they were confronted by members of Hui 'O He'e Nalu, who asserted their sovereignty over the beach. For the Native Hawaiian surfers, the invasion of their beach by white surfers was a performative reiteration of the invasion by white American Marines supporting the white patriarchy that overthrew the Hawaiian monarchy in 1890. Native Hawaiian surfer resistance eventually earned the respect of the International Professional Surfing Organization, which conceded to a reduction in annual competitions at North Shore. Despite the assertion of Native Hawaiian sovereignty over the waves and the beaches, white Australian and South African surfers staked a possessive claim colonizing surfing by riding the waves, "conquering," "attacking," and reducing them to stages on which to perform aggressive acts. This became the dominant form of professional surfing, whereby surfers represented their respective nations, embodying the violent attributes of patriarchal white sovereignty.

By the 1980s, the blonde-haired, barrel-chested, suntanned white male body sauntering in board shorts and thongs had become a new icon of beach culture, reflecting the hedonism of youth in the 1960s and 1970s in Australia. The hedonism of surfing carried with it sex, sun, and surf. This was captured in paintings by artists such as Brett Whiteley, whose reclining nudes and bikini-clad beauties on the beach reflected a theater of indolence. In the catalogue for the Art Gallery of New South Wales exhibition entitled "On the Beach: With Brett Whiteley and Fellow Australian Artists," it states that "it was not only the allure of these inherently erotic bodies [in] languid stupor that compelled Whiteley's fascination for this iconic aspect of Australian landscape; it was also the beautiful vistas of beach and seascapes which provided such fertile ground for his inspirational paintings and drawings."[24] As the embodiment of patriarchal white sovereignty, Whiteley, like the surfers and lifesavers, performatively exhibits the possession

of white women's bodies on "their" beach. While white women are subject to the possessive white male gaze, their presence on the beach is
tied to the heteronormativity of patriarchal white sovereignty. They
can stake a possessive claim to the beach in ways in which Indigenous
women cannot. As I have argued elsewhere, white women have access
to power and privilege on the basis of their race through unequal gendered relations.[25]

After the economic downturn of the 1980s and a decade of multiculturalism and Indigenous rights claims, the militarized white male
body of the digger as the embodiment of nation was returned to the
beach within the national imaginary. Former prime minister John
Howard strategically deployed the memory of Edward "Weary" Dunlop as the quintessential digger, who represented the core national values of mateship and egalitarianism.[26] Dunlop was a fearless and strong
leader, a qualified surgeon who achieved sporting and military success.[27] Taken as a prisoner of war during World War II, he attended to
his comrades, risking his own life by challenging his Japanese captors
to provide medical provisions for the sick and wounded. He continued
to campaign for the rights of soldiers after the war and was a committed humanitarian. Like Howard, former Labor Prime Minister Paul
Keating also used the digger in nationalist rhetoric, but he did so in a
different way. As Nicoll argues, Keating's eulogy to the "unknown"
soldier "presented . . . a figure capable of drawing the diverse threads
comprising contemporary Australian society together in tolerance."[28]
In his attempt to reorient Australia's core values toward a postcolonial
future, Keating performed the digger by walking the Kokoda Trail in
the ex-colony of Papua New Guinea, relocating the white male body
in the Pacific and away from Europe. As the embodied representation
of patriarchal white sovereignty, Keating was also signifying Australia's role as a former colonizing nation that served to displace and negate
the ongoing colonization within the nation.

Following Keating's performance, John Howard visited the majority
of overseas Australian war memorials, where his conveyance of respect
was televised to the nation. In particular, he carried a diary belonging to
a family member when he visited French battlefields, signifying to the
nation that he too had been touched by war. Howard legitimated his
authority as an Australian leader of the nation by vicariously linking
himself to the digger tradition through his family's wartime contribution. He strategically deployed the digger nationalism connecting World

War I to Timor and then Iraq to substantiate our involvement in war by frequently using the term "digger" in his speeches.[29] Howard was at ANZAC Cove, Gallipoli, when a contingent of Australian troops arrived in Muthanna Province, in southern Iraq, on April 25, 2005.[30] Howard's performative reiterations of digger nationalist subjectivity to justify Australia's deployment in Iraq, in the name of patriarchal white sovereignty, perpetuates the historical connection of the white male body to possession and war. Howard's militarization of Australian history through the digger rescripted nationalism and resulted in an unprecedented rise in attendance by predominately white youth at memorial services above the beach at ANZAC Cove during his time in office. The somber respect shown at the memorial service at ANZAC Cove performatively reiterates the relationship between the white male body, possession, and war in the defense of patriarchal white sovereignty signified by the place of encounter: the beach.

In Australia, on December 11, 2005, the beach once again became a place where transgression, violence, and white possession were on display. On that day at Cronulla Beach, approximately five thousand predominately white men rioted over the alleged bashing of a surf lifesaver by an Arabic-speaking youth. The racialized production of the "terrorist" as an internal and external threat to the nation after the 9/11 attacks and the bombings in Bali provides a context within which to understand the Cronulla protesters' rearticulation of white Australians' possessive claims on the beach as their sovereign ground.[31] This is most clearly signified by the pervasiveness of wearing and waving the Australian flag, explicit claims to white possession on T-shirts, inscribed on torsos with body paint, and written on placards waved before media cameras during the protest, such as "We Grew Here: You Flew Here," "We're full, fuck off," "Respect locals or piss off," and the sign written on the beach for the overhead cameras, "100% Aussie Pride." The white male body became the signifier of protest, embedding itself within the material body of the sand through the inscription of the slogan "100% Aussie Pride." These embodied significations construct whiteness as an inalienable property, the purity of which is always potentially at threat from racialized others through contamination and dispossession.[32] At Cronulla, the white male body performatively repossessed the beach through anti-Arabic resentment, thus mimetically reproducing the racialized colonial violence enacted to dispossess Indigenous people.

In response to the events of 2005, one of Australia's leading Indigenous artists, Vernon Ah Kee of the Kuku Yalandji, Waanji, Yidinji, and Gugu Yimithirr peoples, challenged Australian popular culture, racism, and representations of Indigeneity in his exhibit at the Venice Biennale in 2009. The Cronulla riots provided a context for Ah Kee's art installation entitled *Cant Chant*, which offers its audience an Aboriginal man's rendering of the beach, drawing on, but in opposition to, its signification within popular culture as a site of everyday white male performativity and representations of "Australian-ness." Common ownership of the beach looms large in the Australian imagination, but as violent attacks on Cronulla Beach demonstrate, not everyone shares the same proprietary rights within that space. His work frames the beach as an important site for the defense and assumption of territorial sovereignty. It is the place where invaders have landed, and on Australia Day it is reenacted as the place where in 1788 Captain Arthur Phillip planted a flag in the name of some faraway sovereign to signify white possession.

Ah Kee plays with the idea that iconic beaches such as Bondi and Cronulla are white possessions, public spaces perceived within the white Australian imaginary as being urban and natural, civilized and primitive, spiritual and physical. He is acutely aware that the beach is a place where nature and culture become reconciled through the performativity of white male bodies such as lifesavers and surfers. Ah Kee undoes this reconciliation by disrupting the beach as a site of fantasy production where carnival and nature synergize as prehistory in the dialectical image of modernity. He challenges white possession of the beach by making visible the omnipresence of Indigenous sovereignty through the performativity of the Indigenous male body. In this way he brings forth the sovereign body of the Indigenous male into modernity, displacing the white male body on the beach.

The beach is Indigenous land and evokes different memories. As the viewer enters Ah Kee's installation, surfboards hang in the middle of the room, and painted Yadinji shields with markings on one side in red, yellow, and black, the colors of the Indigenous flag, signify our sovereignty and resistance. On the other side of the surfboards, the eyes of Aboriginal male warriors gaze silently at their audience, bearing witness to their uninvited presence. The gaze of Ah Kee's grandfather looks to the east, surveying the coastline in anticipation of invaders. The silent gaze is broken by the text on the walls: "Ah Kee the sovereign warrior speaks his truth. We grew here you flew here, we are the first people, we have to tolerate you, we are not your other, you are dangerous people and your duty is to accept the truth for you will be constantly reminded of your wrong doing by our presence. Aboriginal people are not hybrids and will not comply with what you think you have made us become." Moving out of the first room, the viewer enters another, where a video clip intermittently echoes the sounds of the land and water with the song "Stompin' Ground," sung by Warumpi, an Indigenous band. The song's message to its audience: if you want to know this country and if you want to change your ways, you need to go to the stomping ground for ceremonial business. Ah Kee performatively reiterates Indigenous sovereignty through the use of this song, which offers its white audience a way to belong to this country that is outside the logic of capital and patriarchal white sovereignty. Here Ah Kee also plays with irony because the "Stomp" was the surfers' dance made famous by Little Pattie, one of Australia's original surfie-chick icons. And white Australian youths have continued to stomp all over the beach as shown in video clips for Australian rock bands such as INXS and Midnight Oil, in soap operas such as *Home and Away,* and in the movie *Puberty Blues.*[33] Ah Kee's juxtaposition of the Warumpi band's call to dance for the land and the white performative dancing on the land reiterates Indigenous Australia's challenge to white possessive performances and their grounding in patriarchal white sovereignty.

At the entrance to the second room, Ah Kee invites his audience to bear witness to a seeming anomaly: Aboriginal surfers at the beach. The video shows the Aboriginal surfers walking around the Gold Coast, surveying the beach before entering it with their shield surfboards. The surprised look of a white male gaze is captured on film. This surprise suggests that to the white male beachgoer, Aboriginal surfers are out of place; they are not white in need of a tan, they belong in the landscape in the middle of Australia, not on the beach. Ah Kee plays on this anomaly by taking his audience to the landscape away from the beach, where death is signified by two cemeteries. Suddenly guns are fired repeatedly at two white surfboards encased with barbed wire, one hanging from a tree, the other tied to a rock. The barbed wire evokes the fencing off of the land against Indigenous sovereignty and the wire that was used in the trenches at Gallipoli, both signifying death and destruction. Here Ah Kee brings forth repressed memories of the violence of massacres, incarceration, and dispossession hidden in landscape that is far away from the beach. There is silence as the clip moves back to the beach, where memories of the violence inflicted on Aboriginal people are repressed by its iconic status within the Australian imagination. Suddenly a lone Indigenous surfer appears on his shield surfboard gracefully moving through the water, displaying his skill as he takes command of the waves. He is not out of place. He embodies the resilience of Indigenous sovereignty disrupting the iconography of the beach that represents all that is Australian within white popular culture. Like a stingray barb piercing the heart of white Australia, Ah Kee's masterful use of irony and anomaly reinserts the Indigenous male body at the beach, displacing the white male body as the embodiment of possession 239 years after Captain Cook's originary possessive performance.

Conclusion

The production of the beach as a white possession is both fantasy and reality within the Australian imagination and is tied to a beach culture encompassing pleasure, leisure, and national pride that developed during modernity through the embodied performance of white masculinity. As a border, the beach is constituted by epistemological, ontological, and axiological violence, whereby the nation's past and present treatment of Indigenous people becomes invisible and negated through performative acts of possession that ontologically and socially ground white male bodies. White possession becomes normalized and regulated within society through socially sanctioned embodied performative acts of Australian beach culture. The reiterative nature of these performances is required because within this borderland the omnipresence of Indigenous sovereignty ontologically disturbs patriarchal white sovereignty's possession and its originary violence. Ah Kee's work powerfully demonstrates the resilience of Indigenous sovereignty and its ability to disturb ontologically the performativity of white possession. Continuing the tradition of his ancestors, it is appropriate in the twenty-first century that the silence of the beach becomes the object of Vernon Ah Kee's sovereign artistic warrior-ship.

4 WRITING OFF TREATIES

Possession in the U.S. Critical
Whiteness Literature

WHITENESS STUDIES PROLIFERATED in the United States in the
1990s in response to overt acts of racist violence reported in the press
and the need to reconsider the persistence of racism in light of the proposition that race was socially constructed and not biologically determined. Whiteness studies scholars share in common their commitment
to racial justice, antiracism, and a more humane society. In most of the
literature, prescriptive politics assume a central role; many writers are
committed to the abolition of whiteness through naming it, deconstructing it, resisting it, and betraying it. Their scholarship is informed
by a variety of disciplines, such as literary studies, cultural studies,
anthropology, feminism, postcolonialism, sociology, and history, while
their research methods include textual analysis, ethnography, inter-
views, surveys, and the archival. Whiteness studies has entered Canada and crossed both the Pacific and Atlantic Oceans, providing a new
history of race and modernity in "settler" colonies and empire. However,
the United States remains one of the most productive sites for whiteness
studies—a field of studies that is full of contradictions and ambivalences
as well as sympathetic critics.

Mike Hill argues that "the contradictions surrounding whiteness
studies remain one of its most salient and worthwhile features.... The
study of whiteness was never—and with hard enough work will never
be—an unproblematically unified institutional force."[1] Debates about
the epistemological assumptions and approaches to whiteness within the
field continue to surface. Robyn Wiegman surmises that the contradic-
tory nature of white power has been underplayed by Dyer and other
white studies scholars through claiming its invisibility and universality
as the source of its power. Wiegman argues that the universal serves

to work in the interests of white particularity. This particularity simultaneously distances itself from white supremacy and denies the benefits of white power, which creates a disassociation that takes the form of "liberal whiteness, a colour blind moral sameness."[2] Peter Kolchin critiques whiteness studies for its lack of historical specificity, and the claim that whiteness is everything or nothing leads him to question whether it is a useful tool of inquiry and explanation. He argues that "underlying the new interest in white power, privilege and identity there is evident an intense discouragement over the persistence of racism, the unexpected renewal of nationalism, and the collapse of progressive movements for social change."[3] Stephen Knadler cautions whiteness studies scholars against "an increasing linguistic slippage from the fiction of race into the fiction of racism."[4] The pliable morphology of whiteness, its utilization of the universal, the lack of historical specificity, and the linguistic slippage that fictionalizes racism as problems have shaped this chapter in considering the relationship of this field of study to Indigenous sovereignties.

The field of whiteness studies is not a uniquely white enterprise. African Americans have commented on and written about whiteness since the early 1800s.[5] African American scholarship has been influential, particularly the work of W. E. B. Du Bois and, more recently, Toni Morrison, whose seminal text, *Playing in the Dark: Whiteness and the Literary Imagination,* challenged the naturalized whiteness of American literature by illuminating how the omnipresence of African Americans has historically shaped it.[6] She exposes the embedded racial assumptions that enable whiteness to characterize itself in the literary imagination in powerful and important ways. In her analysis of Ernest Hemingway's *To Have and Have Not,* Morrison illustrates how black men and women were positioned as inferiors within his texts to prop up white masculinity.[7] Morrison further suggests in *Black Matters* that the African American presence has also "shaped the body politic, the Constitution, and the entire history of the [U.S.] culture."[8] Indigenous peoples are outside the scope of Morrison's analysis. Through the centering of the African American presence, Native American texts that have challenged, resisted, and affected the American literary imagination, politics, history, and Constitution remain invisible. This silence is an interesting discursive move, considering that the best-selling novels in the United States in the late eighteenth century were captivity narratives. And as Native American legal scholar Raymond Williams argues, it was the positioning of Indians as incommensurable savages within the Declaration of Independence that enabled "the Founders' vision of America's growth and potentiality as a new form of expansionary white racial dictatorship in the world."[9] The most valuable contribution of Morrison's work for my purposes is her thesis that "blackness," whether real or imagined, services the social construction and application of whiteness in its myriad forms. In this way it is used as a white epistemological possession. Her work opens up a space for considering how this possessiveness operates within the whiteness studies literature to displace Indigenous sovereignties and render them invisible.

White Possessiveness

Most historians mark 1492 as the year when imperialism began to construct the old world order by taking possession of other people, their lands and resources. The possessive nature of this enterprise informed the development of a racial stratification process on a global scale that became solidified in modernity. Taking possession of Indigenous people's lands was a quintessential act of colonization and was tied to the transition from the Enlightenment to modernity, which precipitated the emergence of a new subject into history within Europe. Major social, legal, economic, and political reforms had taken place, changing the feudal nature of persons and property relationship between the sixteenth and eighteenth centuries. "These changes centred upon the rise of 'possessive individualism,' that is, upon an increasing consciousness of the distinctness of each self-owning human entity as the primary social and political value."[10] Private ownership of property, both tangible and intangible, operated through mechanisms of the new nation-state in its regulation of the population and especially through the law. By the late 1700s, people could legally enter into different kinds of contractual arrangements whereby they could own land, sell their labor, and possess their identities, all of which were formed through their relationship to capital and the state. A new white property-owning subject emerged in history and possessiveness became embedded in everyday discourse as "a firm belief that the best in life was the expansion of self through property and property began and ended with possession of one's body."[11] Within the realm of intrasubjectivity, possession can mean control over one's being, ideas, one's mind, one's feelings, and one's body, or within intersubjectivity it can mean the act or fact of possessing something that is beyond the subject, and in other contexts it can refer to a state of being possessed by another. Within the law, possession can refer to holding or occupying territory with or without actual ownership or a thing possessed, such as property or wealth, and it can also refer to territorial domination of a state. At an ontological level, the structure of subjective possession occurs through the imposition of one's will-to-be on the thing that is perceived to lack will; thus it is open to being possessed. This enables the formally free subject to make the thing its own. Ascribing one's own subjective will onto the thing is required to make it one's property, as "wilful possession of what was previously a will-less thing constitutes our primary form of embodiment; it is invoked whenever we assert: this is mine."[12] To be able to assert "this is mine" requires a subject to internalize the idea that one has proprietary rights that are part of normative behavior, rules of interaction, and social engagement. Thus possession that forms part of the ontological structure of white subjectivity is reinforced by its socio-discursive functioning.

White Writing

A number of texts have been written historicizing the acquisition of white identity and the privileges conferred by its status through a trope of migration that is based on the assumption that all those who came after the white folk had taken possession are the immigrants. White possession of the nation works discursively within these texts to displace Native American sovereignties by disavowing that everyone else in the United States are immigrants, whether they came in chains or by choice. The only displacement that is theorized is in relation to African Americans. Theodore Allen's work on how the Irish became white in America illustrates that the transformation of their former status as the blacks of Europe relied on their displacement by African Americans in the new country.[13] David Roediger discusses how the wages of whiteness operated to prevent class alliances between working-class whites and African Americans.[14] Karen Brodkin's excellent book on how Jews became white demonstrates that the lower status of African American workers enabled Jewish class mobility.[15] M. F. Jacobsen illustrates that European migrants were able to become white through ideological and political means that operated to distinguish them from African American blackness.[16] The black/white binary permeates these analyses, enabling tropes of migration and slavery to work covertly in these texts, thus erasing the continuing history of colonization and the Native American sovereign presence. Blackness becomes an epistemological possession that Allen, Roediger, Brodkin, and Jacobsen deploy in analyzing whiteness and race, which forecloses the possibility that the dispossession of Native Americans was tied to migration and the establishment of slavery driven by the logic of capital. Slaves were brought to America as the property of white people to work the land that was appropriated from Native America tribes. Subsequently, migration became a means to enhance capitalist development in the United States. Migration, slavery, and the dispossession of Native Americans were integral to the project of nation building. Thus the question of how anyone came to be white or black in the United States is inextricably tied to the dispossession of the original owners and the assumption of white possession. The various assumptions of sovereignty, beginning with British "settlers," the formation of individual states, and subsequently the United States, all came into existence through the blood-stained taking of Native American land. The United States as a white nation-state cannot exist without land and clearly defined borders; it is the legally defined and asserted territorial sovereignty that provides the context for national identifications of whiteness. In this way I argue that Native American dispossession indelibly marks configurations of white national identity.

Ruth Frankenberg, in the introduction to her edited collection *Displacing Whiteness*, acknowledges that whiteness traveled culturally and physically, impacting on the formation of nationhood, class, and empire sustained by imperialism and global capitalism. She wrote that notions of race were tied "to ideas about legitimate 'ownership' of the nation, with 'whiteness' and 'Americanness' linked tightly together," and that this history was repressed.[17] After making this statement, she then moves on to discuss immigration and its effects.[18] Her acknowledgment did not progress into critical analysis that centered Native American dispossession; instead Frankenberg represses that which she acknowledges is repressed. Repression operates as a defense mechanism to protect one's perception of self and reality from an overwhelming trauma that may threaten one's self-image. Repressing the history of Native American dispossession works to protect the possessive white self from ontological disturbance. It is far easier to extricate oneself from the history of slavery if there is no direct family and material ties to its institution and reproduction. However, it is not as easy to distance one's self from a history of Indigenous dispossession when one benefits every day from being tied to a nation that has and continues to constitute itself as a white possession.

Within the whiteness studies literature, whiteness has been defined in multiple ways. It is usually perceived as unnamed, unmarked, and invisible, and often as culturally empty, operating only by appropriation and absence.[19] It is a location of structural privilege, a subject position, and a cultural praxis.[20] Whiteness constitutes the norm operating within various institutions, influencing decision making and defining itself by what it is not.[21] It is socially constructed and is a form of property that one possesses, invests in, and profits from.[22] Whiteness as a social identity works discursively, becoming ubiquitous, fluid, and dynamic,[23] operating invisibly through pedagogy.[24] What these different definitions of whiteness expose is that whiteness is something that can be possessed, and it is tied to power and dominance despite being fluid, vacuous, and invisible to white people. However, these different conceptualizations of whiteness, which use blackness as an epistemological possession to service what it is not, obscure the more complex way that white possession functions socio-discursively through subjectivity and knowledge production. As something that can be possessed by subjects, it must have ontological and epistemological anchors in order to function through power. As a means of controlling differently racialized populations enclosed within the borders of a given society, white subjects are disciplined, though to different degrees, to invest in the nation as a white possession that imbues them with a sense of belonging and ownership. This sense of belonging is derived from ownership as understood within the logic of capital and citizenship. In its self-legitimacy, white possession operates discursively through narratives of the home of the brave and the land of the free and through white male signifiers of the nation such as the Founding Fathers, the "pioneer," and the "war hero." Against this stands the Indigenous sense of belonging, home, and place in its sovereign incommensurable difference.

Black Writing

Within African American scholarship, whiteness is theorized as a form of power, as supremacy, as hegemony, as ideology and ontology; rarely is the theoretical focus the social construction of white identity, and whiteness is not invisible, unnamed, or unmarked. As Stephen Knadler states, "In contrast to whites who have traditionally located racism in 'colour consciousness and find its absence in colour blindness' peoples of colour have emphasized more how racism involves 'institutionalized systems of power' and racialised practices that are part of everyday experience."[25] Bell hooks argues that whiteness in the everyday is connected to "the mysterious, the strange, and the terrible," and while African Americans may imitate whites, they are still suspicious and afraid of them.[26] Charles W. Smith evaluates whiteness according to a white supremacy paradigm because he argues we are dealing with white systematic domination. He notes that "the idea of white supremacy is intended, in part, to capture the crucial reality that the normal workings of the social system continue to disadvantage blacks in large measure independently of racist feeling."[27] George Yancy examines the social ontology of whiteness, arguing that a central component is the reluctance by whites to discuss their investments in whiteness and its connection to white supremacy and racism, which are perceived as anomalies.[28] Valarie Bhabb illuminates how the ideology of whiteness supports and reinforces systemic privilege and informs the way it is represented in American literature and culture. She argues that "by ascribing common qualities to a select racial group, the ideology of whiteness could accomplish exclusion without explicit rationales of racial superiority."[29] One of the few scholars to connect the formation of whiteness to the appropriation of Indigenous lands is Cheryl Harris. She argues that whiteness became a form of property originally through the appropriation of Indigenous peoples' lands and the subsequent enslavement of African Americans. However, the center of Harris's theory is how "blackness" enabled whiteness as a form of property. What circulates discursively within this literature is the idea that African Americans were possessions that could be bought and sold, and the basis of this status was premised on their being perceived as inferior beings, and freedom from slavery did not bring racial equality.

The theoretical focus on the structural and systematic nature of white supremacy within this literature indicates that the nation is perceived to be a white possession that confers propriety on whites through the racial contract between the state and its citizens. African American scholar Charles W. Mills argues that it is the racial contract that stipulates who can count as full moral and political persons, setting the boundaries for those who can "contract" in to the freedom and equality that it promises and those who must be kept out.[30] White possession operates socio-discursively to produce the racial contract as a regulatory ideal that enables, constrains, and disciplines subjects in various ways. The possessiveness of white subjectivity is thus regulated through its relationship with the nation-state. African Americans have limited access to this proprietariness because the possessive claim to be truly human and a full citizen is underpinned by whiteness.

In the United States, the sovereignty claims of Native American and Pacific Island nations under its jurisdiction are not configured through citizenship rights. They are different from other minority rights at the center of the struggle for racial equality because they are not "based on equality of treatment under the Constitution and the general civil rights laws."[31] Their sovereignty is not epistemologically and ontologically grounded in the citizenship of the white liberal subject of modernity. The coexistence of these different and competing sovereignties complicates white possession and the way in which it shapes knowledge production. The historical amnesia about Indigenous sovereignty occurring in the whiteness literature is tied to a political and epistemological commitment to the idea of the universal white liberal subject. Freedom, liberty, and equality operate discursively, marking critique scoped through the black/white binary in ways that require the exclusion of Native American sovereignties. The relationship between the nation-state, Native Americans, and other Indigenous peoples colonized by it is an outcome of colonization, the establishment of "democracy," and its universal white liberal subject. Indigenous peoples' sovereignty claims are outside the individualized rights framework accorded to this subject. Indigenous rights are collective rights based on an ownership of land that is not configured through the logic of capital.

Outside Whiteness and Race

Despite the colonial history of the United States and the racializing of Native Americans in popular culture, as the embodiment of "redness," the whiteness literature makes a racial demarcation between African Americans and Native Americans. That is, by making blackness synonymous with "race," African Americans are placed in a reified position within the literature. This binary understanding of "race" in one sense places the literature out of colonial history. That is, the theorizing about whiteness does not begin with or center the appropriation of Indigenous peoples' lands and the continuing sovereignty struggles with the U.S. nation-state. This is not to say that Native Americans are not mentioned in the whiteness literature. They are, but they are marginalized within the theories of race and whiteness that whiteness studies offers, despite its epistemological engagement with white race privilege and power. The conceptual links between the privileges and benefits that flow from American citizenship to Native American dispossession remain invisible. Instead, slavery, war, and migration are the narratives by which the historically contingent positionality of whiteness unfolds. This reflects a failure to address the socio-discursive way that white possession functions to produce racism.

White possession was operating socio-discursively when President Bill Clinton established his Advisory Board on Race in June 1997 to counsel and inform him about race and racial reconciliation.[32] No Native American representative was appointed to the board, even though Native Americans are the only racial group required to carry a blood quantum card as proof of their tribal membership.[33] The terms of reference of the advisory board were couched within a civil rights framework that presupposed a particular relationship with the nation-state that did not include Indigenous sovereignties. This exclusion was the catalyst for numerous protests by different Native American groups who argued that Native Americans do share with other racial groups the need for improving their socioeconomic and legal conditions. However, there were other conditions not shared with other racial groups, because of their respective sovereignties and treating with the nation-state. They argued that the racism they experience is predicated on this relationship. Native American sovereignty is constantly under threat by the nation-state and its various mechanisms of governance, such as the plenary powers of the United States Congress. Within their daily lives, Native Americans experience the effects of broken treaties, loss of land and cultural rights, genocide, and breaches of fiduciary duty. They are confronted by the constant battle with congressmen and state governors who wish to diminish their rights by "framing the economic and political empowerment of Indigenous tribes as evidence of a threatening tribal movement to transgress the temporal and spatial boundaries of colonial rule, consume American property and colonise the American political system."[34] Resisting and diminishing Native American sovereignties also include tactics such as positioning their claims

outside racism, which serves to protect and reinscribe possessive investments in the nation as a white possession.

Some twelve months later, in 1998, President Clinton was invited to
discuss his Race Advisory Board with a panel of eight people on a PBS
broadcast. One member of the panel was Native American Sherman
Alexie. The panel discussed with Clinton a number of race issues, including affirmative action. During the show Clinton did not address Native
American sovereignty claims but tried to connect with Alexie by informing him that his grandmother was one-quarter Cherokee. Later in the
program Alexie was asked if he was often engaged by others in discussions about race, to which he replied that a dialogue often takes place
when he is approached by people who "tell me they're Cherokee."[35]
Here Clinton tries to capitalize on a Native American ancestry by staking a possessive claim to a subject position that is not purely white in
order to connect with his native brother while having excluded Native
Americans from the advisory board. This is a classic case of the exercising of white race privilege. Clinton can stake a possessive claim to
Cherokee descent because there is no threat to his investment in his
white identity, which carries a great deal of cultural capital and enables
him to make the claim on biological grounds outside Cherokee sovereignty. What Clinton was also signifying was that race does not matter: even a person of Cherokee descent can be president of the United
States because this is the land of freedom, liberty, and equality. Clinton's executive and personal actions serve to negate Native Americans'
claims that race and racism were operating when Indigenous peoples
were dispossessed, and they continue to mark their everyday lives and
sovereignty claims.

The genealogy of racism toward Native Americans can be traced
back to "Greek and Roman myths of warlike, barbarian tribes and
biblical accounts of wild men cursed by God," which informed
Renaissance-era travel narratives describing them as the embodiment
of primitive human savagery.[36] Enlightenment philosophers such as
John Locke and Thomas Hobbes developed their ideas of the state of
nature using the American Indian as the quintessential example of
"humanity living in its pure, unadulterated savage state."[37] These ideas
operated discursively to inform theories about the rights of man within
the context of the rise of democracy, relegating Indigenous people to a
state of nature without any sovereign rights. These ideas continue to
circulate, preventing Indigenous sovereignties from gaining recognition

as relevant and alternative visions of differently constituted moderni-
ties and global futures. The exclusion of Native Americans from the
Advisory Board on Race correlates with their invisibility within the
whiteness literature. Native Americans are located outside "racism"
because the status of the United States as a former colony and its current mode of colonization are separated from its historical narrative as
being the land of liberty, freedom, and equality.

Indigenous Writing

Few Native American scholars engage theoretically with whiteness studies literature. One exception is Frances V. Rains, who argues that "white
race privilege is the corollary to racism" because the unearned benefits
whites gain are derived from a system based on racial inequality
and stolen land.[38] However, "race" is embedded in the work of Native
American scholars. Robert Williams and Vine Deloria Jr. have written
extensively on the continuing colonization and exploitation of Native
Americans by white America,[39] and Devon A. Mihesuah has challenged
and demystified racialized stereotypes of Native Americans while illuminating the continuing racism in American society.[40] Within the
Native American literature, the racialization of their sovereignty struggles, in its many forms, is denoted by the concept "white man," which
is operationalized extensively as a metaphor for the nation-state and
American culture. The hegemony of white possession is exposed but not
explicitly theorized as such.

When reading the Native American legal history literature, the historical starting point is the invasion of their lands by "settlers" who were
the subjects of other countries and treaty making. Deloria and Lytle
argue that "treaty making became the basis for defining both the legal
and political relationships between Indians and European colonists.
And when the young colonies finally became the United States, the
treaty-making powers that earlier had been exercised by the European
nations were assumed by the Americans with their independence."[41]
However, not all Native Americans have treaties with the U.S. government, and those who seek to reclaim their status as a tribe must do
so under criteria formulated by the nation-state. Many Indigenous people have written about their sovereignty struggles in different ways.[42]
As Robert Warrior, writing about the work of Native American scholars John Joseph Mathews, Vine Deloria Jr., and others, argues: "Both

writers point to the process through which the U.S. government abrogated the sovereign–sovereign relationship with the Natives as a major turning point in the history of that conflict. The multifaceted battle to appropriate Native land, supplant Native religion, and undermine Native traditional social structures is the *mise-en-scène* of American Indian intellectual work of the past one hundred years."[43]

Other Indigenous peoples whose lands are also occupied and possessed by the United States, such as American Samoa, Hawai'i, and Guam, are invisible in the whiteness literature. However, within the academy, analyses of their sovereignty struggles and resistances are being written. In her groundbreaking book, *Aloha Betrayed,* Noenoe Silva has excavated the hidden history of Kanaka Maoli resistance to the invasion of Hawai'i by the United States.[44] Silva's work successfully erases the myth of Hawaiian passivity by revealing their resistance to colonialism and imperialism through examining historical newspaper reports written by Hawaiians in their own language. America's origin story of possession through annexation no longer holds sway; the Hawaiian queen and her people did not ask for "help" from the United States. Instead, it was a group of white capitalists and whites who positioned themselves as "native"-born Hawaiians who wanted "help" to secure possession of Hawai'i. They lobbied the U.S. government to invade and secure their interests by extending its sovereignty beyond its borders. Despite its illegality under international law, the United States complied with their demands. Taking possession of Hawai'i was in the best interests of the United States and its white citizens. The white American claim to Indigeneity to substantiate its possession is not new for Indigenous people of the Americas. Philip Deloria argues that one of the key origin stories for national identity within the United States is the Boston Tea Party. He asks, "Why of all the possible stories of rebellion and re-creation, has the notion of disguised Indians dumping tea in Boston Harbor had such a powerful hold on American's imaginations?" Articulating the paradox of white Americans playing Indian, he concludes:

> The self-defining pairing of American truth with American freedom rests on the ability to wield power against Indians—social, military, economic, and political—while simultaneously drawing power from them. Indianness may have existed primarily as a cultural artifact in American society, but it has helped create these other forms of power, which have then been turned back on native people. The dispossessing of Indians exists in tension with being

aboriginally true. . . . And so while Indian people have lived out a collection of historical nightmares in the material world, they have also haunted a long night of American dreams. As many native people have observed, to be American is to be unfinished. And although that state is powerful and creative, it carries with it nightmares all its own.[45]

Kehulani Kauanui argues that Hawaiian identity is also appropriated by white people as a way of indigenizing their presence within the Hawaiian landscape free from the history of colonial occupation by the United States. Their claims to Hawaiian identity are articulated through a discourse of equality and anti-Hawaiian sovereignty, as was evidenced in the formation of a group that named itself "Aloha for All." This white group supported a number of lawsuits against Native Hawaiians' receipt of government funds. They stated that "it is not in keeping with the spirit of Aloha for the government to give one racial group land or money or special privileges or preferences from which all other racial groups in Hawaii are excluded."[46] In this statement, Aloha for All makes a possessive claim on the nation-state by asserting how government funds can or cannot be used. The nation as a white possession confers privileges on whites living in Hawai'i that remain invisible to its recipients while they simultaneously exercise power. The numerous texts produced within academia by Indigenous peoples, particularly since the 1980s, raises the question of why their work does not surface more within the writing of whiteness studies scholars in the United States. Similarly, much of the Native American literature does not engage with whiteness studies. Perhaps this is because Native American scholarship, like Indigenous scholarship elsewhere, has sought to produce its own epistemological boundaries and knowledges to critique white possession in its multiple forms.

Australian Engagements with Whiteness Studies

This epistemological and ontological predisposition exists within a small number of monographs within the Australian context that explicitly engage with whiteness. Warwick Anderson's book *The Cultivation of Whiteness: Science, Health, and Racial Destiny in Australia* provides insights about how the white body was the principal research interest of medicine, which itself was a "discourse of settlement," in the antipodes.[47] Anderson's discourse of settlement fails to engage with the assumption of white sovereignty and Indigenous sovereignty in any critical way.

Instead, the indigenous body becomes the measure of white men's lack within the tropics. Ghassan Hage's seminal text, *White Nation: Fantasies of White Supremacy in a Multicultural Society*, illuminates fantasies of white supremacy and national loss, providing a window on the way whiteness uses both liberal and racist discourses in order to maintain its dominance by focusing on the multicultural nature of Australian society.[48] While Hage's book does address the relationship between multiculturalism, whiteness, and Indigenous sovereignty, it fails to consider in depth how Indigenous sovereignty shapes Australian politics and nationhood. Jon Stratton's *Race Daze: Australia in Identity Crisis* engages with whiteness as constituting the core element of Australian Anglo-Celtic identity to show how race still patrols the borders of multiculturalism, but he fails to excavate how migration is also a product of colonization and Indigenous dispossession.[49] However, there is an emerging body of work that explicitly engages in a variety of ways with colonization, migration, and Indigenous sovereignty.[50] In particular, the works of Ravenscroft, Nicoll, and Vassilacopoulos and Nicolacopoulos consider the relationship between Indigenous sovereignty and the psychosocial and ontological realms of white subjectivity, while others, such as Kate Foord, illustrate that the white fantasy of *terra nullius* and the disavowal of Indigenous sovereignty are fundamental to the narration of Australian identity and nation building.[51]

Conclusion

I have shown that tropes of migration and slavery are indelibly inscribed as the master narrative of white American national identity within the whiteness literature. This raises some interesting questions: Why are the appropriation of Indigenous peoples' lands and ensuing wars not perceived as having anything to do with the ongoing praxis of the United States as a white nation-state? Why is this continuing history written out of the whiteness literature? Does the historically constructed narrative of the nation as "liberator" rather than "colonizer" operate discursively in most of the whiteness literature because the legitimacy of the sovereignty of the United States is taken for granted? These questions cannot be answered in this chapter, but they highlight an epistemological and ontological a priori at the heart of the whiteness literature: the unequivocal acceptance that the United States is a white possession.

The work produced in the field of whiteness studies in the United States is written on and yet over the sovereign ground of Native Americans and Indigenous people from its other territories. The failure of this literature to address the explicit colonial and continuing imperial position of the nation-state results in the writing off of Indigenous sovereignties as fundamental to its establishment and existence in the service of white possession. Perhaps the selective historical amnesia displayed within the whiteness literature is partly the result of scholars not being epistemologically and ontologically open to being a disoriented, displaced, and diasporic racialized subject whose existence within the nation-state is predicated on the continuing divestment of Indigenous peoples' sovereign rights. As long as the field of whiteness studies remains locked in to the black/white binary and tropes of migration and slavery, the nation as a white possession will continue to operate discursively and invisibly within knowledge production of the United States academy. And the silence and marginalization of Indigenous sovereignties that work to exclude and reinscribe the black/white binary services a particular way of being in the United States.

II. Becoming Propertyless

5 NULLIFYING NATIVE TITLE

A Possessive Investment in Whiteness

For those in power in the West . . . Whiteness is felt to be the
human condition . . . it alone defines normality and fully inhabits
it. . . . White people have power and believe that they think, feel
and act like and for all people; White people, unable to see their
particularity, cannot take account of other people's; White people
create the dominant images of the world and don't quite see that
they thus construct the world in their own image; White people
set the standards of humanity by which they are bound to succeed
and others bound to fail. Most of this is not done deliberately and
maliciously; there are enormous variations in power amongst
White people to do with class, gender and other factors; goodwill
is not unheard of in White people's engagement with others.
White power none the less reproduces itself regardless of intention,
power differences and goodwill, and overwhelmingly because it is
not seen as Whiteness, but as normal.

—Richard Dyer, *White: Essays on Race and Culture*

The Legal legacy of . . . the seizure of land from [Indigenous] peoples
is not merely a regime of property law that is (mis)informed by
racist and ethnocentric themes. Rather, the law has established
and protected an actual property interest in whiteness itself, which
shares the critical characteristics of property and accords with the
many and varied theoretical descriptions of property.

—Cheryl Harris, *"Whiteness as Property," in Black on White:
Black Writers on What It Means to Be White*

WHITENESS IN ITS DOMINANT contemporary form in Australian
society is Anglicized, institutionalized, and culturally based. Australian
culture is less white than it used to be, but Anglicized whiteness forms
the center where white men established institutions encouraging a

possessive investment in whiteness.[1] Colonial and subsequent governments legitimated the appropriation of Indigenous lands, racialized
incarceration and enslavement, and limited naturalized citizenship to
white immigrants.[2] While blackness was congruent with Indigenous
subjugation and subordination, patriarchal whiteness was perceived
as being synonymous with freedom and citizenship.

This chapter argues that patriarchal whiteness is imbued with power.
It confers dominance and a property right that has consequences for the
distribution of wealth, status, and opportunity in Australia for Indigenous people. I will demonstrate this through an analysis of the discourse
about native title with reference to the *Mabo* and *Wik* decisions, amendments to the Native Title Act 1993, and recent decisions made by the
United Nations Committee on the Elimination of Racial Discrimination.

Patriarchal whiteness is an invisible unnamed organizing principle
that surreptitiously shapes social relations and economic development.
Indigenous people continue to be the most impoverished group in Australian society in critical areas such as housing, health, education, criminal justice, employment, and economic development. Race and gender
are salient in determining who rules and who accumulates property and
wealth.[3]

The patriarchal Australian State has a long history of a possessive
investment in whiteness. White women, Indigenous women, and Indigenous men were excluded from designing and establishing the legal
and political institutions that control and maintain the social structure
under which Australians now live. The application of the legal fiction
terra nullius ("land belonging to no one") was tantamount to the recognition of British sovereignty and the subsequent investment of property
rights in men.[4] Indigenous People and some white women experienced
the power of white property as acts of violence sanctioned by the law.
Simultaneously, these laws were perceived as customary, normal, and
natural by white male colonizers. Patriarchal whiteness manifested
itself in Australian law by defining who was and who was not white
and conferred privilege by identifying what legal entitlements accrued
to those categorized as white. Whiteness became a form of property.

Although the concept of "property" commonly refers to things owned
by persons, or the rights of persons with respect to a thing, it is more
than a relationship to the tangible and embraces metaphysical rights
such as reputation. As Cheryl Harris notes, "Property rights and interests embrace much more than land and personality. Thus, the fact that

whiteness is not a 'physical' entity does not remove it from the realm of property."[5] In other words, patriarchal whiteness can be deployed simultaneously or separately as status, identity, and property. As a form of property, patriarchal whiteness is a valuable possession warranting protection. Patriarchal whiteness invests in property rights and is possessive and protective about asset accumulation and ownership. Here I use the term "possessive" to mean having an excessive desire to own, control, and dominate, and I use the term "invest" to denote the effort spent toward a given end.

Misunderstanding the *Mabo* Decision

After a sustained effort over a number of years by Koiki Mabo and others, the existence of indigenous proprietary rights in land was recognized in 1992 by the High Court of Australia in *Mabo and Others v. Queensland (No. 2)* (1992). The High Court decisions were proclaimed by the media and lawyers as reversing the legal fiction of *terra nullius* through the recognition of native title. However, Professor Kent McNeil, whose groundbreaking work on native title in Canada was relied upon by the plaintiffs, argues that the rule of extinguishment used by the High Court in the *Mabo* decision is inconsistent with the broad rule of common law. The High Court's interpretation that "at Common law, native title can be extinguished or impaired by a valid exercise of sovereign power, inconsistent with the continued enjoyment or unimpaired enjoyment of native title," transgresses the common-law rule that the Crown cannot derogate from the vested interests of its subjects.[6] This rule is encapsulated in the Privy Council decision in *Attorney General of the Isle of Man v. Mylchreest*.[7] In this case the traditional owner, Mylchreest, sought an injunction to prevent the Crown from granting a lease of a portion of his land to a third party. The Court of Chancery granted the injunction holding that the Crown grant is invalid because it interfered with Mylchreest's customary rights. However, Mylchreest then leased his land to the third party. The Crown subsequently decided that it would challenge this, and the Privy Council found that "customary rights are to be protected against Crown grants, and that was the case in 1405 when the first grant was made and it was true in 1610 when the second grand was made and it was also true in 1867, when the Crown attempted to grant the sand and clay to the defendants in this action."[8]

In other words, the common law recognizes and protects customary rights and as such the Crown cannot derogate from the vested rights of its subjects. McNeil argues that "it is doesn't matter whether those rights were derived from Crown grant or adverse possession or customary law. That is a fundamental limitation on the executive power."[9] Effectively what the High Court did in *Mabo* was invent a rule of extinguishment that did not exist under common law, to allow for inconsistent grants to extinguish native title prior to the Racial Discrimination Act 1975. That is, it invented a rule of extinguishment that allowed the Crown to retrospectively derogate from the vested rights of its Indigenous subjects. In doing so, the High Court judges made a decision based on politics and economics rather than the rule of the law. The decision protects the property interests of patriarchal whiteness by reinscribing the legitimacy of the sovereignty of the white patriarchal nation-state. The decision affirms white identity by creating in law a hybrid of settlement that diminishes but does not erase *terra nullius*.

In *Mabo*, the common law ensured the continuance of patriarchal whiteness as a system that protects the property and privileges of whites by allowing the vested rights of Indigenous people prior to 1975 to be diminished. Despite the High Court's decision in favor of white patriarchal property rights and the Keating Government's promotion that justice had prevailed, the decision was strongly protested by the National Party as well as mining and pastoralist groups. These bastions of patriarchal whiteness lobbied the Keating Government to either legislate away the decision or ensure "certainty of tenure," which became a key catch phrase within the discourse on native title. Mining Company chief executives made comments such as: "If there is any uncertainty about land-holder titles, that should be cleared up. Company Directors needed some comfort that they were signing secure land titles. . . . The [*Mabo*] decision had considerable uncertainty and needed to be addressed by the government as a matter of urgency."[10]

The possessive relationship between patriarchal whiteness and asset accumulation underpinned the "certainty of tenure" politics. Fear was strategically deployed as a tool to mobilize public support. The message was clear: white property rights were being eroded by native title. The Commonwealth responded to the "certainty of tenure" politics by holding consultation with all relevant stakeholders in the process of developing its legislative responses to the *Mabo* decision. The outcome was the Commonwealth Native Title Act 1993 and, due to the inclusion and involvement of the National Indigenous Working Group in delibera- tions, native titleholders gained some concessions at the expense of some losses.

Under the act, our customary rights were recognized and an Indig- enous land fund was established for Indigenous groups that, through various acts of dispossession, could not make a native title claim. We retained a right to negotiate subject to arbitration and ministerial veto in the national interest, and the "freehold standard" was to be applied to native title after 1993.[11] The Native Title Act 1993 delivered to pas- toralists a guarantee that they would be able to renew their existing leases on identical terms and conditions without ever consulting with a native titleholder. And it allowed the validation of land grants made after 1975, which might have been invalid because of the Racial Dis- crimination Act 1975. The Native Title Act 1993 gave Indigenous peo- ple limited political and economic power, but the terms and conditions were shaped by a possessive investment in patriarchal whiteness.

Pursuant to the *Mabo* decision and the subsequent Native Title Act 1993, Indigenous people are in effect trespassers in the land until they prove their native title.[12] The law places the burden of proof for native title on the Indigenous people to demonstrate to courts of law con- trolled by predominantly white men. Since courts regard the written word as more reliable than oral testimonies, all claimants must be able to substantiate their oral histories with documents written by white people, such as explorers, public servants, historians, lawyers, anthro- pologists, pastoralists, and police. These documents are often in con- flict with Indigenous representations; lawyers and judges usually seek to resolve the disjuncture by introducing the texts or oral testimonies of additional white experts.[13] Thus, patriarchal whiteness sets the cri- teria for proof and the standards for credibility. Confirmation of the Indigenous presence in the landscape is dependent on the written words and oral testimonies of white people, which is a direct manifes- tation of the law's legitimation of whiteness as a form of property. As Harris argues that "by recognising the reputational interest in being regarded as white, as a thing of significant value, which like other repu- tational interests, [is] intrinsically bound up with identity and person- hood . . . a property interest [can] be asserted. In this context, [patriarchal] whiteness [is] a form of status property."[14]

Whitewashing the *Wik* Decision and Negating the Native Title Act 1993

Almost three years after parliament passed the Native Title Act, the High Court in June 1996 ruled on *Wik Peoples v. State of Queensland and Ors*. The Court held that pastoral leases did not give pastoralists exclusive possession of their land and that native title is not necessarily extinguished on pastoral leases. Instead, native title coexisted with pastoral leases, but only to the extent of any inconsistency between the two titles, which would be resolved in favor of the pastoralist. In response to this, the bastions of patriarchal whiteness deployed an overt oppositional campaign demonstrating their possessiveness. The National Farmers Federation and the mining industry were the main protagonists utilizing the "certainty of tenure" mantra to undermine native title rights. Native title claimants were positioned as a threat to industry, development, and the interests of the nation. Such a positioning is predicated on the idea that the real property interests of the nation are white, and they must be protected. The National Farmers Federation, the Mining Council, and the National Party reacted to the *Wik* decision by demanding exclusive possession through upgrading leasehold to freehold title. Martin Taylor argues:

> Beginning in 1957, most leases could readily be converted into freeholding leases, by signing onto a mortgage agreement for eventual freehold rights. Many pre-1994 freehold leases were interest-free and *continue to be so*. Payments did not even cover the cost of collection. . . . Queensland has the largest proportion of pastoral lands under leasehold titles. Hence Queensland is the state where pastoralists are the loudest opponents of native title. A long period of exclusive occupancy in combination with token rents has cemented in the minds of many pastoralists a perception of "ownership" that is not legally justified.[15]

Prior to *Wik*, pastoralists assumed that the relationship between patriarchal whiteness and asset accumulation was protected by law.[16] Pastoralists relied on the system protecting their privilege and property by excluding it from others.

The National Farmers Federation and the mining industry lobbied the new Howard-led Commonwealth government, demanding amendments to the Native Title Act 1993. The government complied and Prime Minister John Howard excluded Indigenous people from the negotiations over amendments. And on national television on September 4,

1997, he displayed a map claiming that Indigenous people could veto development over 79 percent of Australia's landmass.[17] Later in the same week in parliament, he stated that it was possible for native title claims to be made over 79 percent of Australia.[18] The map Howard displayed was developed by the National Farmers Federation and conflicts with advice given to the National Indigenous Working Group that only 40 percent of land under pastoral lease is claimable.[19]

Collusion between white interest groups and the prime minister in the campaign of misinformation reveals that there is a possessive investment in patriarchal whiteness, which will act to reinforce white privilege, protect property, and preserve dominance. Howard agreed to amend the Native Title Act, stating that "it was simply not possible for the state of the law immediately post-Wik to be maintained. I have never denied that major changes to the right to negotiate were essential. . . . The fact is that the Wik decision pushed the pendulum too far into the Aboriginal direction. The 10 point Plan will return the pendulum to the centre."[20] Howard's premise that the law favored Indigenous property rights and that it had to be corrected reveals his possessive investment in patriarchal whiteness. He is selective about whose proprietary rights are to be protected and entrenched within existing regimes of power. His possessive investment in patriarchal whiteness endorses white accumulation of property by diminishing Indigenous property rights.

Although the National Indigenous Working Group was excluded from negotiations concerning the amendments to the Native Title Act 1993, the group established the Wik Summit to discuss and resolve the concerns of all stakeholders and developed the "Co-Existence: Negotiation and Certainty Document" for consideration by government and stakeholders. Representatives of government did not attend the Wik Summit, nor did they provide a response to the "Co-Existence" document.[21] The right to negotiate with government was reserved for those who held a possessive investment in patriarchal whiteness, which confers on its owners aspects of citizenship that can be denied to others.[22]

Deliberations on the 10-point Plan began in the Senate on November 28, 1997. The bill was passed, amended, and returned to the House of Representatives, where Howard moved a motion rejecting the majority of proposed amendments made by the Senate on the basis of four points:

The registration test;
The right to negotiate;
The proposal to make the NTA subject to the provisions of the RDA;
The sunset clause.[23]

Another motion was later passed in the House of Representatives that outlined amendments that were acceptable to the government. Howard argued:

> The whole basis of the legislation is to give effect to the Wik decision in relation to the common law. What it does is to confirm what the Wik decision said—that is that the grant of an exclusive possession over property extinguishes native title. . . . The right to negotiate is not a common law right. It was a special addition put into the Native Title Bill [in 1993] which no other title-holder, let alone claimant in Australia has. . . . Those people who agreed to it at the time said it was a trade-off but that doesn't give it the status of a common law right. It was a trade-off of the validation of a small number of post-1975 leases, but whatever it was, whatever the circumstances that gave rise to it in the first place is immaterial to an examination of what it represents. It is a procedural right conferred by statute. And to suggest that you're violating the rights of Aborigines by doing that [removing it] is just absurd. . . . Now just because you are taking away the right to negotiate doesn't means you've [*sic*] behaving in a racially discriminatory way. I mean, you may not agree with it, you may argue that it should stay there, but it's not an act of racism to take it away because it is not a property right.[24]

In the negotiations surrounding the original act, native titleholders conceded a common-law property right to acquire the right to negotiate under statute law by agreeing to the validation of leases that were rendered invalid under the Racial Discrimination Act 1975. Prime Minister Howard ignored the basis of the trade-off to justify his actions; by reneging on the trade-off, he in effect sacrificed native titleholders' prior common-law property rights to validate the property rights of white pastoralists. He was willing to amend the Native Title Act 1993 to ensure that white property interests were protected under statute law. This is an expectation of the law and its makers upon which white interests have come to depend. "When the law recognizes, either implicitly or explicitly, the settled expectations of whites built on the privileges and benefits produced by white supremacy, it acknowledges and reinforces a property interest in whiteness that reproduces [Indigenous] subordination."[25] After threats to call a double dissolution based on race, the Government's Native Title Amendment Bill was passed in the Senate in June 1998. On September 28, changes to the Native Title Act 1993 were implemented.

Lobbying the United Nation's Committee on the Elimination of Racial Discrimination (CERD)

In response to the Native Title Act amendments, the National Indigenous Working Group, FAIRA, and Australians for Native Title and Reconciliation (ANTaR) began lobbying the United Nations. In 1998 and 1999, they provided detailed submissions to the United Nations Committee on the Elimination of Racial Discrimination (CERD), outlining the amendments and how they contravened the International Convention on the Elimination of All Forms of Racial Discrimination. CERD requested that the Australian government provide information addressing the claims made in the submissions. On the basis of this information and her own research, the special country rapporteur to CERD gave the following advice in March 1999:

1. Australian common law is racially discriminatory because native title is a vulnerable property right that is less protected from interference and forced alienation than other land titles.
2. The main aims of the original Native Title Act, the protection and recognition of Native Title have been diminished to the extent that the new provisions impair or extinguish Native Title rights and interests.
3. The increased criteria for registration under the amended Act reduce the ability of Native title claimants to assert their native title rights.
4. With regard to the validation of certain past invalid acts the new amended act is discriminatory because it only provides for extinguishment of native title and no other titles.
5. Native title is extinguished by the confirmation of certain previous exclusive possession Acts, of which the schedule of tenures is 50 pages long and relates back to grants made in 1826 and legislation in the 1860s. Many titles listed in the schedule did not extinguish native title at common law. The amended act creates a situation of discrimination and divestment that did not exist under common law. The provisions operate specifically to divest native titleholders and have no impact on other property owners.

6. Pastoral leaseholders can upgrade the range of primary production activities regardless of the effect of those activities on native title interests in the land and without the consent of native titleholders. The provisions discriminate by giving unwarranted preference to non-native titleholders. The provisions appear to erase the freehold standard in the original act and place Indigenous people in an unequal position.

7. The emended Act does not allow the right to negotiate in certain circumstances and reduces it to one of consultation and objection. It also allows States and Territories to replace the right to negotiate with their own regimes.

8. The exclusion of Indigenous people in the process of developing amendments raises concerns about Australia's compliance with the Convention because of CERD's general recommendation No. 23, which calls on states to "recognize and protect the rights of indigenous people to own, develop, control and use their common lands, territories and resources." And that "members of the Indigenous people have equal rights in respect of effective participation in public life and that no decisions directly relating to their rights and interests are taken without their informed consent."[26]

9. [T]hat the principle of parliamentary sovereignty places the Racial Discrimination Act in an inferior relationship with subsequent legislation of the federal parliament that conflicts with provisions of the Racial Discrimination Act. So, unfortunately, it appears that the Racial Discrimination provisions are overridden by conflicting provisions of both the original and the amended Act and further the State legislation authorized by the amended Act is also immune from challenge based on the Racial Discrimination Act. . . . This means that where the Act authorizes the States and Territories to conduct activities which would conflict with the RDA, and therefore breach Australia's obligations under CERD, those activities will be valid as a matter of Australian Law.[27]

In effect, the Native Title Amendment Act 1998 discriminates against Indigenous native titleholders by validating past acts, extinguishing native title, upgrading non-Indigenous title, and restricting the Indigenous right to negotiate. The diminution of Indigenous property rights reinforces a possessive investment in patriarchal whiteness because advantages are accorded to "those who have profited most from present and post racial discrimination . . . especially through intergenerational transfers of inherited wealth that pass on the spoils of discrimination to succeeding generations."[28] In March 1999, CERD made the following decision:

> . . . having considered a series of new amendments to the Native Title Act, as adopted in 1998, [CERD] expresses concern over the compatibility of the Native Title Act, as currently amended, with the State Party's International obligations under the Convention. . . . The Committee notes, in particular, four specific provisions that discriminate against Indigenous title-holders under the newly amended Act. These include: The Act's "validation" provisions; the "confirmation of extinguishment" provisions; the primary production upgrade provisions; and restrictions concerning the right of Indigenous title holders to negotiate non-indigenous land uses. . . . [T]he Committee urges the State Party to suspend implementation of the 1998 amendments and re-open discussions with the representatives of the Aboriginal and Torres Strait Islander peoples with a view to finding solutions acceptable to the indigenous peoples and which would comply with Australia's obligations under the Convention. . . . [T]he Committee decides to keep this matter on its agenda under its early warning and urgent action procedures to be reviewed again at its fifty-fifth session.[29]

The Australian government reacted by claiming the CERD hearing was unfair, and in April it rejected an application by the Committee to Eliminate Racial Discrimination to visit Australia and "see for itself the discriminatory provisions of Native Title Laws."[30] In July 1999, the Australian government presented a submission to the CERD committee for its consideration at the 55th session because

> the Australian government was disappointed that the written views of the Committee did not record the substance of the Government's submission and evidence on key issues. . . . The following comments seek to redress what the Australian Government considers to have been the unfortunate omission of relevant material from the Committee's report that, by its absence, supports a point of view on the issues before the committee which the Australian government contests. As a general point, the Australian government does not believe that past discrimination against Australia's [I]ndigenous peoples in relation to their land has endured. Indigenous land rights legislation operates in various States and Territories of Australia. The Australian High Court has recognised the native title rights of Australia's indigenous people to their lands (in Mabo 1992 and Wik 1996) decisions, and the Australian Parliament has enacted laws to protect those rights (in the Native Title Act 1993 in response to the Mabo decision, as amended in 1998 in response to the Wik decision).[31]

Here the Australian government positions white supremacy and racism as belonging in the past, as demons that have been put to rest by the *Mabo* decision and subsequent legislation. This is an attempt to mask its possessive investment in whiteness. The Australian government also advised CERD that there was no basis for suspending the implementation of the Native Title Amendment Act 1998 because "the Act was made by Parliament of Australia, and operates as the law of Australia, to which the Government is subject. The constitutional validity of the Act can be challenged in Australian courts, though no such action has been taken yet, and its operation will be determined by those courts."[32]

At its 55th meeting on August 16, 1999, the special rapporteur to CERD advised that the Australian government had not acted upon the committee's decision. Instead, amendments to the act were being brought into effect and there was no progress concerning Indigenous land titles in Australia. The Committee reaffirmed its decision of the 54th session in March 1999 and reported on the matter to the General Assembly. During its 56th session in March 2000, the committee expressed concern at the unsatisfactory response to decisions 2 (54) of March 1999 and 2 (55) of August 1999. It reiterated the content of these decisions to the Australian government and noted that it "is concerned over the absence from Australian law of any entrenched guarantee against racial discrimination that would override subsequent law of the Commonwealth, states and territories."[33] The Australian government has not sought to implement CERD decisions. Instead, the prime minister has referred the issue of compliance with the CERD Convention to the Parliamentary Joint Committee on Native Title and the Aboriginal and Torres Strait Islander Land Fund. The prime minister has not accepted the formal offer of cooperation by the National Indigenous Working Group to begin renegotiations and has not addressed the issues raised by CERD within Australia.[34]

Conclusion

By asserting its sovereignty, the Australian government officially protects and reaffirms a possessive investment in whiteness, and in doing so it endorses the racial hierarchy reified in Australian law. The possessive investment in patriarchal whiteness is invisible, unmarked, and unnamed in the discourse on native title. It is never a point of discussion, focus, or examination despite being omnipresent; its transparency is part of its power. The patriarchal state reinforces the invisibility of a possessive investment in patriarchal whiteness by normalizing it in discussions about economic development and commitments to the nation. Visibility is reserved for Indigenous people and their native title rights, which are the objects of scrutiny and divestment. Patriarchal whiteness can shift from being an inactive component of identity to a mobile entity that, resembling other forms of property, is deployed to execute intention and to exert power. The patriarchal state's official sanction of "privileged rights in property based on race elevate[s] whiteness from a passive attribute to an object of law and a resource deployable at the social and institutional level to maintain control."[35]

I have argued that patriarchal whiteness is usable property that the law protects and values. For over two hundred years, patriarchal whiteness in Australia has been the defining attribute for personhood and property in law. However, not all white men and white women benefit from it in the same way and to the same degree. Racial inequities that are accomplished and replicated by the law are a part of the social order and the structuring of social relations. The intimate relationship between whiteness and asset accumulation in Australian society is reinforced by a consistent pattern of expectations and interests. While appearing to be color blind and power evasive, patriarchal whiteness is a system that protects the privileges of whites through diminishing Indigenous entitlements. As a form of property, patriarchal whiteness surreptitiously denies Indigenous people the opportunity for asset accumulation and economic development. The nullification of our native title rights continues to be a further dividend for a possessive investment in patriarchal whiteness.

6 THE HIGH COURT AND THE YORTA YORTA DECISION

> Is there any knowledge in the world which is so certain that no reasonable [person] could doubt it?
>
> —Bertrand Russell, *The Problems of Philosophy*

AFTER THE *MABO* DECISION, the subsequent introduction of the Native Title Act 1993, and extensive community consultation, the Yorta Yorta people decided in January to lodge an application for determination of native title with the national Native Title Tribunal.[1] The Native Title Tribunal accepted the application and began mediation with interested parties to the claim. As no mediated agreements could be reached through the Tribunal's processes, in April 1995 the application was lodged in the Federal Court. In preparation for the arduous task before them, the Yorta Yorta prepared for trial by collecting as much evidence as possible to substantiate their case. They carried out extensive archival and field research as well as employing experts to assist in developing different forms of evidence. *The Age* newspaper reported that the evidence occupied fifteen meters of shelf space in the judge's chambers.

In December 1998, the primary judge of the Federal Court, Justice Olney, found that "the facts in this case lead inevitably to the conclusion that before the end of the 19th century the ancestors through whom the claimants claim title had ceased to occupy their traditional lands in accordance with their traditional laws and customs. The tide of history has indeed washed away any real acknowledgement of their traditional lands in accordance with their traditional laws and any real observance of their traditional customs."[2] On the basis of this determination, the Yorta Yorta appealed to the Full Court of the Federal Court, where two of the three judges dismissed the appeal. By special leave, the Yorta Yorta then appealed to the High Court, which gave its determination on December 12, 2001. Five of the seven justices agreed that "the forebears of the claimants had ceased to occupy their lands in accordance with traditional laws and customs and that there was no evidence that they continued to acknowledge and observe those laws and customs."[3]

Apart from reports in the press, there has been little engagement with the High and Federal Courts' decisions regarding the Yorta Yorta. There appears to be virtually no critique from bodies such as law societies, bar associations, and the international Commission of Jurists, which is part of the normative system of law. Only a few critiques by individual lawyers, historians, and political scientists have been made addressing legal, political, and historical issues.[4] However, their work tends to overlook the fundamental role that race played in the development of the decision. Perhaps this is because politicians and the media believe that "race" no longer matters in "settler" democracies such as Australia. Public discourse promotes the idea that Australia as a nation has become race-blind, inclusive, and tolerant, as the racial barriers and laws that explicitly discriminated against Indigenous people and kept Australia white have been eliminated. Australia promotes itself as an egalitarian society based on a fair go for all, a society in which equal opportunity enables meritocracy to flourish. Therefore "race" appears to matter little in the distribution of resources such as jobs, power, wealth, land, and social prestige. The assumption is that society operates according to neutral, rational, and just ways of distributing resources.

As a civilized nation Australia has the Racial Discrimination Act 1975 to deal with the misconduct of individuals who have transgressed the norm by their overtly racially discriminatory behavior. By reducing racism to the transgressive behavior of a few individuals, Australian law acknowledges racism while insisting "on its irregular occurrence and limited significance. Liberal race reform [in the form of the Racial Discrimination Act 1975] has thus served to legitimise the myth of [Australian] meritocracy" and equal opportunity.[5] Racial discrimination in Australia is not associated with the unacknowledged culturally sanctioned beliefs that defend the advantages white people have because of the theft of Indigenous lands. The Racial Discrimination Act 1975 provides no legal redress for the extinguishment of native title in the context of the Native Title Act 1993, as amended, where native title is the only title that can be extinguished by other tenures.[6]

Race has shaped the development of Australian law just as it has influenced the morphology of law in other former colonies, such as the United States, where a body of critical race theory has emerged to reveal the racialization of law. In this chapter, I reveal how the possessive logic of patriarchal white sovereignty works ideologically (that is, how it operates at the level of beliefs, and discursively at the level of epistemology) to naturalize the nation as a white possession. Australia was acquired in the name of the king of England. As such, patriarchal white sovereignty is a regime of power that derives from the illegal act of possession and is most acutely manifested in the form of the Crown and the judiciary. The Crown holds exclusive possession of its territory, which is the very foundation of the nation-state. The nation-state in turn confers patriarchal white sovereignty on its citizens through what Carol Pateman argues is the sexual contract.[7] However, not all citizens benefit from or exercise patriarchal white sovereignty equally. Race, class, gender, sexuality, and able-bodiedness are markers that circumscribe the performance of patriarchal white sovereignty by citizens within Australian society. The possessive logic of patriarchal white sovereignty is predicated on exclusion; that is, it denies and refuses what it does not own—the sovereignty of the Indigenous other. Here I use the concept of "possessive logic" to denote a mode of rationalization, rather than a set of positions that produce a more or less inevitable answer, that is underpinned by an excessive desire to invest in reproducing and reaffirming the nation-state's ownership, control, and domination. As such, it is operationalized to circulate sets of meanings about white ownership of the nation as part of commonsense knowledge, decision making, and socially produced conventions.

The possessive logic of patriarchal white sovereignty is deployed to promote the idea of race neutrality through concepts attached to the ideals of democracy, such as egalitarianism, equity, and equal opportunity. This allows patriarchal white sovereignty to remain transparent and invisible—two key attributes of its power. Yet as the premise of white national identity, it defines "the human condition. . . . It alone defines normality and fully inhabits it."[8] The law in Australian society is one of the key institutions through which the possessive logic of patriarchal white sovereignty operates. White patriarchs designed and established the legal and political institutions that control and maintain the social structure under which we now live. White Anglo heterosexual, abled, and middle-class males are overrepresented in government, legislatures, bureaucracies, the legal profession, and the judiciary, where "they shape legislation, administration and judicial texts in their own image and to their own advantage."[9]

For over two hundred years, the possessive logic of patriarchal white sovereignty has served to define the attributes of personhood and property through the law. "The theft of Indigenous lands was ratified by bestowing and acknowledging the property rights of whites in [Indigenous lands]. Only white possession and occupation of land was validated and therefore privileged as a basis for property rights."[10] The possessive logic of patriarchal white sovereignty was deployed in defining who was, and who was not, white, conferring privilege by identifying what legal entitlements accrued to those categorized as white. At the beginning of the twentieth century, this same logic was operative, making whiteness itself a visible form of property in Australian law through the Immigration Restriction Act 1901. And at the commencement of the twenty-first century, it continues to function invisibly, informing the legal exclusion of refugees. The possessive logic of patriarchal white sovereignty operates to discriminate in favor of itself, ensuring that it protects and maintains its interest by the continuing denial and exclusion of Indigenous sovereignty. This logic is evident in the High Court's *Yorta Yorta* decision.

The High Court decision on the Yorta Yorta's appeal of the Full Federal Court's determination on their native title consisted of four separate judgments. The majority decision was a combination of three judgments: a collective judgment by Gleeson, Gummow, and Hayne, and individual judgments by McHugh and Callinan. Gaudron and Kirby together gave a dissenting judgment upholding the Yorta Yorta's appeal. I begin by summarizing some of the key points made in each of the judges' determinations regarding "tradition," "occupation," "continuity," and the role of the common law.

Gleeson et al. began their judgment by stating that "much of the argument of the present appeal was directed to what is meant by par (C) in section 223(1) of the Native Title Act."[11] This section states that native title rights and interests are defined as:

> The communal, group or individual rights and interests of Aboriginal peoples or Torres Strait Islanders in relation to land or waters, where:
>
> (a) the rights and interests are possessed under the traditional laws acknowledged, and the traditional customs observed, by the Aboriginal peoples or Torres Strait Islanders; and

(b) the Aboriginal peoples or Torres Strait Islanders, by those laws and customs, have a connection with the land or waters; and
    (c) the rights and interests are recognised by the common law of Australia.[12]

Gleeson et al. stated that the Yorta Yorta argued on appeal that the Full Court of the Federal Court had made the same error in law that Olney J had made in his decision. That is, it misconstrued and misapplied the definition of section 223(1) of the Native Title Act. The error was the requirement of positive proof of continuous acknowledgment of traditional laws and customs. In arguing their case, the Yorta Yorta stated that "attention should be directed to the rights and interests presently possessed under traditional laws presently acknowledged and customs presently observed, and to a present connection by those laws and customs."[13]

    Gleeson et al. responded to the Yorta Yorta submission in a number of ways. Because they found that native title is not a creature of the common law, they argued that it is the Native Title Act that should be used to determine native title. They reasoned that after the Crown acquired sovereignty there could be no parallel law-making system operating in Australia. Therefore the rights and interests to which the Native Title Act refers are those derived from a normative system of Indigenous society, which existed before white sovereignty. According to Gleeson et al., the concept of society "is to be understood as a body of persons united in and by its acknowledgement and observance of a body of law and customs."[14] They held that if the normative system ceases to exist, then so does native title. However, should the content of the laws and customs be adopted by a new society, then they are not the same as those that existed at pre-sovereignty. Gleeson et al.'s reasoning supported the findings of the primary judge and the Full Federal Court. They disagreed with the dissenting judge of the Federal Court's argument that "no proper allowance [had been made] for adaptation and change in traditional law and customs in response to European settlement." They maintained that "what is the most reliable evidence about that subject was quintessentially a matter for the primary judge. . . . The assessment he made of the evidence was one which no doubt took account of the emphasis given and reliance placed by the claimants on the writings of Edward Curr [Curr was a squatter on Yorta Yorta lands; his recollections of squatting and Aboriginal people in Victoria were published in 1883].[15] They support Olney's view that as Curr's evidence did not concur with the testimony of many claimants regarding traditions and customs, his testimony could be considered credible and compelling. And they agreed that when the Yorta Yorta moved on to the Maloga mission and presented the Crown with a petition for land, in which they acknowledged their lands were inhabited by whites, their connection to land was interrupted.[16] This was further supported by Olney's findings of the Yorta Yorta: that while at Maloga "the evidence was silent about the continued observance . . . of those aspects of traditional lifestyle to which Curr had referred."[17] Gleeson et al. accepted Olney's findings that some of the claimants were identified as having been descended from the Indigenous inhabitants who were in possession of the area under claim in 1788.

Despite this acknowledgment of descent, the assumption that the nation is a white possession manifests itself in Gleeson et al.'s decision in a number of ways. First, they rationalize that only the law-making system of patriarchal white sovereignty can exist as such once sovereignty has been asserted. This is done by arguing contrary to the reasoning in *Mabo*, where it is acknowledged that native title was progressively extinguished by freehold title and, as such, Indigenous law-making systems continued to function. Thus there is a refusal to acknowledge the Indigenous sovereignty that was implicit in *Mabo*. Second, they assume that Indigenous law and custom is only constituted through a normative system made up of a body of persons who acknowledge and observe them collectively and was used to negate native title. This assumption is inconsistent with Indigenous knowledge about how law and custom work. Traditional law and custom in Indigenous societies does contain a normative system of rules, but they are intrinsic to an intersubstantiation of humans, ancestral beings, and land. Indigenous people are the human manifestations of the land and creator beings; they carry title to the land through and on their bodies. Thus the physicality of Indigenous people is testimony to the existence of particular tracts of country. The relationship between people and their country is synonymous and symbiotic. This is why the connection to land is never broken and why no other Indigenous group claimed, or could claim, Yorta Yorta country. Third, Gleeson et al.'s reliance on the primary judge's interpretation of the evidence, despite not having assessed it themselves, is based on the assumption that he knew what were traditional law and customs and whether there was a continuity between them, albeit in evolutionary form. Rather than the appellate Court's receiving and making its own assessment of the evidence, as a matter of orthodoxy it relied on the primary judge's assessment to inform its decision. Despite their insistence upon objectivity, Gleeson et al. based their findings on the primary judge's interpretation of Curr's interpretation of Yorta Yorta culture.[18] They cloaked their possessiveness through assuming the epistemological privilege of defining who Indigenous people are and that to which they are entitled. This is also evident in their findings that the petition for the return of land put forward by the Yorta Yorta at Maloga revealed the Yorta Yorta's acknowledgment of their dispossession. The Yorta Yorta did not cede their sovereignty anywhere in writing in the petition; instead, they asked for the return of their property, which was illegally taken. Under the law of patriarchal white sovereignty, when a thief steals someone's property, ownership is not assumed or inferred as being ceded to the thief. To the contrary, the law preserves ownership and guarantees return of the property to the owner. This principle in law was not applied to the Yorta Yorta's use of the petition. Instead, the findings by Gleeson, Gummow, and Hayne fundamentally represented the Yorta Yorta as a people without any proprietary rights in land.

Unlike Gleeson, Gummow, and Hayne, Justice McHugh presented a very short determination in which he argued that the High Court had narrowly interpreted section 223 of the Native Title Act because parliament believed that native title would depend on the developing common law.[19] He held that "parliament intended native title to be determined by the common law principles laid down in *Mabo v. Queensland [No 2]* [68], particularly those formulated by Brennan J[ustice] in his judgement in that case. When s 223 (1) (c) of the 1993 Act referred to the rights and interests 'recognised by the common law of Australia,' it was . . . referring to the principles expounded by Brennan J in Mabo [No 2]."[20] However, he states that "this Court has now given the concept of 'recognition' a narrower scope than [he thinks] the Parliament intended, and this Court's interpretation of section 223 must now be accepted as settling the law."[21] McHugh could have dissented on this determination but choose instead to follow Gleeson et al. By restricting the concept of "recognition" to statute law, McHugh and Gleeson et al. denied the Yorta Yorta's argument based on recourse to the common law that has recognized Indigenous sovereignty in countries such as Canada. McHugh's rationalization for adhering to this narrower interpretation is tied to his desire to maintain the national status quo rather than following precedent. McHugh's investment in possession operates discursively, ensuring compliance and solidarity when it is perceived that the nation requires protection from the threat of Indigenous sovereignty in international common law.

Justice Callinan presented a lengthy determination, quoting extensively from the primary judge, Justice Olney. Callinan agreed with the findings of the Full Federal Court, arguing that the Yorta Yorta did not identify their rights and interests in land according to traditional laws and customs that could be recognized by the common law.[22] He stated that the Yorta Yorta were disadvantaged by

> [l]oss of traditional knowledge and practice because of dislocation and past exploitation; and, by reason of the lack of a written language and the absence therefore of any indigenous contemporaneous documents, the need to rely extensively upon the spoken word of their forbearers, which, human experience knows is at risk of being influenced and distorted in transmission through the generations, for example, fragility of recollection, intentional and unintentional exaggeration, embellishment, wishful thinking, justifiable sense of grievance, embroidery and self-interest. Anthropologists' reports, which also relied to a large extent on transmitted materials were liable to suffer from similar defects as well, in this case, as his Honour held, as some lack of objectivity ordinarily to be expected of experts. A further complication was that some witnesses on behalf of the appellants, understandably resentful of past dispossession, made emotional outbursts and failed to give evidence which could be of assistance to the Court.[23]

Justice Callinan further held that, as there was no precision in identifying traditional laws and customs, then the common law could not give effect or enforcement to them. He found too that native title is not a creature of the common law but, combined with the role of the Native Title Act, protects and gives effect to it. In relation to section 223(1), he states that the "use of the word 'connection' contemplates at least a degree of continuity either of acknowledgement or observance, and possession, except arguably perhaps in exceptional cases, of which this does not appear to be one."[24] And as the act "makes for no provision for nonextinguishment, or revival of native title . . . this is an indication of a need for continuity."[25] In relation to "tradition," he notes that the act sets out the process by which an application can be made for native title. It includes the Registrar of the Native Title Tribunal being satisfied that there is a traditional physical connection with land or water that suggests there is a "need for an actual presence on the land."[26] Referring to the *Oxford English Dictionary* for a definition of "tradition," he offers the following advice: "Tradition, myth and legend are often indistinguishable, but mere existence of either of the latter, in the sense of a fictitious narrative, or an unauthentic or nonhistorical story, however venerated by repetition, will not suffice of itself to establish native title rights and interests possessed under traditional laws or customs by people claiming a relevant connection to land."[27]

Callinan maintained that in order for the common law to recognize rights and interests, they must be found in traditional laws or customs, and they must be connected to land, "for their enjoyment a physical presence is essential."[28] He notes that the traditional laws and customs that existed at sovereignty must be the ones that have continued, and "the extent to which longstanding law and custom may evolve without ceasing to be traditional raise difficult questions."[29] Callinan asserted that the matter went uncontested in *Yanner v. Eaton*. Referring to the Yanner case, he reasoned: "[F]or myself I might have questioned whether the use of a motor boat powered by mined and processed liquid fuel, and a steel tomahawk, remained in accordance with a traditional law or custom, particularly one of alleged totemic significance."[30] Then, without exploring any evolutionary aspect of Yorta Yorta tradition and customs, he concurs with Justice Olney and the Full Federal Court that the appellants could not establish continuity. In conclusion, he reiterates, in relation to the oral evidence as assessed by the trial judge, that due weight had been given to the oral evidence but that it was not sufficient to refute contemporaneous records to the contrary.[31] He found that Olney had not made an error in finding a lack of continuity because farming on both sides of the Murray River were incompatible with the traditional way of life or any evolution of it. He further held that Olney did not have to refer to all the evidence upon which the parties relied and it was sufficient for Olney to refer only to that evidence that he assessed as relevant or necessary for his decision.[32]

Callinan's perceptions of the disadvantages the Yorta Yorta faced are not predicated on the rule of law; rather, they are connected to an epistemological privilege tied to possession, which served to undermine both the oral testimony of the Yorta Yorta and the expertise of white anthropologists. His claim that there was a lack of objectivity is based on the assumption that where the oral evidence is not corroborated by the white written record, it is unreliable. Despite the basis of Curr's evidence—his observations and judgments as an amateur ethnographer—being outside Yorta Yorta culture, his written words are granted authority. Callinan does not convincingly explain why Curr is treated as such an authority; instead, he accepts this authority to suit his investment, which is also evident in how he diminishes the testimony of the Yorta Yorta and anthropologists. He implies that the Yorta Yorta and their experts are unreliable witnesses prone to embellishment, emotion, and self-interest. And where he concludes that the trial judge found no written evidence at all to suggest that the Yorta Yorta continued their traditions and customs, such as at the Maloga mission, he held that they were discontinued. For Callinan, the lack of evidence becomes evidence in itself. Callinan selectively chooses evidence to suit his self-interest—the refusal of Yorta Yorta sovereignty. For example, he refers to an administrative procedure, based on an interpretation of the Native Title Act, to state that a physical presence is required to prove connection to land when the act makes no such stipulation. By elevating an administrative procedure to a legal criterion, he is able to dismiss the Yorta Yorta's claims on the basis of no physical presence. The idea that you have to have a physical presence on the land to enjoy one's entitlements is based on conceptions of white property ownership, which requires evidence of human occupation in the form of fences, title deeds, or residences. For Callinan, signifiers of white possession are imputed as the only measure of Indigenous possession. His investment in white possession is further revealed through the way in which he deploys "tradition." He refers to the *Oxford English Dictionary*'s definition, which he finds is insufficient to establish Indigenous possession. Then, although alluding to the idea that he may not know what the evolving tradition and customs might be, he authoritatively states that it is questionable to apply it to the use of a motorboat and steel tomahawk as in the Yanner case. In effect, he defines "tradition" by what it is not, rather than providing a definitive statement of what it is, as a way of refusing Indigenous possession and therefore Indigenous sovereignty. Callinan's static construction of Indigenous culture effectively denies traditional laws and customs as they are now practiced. He privileges certain written documentation over the oral and written evidence presented on behalf of the Yorta Yorta and represents them as being self-interested, highly emotive, and mendacious. Callinan's refusal of Yorta Yorta sovereignty penetrates his findings.

Justices Mary Gaudron and Michael Kirby in their determination also reasoned that native title is not a creature of the common law and held that statutory interpretation of the Native Title Act was required for any determination of native title, particularly section 223(1). They disagreed that it was necessary "to establish that those rights and interests have been continuously availed of in relation to land, or, even that they are presently availed of."[33] They further argued that section 223(1)(b) "requires only that there be a present connection to land and waters." The terms of section 223(1)(b) also indicate the nature of the requisite connection—namely, "by [the traditional] laws and customs [acknowledged and observed]," not a physical connection or continuing occupancy. They argued that "spiritual connection by laws acknowledged and customs observed falls comfortably within the words of s 223 (1)(b)."[34] They found that section 223(1)(c) does not give expression to the "notion of continuity as a traditional community," only that the rights and interests be recognized by the common law.[35] In their view, continuity of a community is "primarily a question of whether, throughout the period in issue, there have been persons who have identified themselves and each other as members of the community in question."[36] They found that the preamble to the Native Title Act acknowledged the history of dispossession. Traditional laws and customs should have their origins in the past. However, "to the extent that they differ from past practices, the differences should constitute adaptations, alterations, modifications or extensions made in accordance with the shared values or the customs and practices of the people who acknowledge and observe those laws and customs."[37] They held that Justice Olney was misdirected in requiring the Yorta Yorta "to identify acknowledgement of laws and observance of customs with respect to the utilisation or occupation of land."[38] They stated that section 223(1)(a) and (b) of the Native Title Act does not contain a requirement that "the traditional connection with the land . . . be substantially maintained."

The dissenting judgment by Gaudron and Kirby constituted nine pages out of the eighty-four pages of the decision, and it appears to contest the possessive logic of patriarchal white sovereignty. Their broad approach to interpreting the Native Title Act acknowledged several possibilities for the existence of native title in modern form. However, they, like the other judges, reaffirmed white possession of the nation in their decision making by denying the fundamental role of the common law. Perhaps this is because Gaudron and Kirby hold that the nation, as the anchor of patriarchal white sovereignty, is destabilized by the incremental process of native title claims. Neither Gaudron nor Kirby is able to detach the technicalities of legal argument posed by the common law from the legitimacy of the nation as such. By not drawing on any common law cases as precedent, including the *Mabo* decision, they restricted native title to statutory interpretation. In doing so, they refused the finding in the *Mabo* decision: the Crown's acquisition of sovereignty provided Indigenous people with common law rights as British subjects.

Noel Pearson argues that section 223(1) of the Native Title Act does not diminish, but preserves, the common law meaning of native title. The High Court's interpretation of this section fundamentally abridges its meaning and mitigates the intention of parliament as stated in McHugh's decision and the preamble to the act. Pearson argues that "at the heart of this whole misconception is our understanding of how the common law treats traditional indigenous occupants of land when the Crown acquires sovereignty over their homelands."[39] In the *Mabo* decision, the justices held that when the Crown asserted sovereignty, the Indigenous people of Australia became subjects of the Crown and as such were entitled to the protection of the imported common law, which extended to the protection of existing property rights. Pearson argues that "it is the fact of occupation that excites recognition and protection by the common law. Possession is the conclusion of law that follows from the fact of occupation. . . . [I]t is the occupation of land that the common law recognizes and protects in the first instance," not traditional laws and customs.[40] Traditional laws and customs identify entitlement and territory, allocate rights, interests, and responsibilities within communal possession and regulate their exercise by community members. According to Pearson: "When you approach the question of what continues after annexation by answering the rights and interests established by traditional law and custom—rather than by answering that it is the right to occupy land by authority of, and in accordance with, one's traditional laws and customs—this has profound implications for the way in which one conceptualises native title and ultimately, how one deals with proof."[41]

The High Court, by not discussing the body of case law dealing with native title within the common law, avoided legal definitions of "tradition," "continuity," and "connection" established within such case law. In dealing with native title as defined in section 223(1) of the Native Title Act, the High Court ruled on "important questions and principles on the basis of bare assertion, rather than . . . 'the time-honoured methodology of the common law' whereby cases are ruled upon according to established and developing precedents."[42] The possessive logic of patriarchal white sovereignty inherent in the High Court's decision has produced an outcome whereby its accumulation of titles is unaffected and Indigenous people's property rights are reduced to a coexisting and deferential title. Indigenous people now face an unrealistic and inflexible burden of proof to meet "white Australia's cultural and legal prejudices about what constitutes 'real Aborigines.'"[43]

Conclusion

The possessive logic of patriarchal white sovereignty operated discursively and ideologically in the *Yorta Yorta* decision to produce legal and political resistance to native title by creating judicial and legal impediments that were presented as though they are race blind. Yet the origin and assertion of property law in Australia continues to be based on racial domination. The intersection between race and property continues to play a definitive role in constructing and affirming Indigenous dispossession. The denial of the Yorta Yorta's native title was based on a regime of statutory interpretation that usurped the common-law property rights of Indigenous people. By the fact of occupation under Australian common law, the Yorta Yorta proved their native title. This is inconsistent with the High Court's majority decision that "only white possession and occupation of land was validated and therefore privileged as a basis for property rights."[44] The High Court required evidence of traditional law and customs derived from Indigenous sovereignty that existed prior to patriarchal white sovereignty, but it chose to define them by what they are not through the Native Title Act. The High Court refused the continuity of Indigenous sovereignty as the precondition and genesis of all concomitant rights, interests, entitlements, responsibilities, obligations, customs, and law.

This refusal resulted in the High Court's majority decision, which reinterpreted Olney's decision through the appeal by the Yorta Yorta, to validate divesting the Yorta Yorta of their land. The High Court majority decision rationalized Yorta Yorta adaptation of white culture, which was necessary for their survival as a society and nation, as proof that they had surrendered both their Indigeneity and sovereignty. In doing so, the High Court imputed reified white social standards to the Yorta Yorta that "not only denied their right to historical change but also the reality of their paradoxical continued existence" in white Australia.[45] In the High Court's majority decision, concepts such as "tradition," "continuity," and "connection" became sociolegal constructs that took on a pseudo-objective form, which holds no form in the law of the Yorta Yorta. The High Court's decision holds the "definition from above can be fair to those below, that beneficiaries of racially conferred privilege have the right to establish norms for those who have historically been oppressed pursuant to those norms."[46]

In the High Court's decision, the evidence and legal interpretation by and of white men were raised to a sublime position of authority, thus "reflecting the power inherent in legal discourse to corrupt meaning as well as the role of legal translation in that process."[47] The High Court's judges' claims to objectivity served to mask the racialization of their knowledge and its partiality. The possessive logic of patriarchal white sovereignty was omnipresent, but invisible, unnamed and unmarked in this decision, appearing to be disinvested when protecting its sovereignty. Despite the High Court's decision, the bloodline to country of the Yorta Yorta continues to carry their sovereignty. Indigenous sovereignty invokes different sets of relations, belonging, and ownership that are grounded in a different epistemology from that which underpins the possessive logic of patriarchal white sovereignty. This is why Yorta Yorta sovereignty will continue to unsettle and challenge the possessive logic of patriarchal white sovereignty and its premise that adverse possession is nine-tenths of the law.

7 LEESA'S STORY

White Possession in the Workplace

> Possession: the act or fact of possessing; the state of being
> possessed; ownership; Law actual holding or occupancy, either
> with or without rights of ownership; a thing possessed; plural
> property or wealth; a territorial domination of a state; control
> over oneself, one's mind, etc. the feeling or idea itself.
>
> —*The Macquarie Concise Dictionary,* 1998

"POSSESSION" IS ONE OF THOSE LITTLE WORDS with lots of
meanings: ownership, rights, containment, domination, and control. In
Australia, taking possession of Indigenous lands and people by the British Crown was a proprietary right exercised under its law. The Crown
"owned" and continues to "own" the land inhabited by its subjects and
confers on them proprietary rights that are intangible and tangible. The
colonists were formally deemed to be property-owning subjects through
their relationship to the Crown regardless of whether or not they came
in chains. The development of civil rights had occurred in Britain in
the eighteenth century and was instrumental in changing the nature
of the feudal system to one of mercantile capitalism. Civil rights were
composed of those necessary "for individual freedom—liberty of person, freedom of speech, thought and faith, the right to own property
and conclude valid contracts, and the right to justice."[1] This contractual relationship between white subjects and the Crown is the foundation upon which the colony and subsequent nation was built as a white
possession. Since the *Mabo* decision, it has become popular within
legal discourse to argue that Indigenous people too were subjects of
the Crown under British law. However, this "fact" of British subjecthood was disputed by the colony of New South Wales, which turned

that status into one of wardship, thus setting the precedent for subsequent governments to follow.[2]

Indigenous people have never been recognized as property-owning subjects in our own right as Indigenous peoples, and this continues in current law and policy. Native title is not Indigenous sovereignty because it is nothing more than a bundle of rights to hunt, gather, and negotiate as determined by Australian law. Indigenous ownership of the territory, now called Australia, constituted more than a bundle of rights long before it was colonized by white men. The refusal to recognize Indigenous people as property-owning subjects is one of the reasons why our existence has always been tied to welfare dispensed at the discretion of colonial, state, and national governments and our sovereign claims denied.[3] At an ontological and epistemological level, the Crown and subsequent governments have treated us as their property. We have been represented within popular and legal discourse as not owning anything, not even our bodies; we are propertyless. This is in contrast with how whiteness became a form of property in law as a possession constitutive of white subjectivity. As Cheryl Harris argues in the U.S. context, upon the Crown's assumption of sovereignty, only white property rights were validated by the law: "Possession—the act necessary to lay the basis for rights in property—was defined to include only the cultural practices of whites. This definition laid the foundation for the idea that whiteness—that which whites alone possess—is valuable and is property."[4]

Similarly, in Australia, the nation has been operating as a white possession reinforcing its investments. This is why, as Stratton has argued throughout the nineteenth and twentieth centuries, homogeneity of race, language, and culture was the most important concern of the nation.[5] The pervasiveness of the nation's white possessiveness functions through social institutions such as the workplace, operating in everyday intersubjective relations between Indigenous and white subjects. These daily intersubjective relations are the mechanisms by which the exercising of white possession is experienced by Indigenous people as racism. As I have argued elsewhere:

> Under Australia's white anglicised legal regime Indigenous peoples are homeless and out of place because of the hybrid of settlement, which now exists in common law, and continues the legal fiction of Terra Nullius through positioning us as trespassers. Who belongs, and the degree of that belonging, is inextricably tied to white possession. The right to be here and the sense

of belonging it creates are reinforced institutionally and socially; personal profound sentiment is enabled by structural conditions.[6]

In this chapter, I examine a racial discrimination case to unpack the ways by which the gendered nature of white possession operates discursively, manifesting as racism within the workforce.

Whitewashing Racism

Since the repeal of the Commonwealth government's Immigration Restriction Act 1901 and the dismantling of the White Australia Policy in 1972, politicians, the media, academics, and religious leaders have expressed the view that racism either exists only in small pockets of society or not at all. The federal government enacted the Racial Discrimination Act 1975, affirming the Australian nation's intolerance of racism, and each state government has subsequently enacted some form of antidiscrimination legislation. Australians' belief in a fair go for all, an attribute of the national character, means legal measures such as these are seen to be in place to protect the "raced" population (in other words, the nonwhite) from such discrimination. The Racial Discrimination Act 1975 and subsequent antidiscrimination legislations function discursively, informing white commonsense understandings of Australia's tolerance: "we" have antiracist legislation in place so "we" as a nation cannot be racist; "we" allow nonwhite migrants into the country, therefore "we" are not racist. Despite seventy-five years of an explicit white Australia policy, white subjects now rationalize that "race" no longer matters or functions as an exclusionary tool in Australian society. In the 1990s, in the wake of Pauline Hanson and the call for more economic engagement within the Asia-Pacific region, Schech and Haggis argue:

> There has clearly been a substantial shift in Australia's sense of itself since the 1960s, as reflected in the changing policies on aid, to a greater openness and willingness to engage with its neighbours and achieve an integrated regional presence. We argue, though, that the economic paradigm within which this has occurred has placed constraints on the extent to which this has involved a fundamental reordering of Australian identity. The ambivalence expressed in recent government statements and initiative clearly echoes reservations amongst white Australians about the extent to which they are prepared to see home both culturally and psychologically as the Asia–Pacific region. There remains a gap between geography and identity.[7]

This sense of separation between our geography and Australia's identity and history are peppered throughout the speeches of Prime Minister John Howard, who continues to praise Australia's tolerance
while advocating Anglo-Saxon culture as holding the core values of our
nationalism.[8] Since his time in office, Howard has continually reaffirmed the nation as a white possession, one that is tolerant but secure
in its white identity. This is evident in his response after the Cronulla
riots,[9] and in particular to New South Wales Premier Morris Iemma's
initial statement that the riots showed "the ugly face of racism in this
country." Howard said he was not going to "rush to judgment about
these events. . . . I do not accept that there is underlying racism in this
country. . . . I take a more optimistic view of the Australian people."[10]
He did not want to invoke racism as having any bearing on the events
that took place at the beach, and the popular media predictably followed suit by characterizing the behavior of the young men as simply
thuggery born of too much alcohol. The fact that those involved in the
riot were clearly divided along race lines (Anglo vs. other) was but a
mere coincidence.[11] The way in which racism became written out of
the event is indicative of how neoliberalism functions discursively to
produce a race-blind and power-evasive discourse.[12]

This discourse involves "color-blindness," or a mode of thinking about
race organized around an effort not to "see," or not to acknowledge,
race differences.[13] It involves a selective engagement with difference
rather than no engagement at all. "We" are all Australians and "we"
all have the same chances. Any failure to achieve is the fault of the
individual. It denies the existence of the privileges conferred on white
citizens through generations of white possession while simultaneously
enhancing the benefits they enjoy.

Howard's discourse is reflected in our everyday encounters with
white citizens: Indigenous people regularly told by white people that
there is no racism and that "race" does not matter in how they judge
other people. As evidence of their "race blindness," white people will
usually begin by identifying the people they worked for, or had contact with, or fallen in love with, or mention that they are friends with
people who come from cultural and ethnic backgrounds different from
their own. They assure us that they treat everyone equally and everyone is treated the same within Australian society; this is the lucky country, the land of a fair go for all. In this way, race blindness functions
discursively to hide the power imbalance between those who are marked

by "race" and those who do the marking. It is a powerful and pervasive discourse that supports a national identity founded on white possession and promotes the idea that merit underpins the success of white individuals, as though this success has nothing to do with the inherited race privileges conferred by previous generations, whose wealth was built on the British government's theft of Indigenous lands. This leads me to ask: If race does not matter, then how do white people "know" how to identify who the Indigenous people are? Why do white people think they are not "raced"? And how do Indigenous people "know" who the white people are? Why do most white people believe racism does not exist and most Indigenous people believe that it does? Why is the dominant representation of Indigenous socioeconomic disadvantage within the media attributed to our pathology and the existence of white people on welfare attributed to a lack of opportunity, training, and market forces?

The law does finds racism from time to time, usually with reference to the overt behavior of individuals. To my knowledge, there has never been a finding of systemic racism in any racial discrimination case. However, individually based definitions do not sufficiently explain or expose how white possession enables racism to flourish. Instead, racism becomes reduced to the behavior of a few individuals, which is why it is only found sometimes.[14] Racism conceptualized in this way does not include "the culturally sanctioned beliefs which, regardless of the intentions involved, defend the advantages whites have because of the subordinated position of [Indigenous peoples]."[15] White race privilege and advantage are unearned invisible assets that benefit white people in their everyday lives; they are possessions. These assets include simple things such as not having to educate white children about systemic racism for their protection and having white identity affirmed in society on a daily basis through positive representations in the media, government policies, legislation, and the education system. These representations provide white people with a sense of pride and investment in their ownership of the nation, its institutions and public spaces. They have a right to worry about, and contribute to, their management on a daily basis.[16] Assets such as these are derived from and contribute to the normalization of white possessiveness, which remains invisible to white people in everyday practice.

Race informs assumptions and influences social practice just as it shapes the contours of everyday life. Race therefore does not belong

just to people who are racialized according to a continuum of "blackness"; all contexts are racialized, just as they are gendered. This has
been revealed by scholarship developed in the field of critical race and
whiteness studies in the United States, Britain, and Australia since the
1990s. This body of literature provides a form of critique that approaches
whiteness as an analytical object of research by investigating the relationship between whiteness, law, and the reproduction and maintenance of racial hierarchies.[17] Legal scholars have not developed a
similar body of critical race scholarship within the Australian context,
and perhaps the paucity of literature is indicative of how white possession operates through the agency of legal scholars located within the
discipline of law and its function as a social institution.[18] The invisibility
of white possession in policies, legislation, and everyday practice functions discursively through discourse to designate "race" as the possession of the nonwhite other. So how does white possession reveal itself
to Indigenous people in the everyday, and how is it tied to racism?

The Workings of White Possession in the Workforce

In 2005, I was asked to be an expert witness for a case of racial discrimination that was lodged in the Anti-Discrimination Tribunal in
Queensland. The complainant in the matter was an Indigenous nurse
whom I shall call Leesa. I was asked to analyze Leesa's affidavit and
the affidavits of twenty-five respondents. Leesa gave me permission to
use her affidavit in this chapter. I do not have permission to use the other
affidavits, but I can reveal that in the statements made by the white
nurses there was consistency in each other's recollection of events,
even when many did not witness those that took place. The obvious
collaboration of testimonies and the institutional support for the white
nurses' defense illustrates how white possession discursively shapes the
ground of their unity on the basis of race. The hospital and the nurses
were the major stakeholders, whose interests required protection. This
indicates that when white possession is under threat, it becomes a catalyst for the collective closing of ranks, support, and defense. The case
was settled outside the tribunal prior to the exposure by the media of
the "culture of bullying" within the Queensland health system. The
culture of bullying is not gender, race, class, status, or sexually neutral.
All of these factors are operationalized within it, but they are seldom
recognized as such. Bullying can take many forms, some of which are

invisible and hard to prove in a court of law. Psychological abuse in the form of insult and humiliation is commonly experienced by Indigenous people in the workforce in this country on a daily basis.

When Indigenous people raise issues of racism within the workforce, they are more often than not positioned as "troublemakers" or are represented as being "too sensitive." What is often not understood by one's "white workmates" is the way in which the work environment supports and normalizes their behavior and attitudes. Indigenous people tend to judge the behavior and attitudes of white people on the basis of their observations of how white people treat other white people. This then becomes the measure for our expectations of how we should be treated. We have to learn what is considered "normal" behavior within the work environment so that we can participate. Many of us work in white male-dominated environments, often belonging to the first generation of Indigenous professionals, and we have to manage and negotiate white systems, knowledges, practices, and people. The workforce can be a place of great stress and anxiety because of the added burden of being the known and knowing stranger in a space where we are both in and out of place. We have to contend with white people's knowledge and representations of and about us; in this way, we are already "known" by them. While Indigenous people "know" this about white people, we also know that our knowledges about ourselves have very little impact on the work environment because we are not in control. Instead, we have to endure the white gaze in all its manifestations as we try to earn a living for our families.

Like many Aboriginal people of her generation, Leesa, who was born in 1962, was raised on an Aboriginal reserve that was governed by the Queensland Government's Aborigines Act,[19] which separated Aborigines from the rest of Queensland society. Leesa was first employed in 1978 as a casual domestic, and after many years of casual and part-time employment she enrolled in tertiary studies, graduating from the Queensland University of Technology in 2001 with a degree in nursing. In 2002, Leesa was employed as a registered nurse (graduate) in Charters Towers. However, in order to take care of her grandson, she requested a transfer to Townsville, where she began employment in Queensland Health in April 2002. Leesa experienced alienation and inferiorization when she encountered the workings of white possession. She experienced mental anxiety, loss of self-esteem, and depression as a result of her treatment and believes that she was discriminated against because of her Aboriginality. Leesa observed that white registered and graduate nurses were spoken to in a normal voice and treated in a respectful manner by their white preceptors. Leesa's observations of this normality are based on her experiences of consistently being treated differently.

The Inferiorization and Exclusion of Leesa

During orientation day at a Townsville nursing home, Leesa experienced an incident with Nurse A, a level-2 clinical nurse, who queried Leesa's credentials and physically handled her personal effects in front of the other graduate nurses. Nurse A queried whether Leesa was a registered nurse, asking, "Are you sure? When did you do your training? She then reached out and grabbed Leesa's badge, which was attached to her uniform, to check its details without Leesa's consent. Leesa notes that "none of the other six nonindigenous enrolled nurses' qualifications were queried by [Nurse A]. Her questioning made me feel uncomfortable and embarrassed."

When Nurse A grabbed Leesa's badge, she exercised her "right" to invade Leesa's personal space without permission. Nurse A's actions imply that Aborigines are not worthy of being in a professional domain controlled and owned by white people. As such, Leesa as an Aborigine is out of place in this domain and she must be made accountable for being in it. Leesa is not accorded her own personal space and her body is not perceived to be her property, thus she can be treated accordingly. Leesa is Nurse A's property. Nurse A did not behave in the same way toward the other white nurses because they have a "right" to be in the same space. It is normal for them to be there, so they do not have to be subjected to such scrutiny. The other white graduate nurses did not object to Nurse A's behavior or, it appears, to show any empathy for Leesa. While it can be argued that they were all intimidated by Nurse A as an authority figure, their silence makes them complicit in Nurse A's possessive behavior. In turn, Nurse A's behavior also conveys to her graduate nurses that treating Aboriginal people in this way is normal and acceptable.

On or about April 11, 2002, Nurse B requested Leesa to carry out a procedure. Leesa had only seen the procedure performed once before and therefore sought direction. In response, Nurse B said the continuous ambulatory peritoneal dialysis procedure was outlined step-by-step on a poster. Nurse B commented that the poster was designed for people who were mentally retarded, and if you could not follow it then there was obviously something wrong with you. Leesa took issue with Nurse B's words, stating, "No, that wouldn't mean there's something wrong with me. I'm new. This is my second shift here and I've only seen it done once. I feel offended that you should say something like that." Nurse B responded with words to the effect, "Oh, for heaven's sake! Don't take things too personal. Stop being so sensitive." Leesa said, "I did not witness Nurse B treat white nurses in a similar way."

Nurse B's use of the words "mentally retarded" while addressing Leesa implied that she thought Leesa was incompetent and not very intelligent. While Nurse B used the term "people" when referring to being "mentally retarded," it was Leesa she was addressing, not anyone else in this context. In responding to Leesa's displeasure, Nurse B deployed a strategy to recuperate her offensive statement, not by way of an apology, but by blaming Leesa's sensitivity. Nurse B's capacity to abdicate responsibility and blame Leesa illuminates the cultural safety of the institution for white nurses to exercise their race privilege. To whom was Nurse B accountable within the institution? Who would interpret her statement as a racial slur besides Leesa, a junior graduate Aboriginal nurse? Similarly, Leesa's observation that the conversation was not repeated with other white nurses illustrates that Nurse B's sense of racial superiority need only be wielded when people are not considered to be of the same race.

On or about April 23, 2002, Leesa was rostered on a shift with Nurse C, a registered nurse whose previous behavior, attitude, and statements about Leesa's presence were racially explicit. Nurse C stated quite openly to Leesa that she did not want to work in the same public space in the hospital with her, and when the shift was over she told Leesa that she was glad it had finished. In a second incident, Leesa is rostered on a shift with Nurse C and Nurse D on a public holiday. After Nurse C holds a conversation with Nurse D, Leesa is informed by Nurse D that there has been a mistake as she is not rostered on the same shift. When Leesa reports the incident to Nurse E, the Nursing Practice Coordinator, he confirms that Leesa was rostered on the shift and Nurse D did not have the authority to instruct Leesa not to work.

Nurse C's resentment of Leesa's presence is predicated on the assumption that the hospital space should only be occupied by white nurses because graduate Aboriginal nurses are not their equal; they are inferior, lack sufficient intelligence, and therefore are incompetent. In the second incident, through Nurse D's intervention, Nurse C does not have to work with Leesa. Nurse D obviously felt safe to behave in a deceitful manner because, despite acting beyond her authority, the risk of censure was insignificant. Nurse E told Nurse D not to do it again, and no apology was made to Leesa. The alliance between Nurse D, Nurse C, and Nurse E illustrates that they, as members of a racially dominant group, hold similar views about Aborigines and will act to exclude them. This scenario reveals how Nurse C's and Nurse D's exercising of white race privilege ensured that Leesa did not work with them and that the penalty pay rates for the public holiday were the preserve of the white staff. Nurse C and Nurse D and other white staff also practiced these exclusionary tactics in the meal room, where Leesa was not included in conversations, and are evidence of the possessive nature of racialized power relations working within the hospital as everyday practice.

On or about July 23, Leesa was transferred to Townsville Hospital Renal Unit, where she was placed under the supervision of two preceptors, Nurse E and Nurse F. Nurse E's supervision of Leesa entailed speaking loud and slowly to her when giving instructions or providing quick and inadequate instruction. The other preceptor, Nurse F, spoke in an abrupt way to Leesa, indicating that she disapproved of supervising someone not deserving of her time and effort. Nurse E's and Nurse F's behavior suggests that they hold certain racist assumptions about Aboriginal people, namely, that they are inferior, unable to comprehend instructions, and should not be in the same professional space. Nurse E and Nurse F have the power to include and exclude within an environment where they dominate. As members of the racially dominant group, they can exercise their power deliberately and subconsciously, individually and collectively, as it operates normatively in everyday practice.

In or about early August 2002, Nurse G spoke in a loud, angry, and abrupt way to Leesa in response to her questions and communications in general. Leesa then made a complaint to Nurse H, who requested that Nurse G explain her behavior. Nurse G defended her position by stating she was unaware of how she spoke and that it was just Leesa's opinion. Nurse G's referral to the complaint just being a matter of Leesa's opinion illustrates two things: one, because of Leesa's Aboriginality, it did not hold any weight, and two, it is Leesa's interpretation that is the problem. Nurse G abdicates responsibility for her abusive behavior and Nurse H excuses her on the basis of her word. Leesa is

then counseled by Nurse H about being overly sensitive. Nurse H col-
ludes in Nurse G's abdication of responsibility through the excuses she
gives for her behavior. In effect, Nurse H favors Nurse G's explanation
and, conversely, is dismissive of Leesa's. There is no attempt to denounce
or criticize Nurse G's behavior, which sends a message to the staff that
it is acceptable to be abusive to Indigenous people because there will be
no repercussions. The race-blind discourse works invisibly to produce
these interactions as a form of personality clash and positions Leesa as
the person with the problem.

Subsequently, Nurse H convenes a meeting with an Indigenous
health manager, Mr. W, and the Director of Nursing, Nurse I, to discuss
Leesa's complaint. At the conclusion of the meeting, Nurse H encour-
ages Leesa to address her concerns to Nurse J, a young graduate nurse.
Leesa is also moved to a different division, where she experiences isolation and inadequate instruction. Clearly Leesa's complaint is not
taken seriously and she is perceived to be the problem that needs to be
dealt with. Her relocation and isolation can be seen as a form of punishment in retribution for her complaint. Nurse G, in contrast, is left
to continue her work, unscathed by the incident. The racialized power
relations within the institution worked against Leesa's interests but in
the interests of white staff. After the transfer, Leesa brings to the attention of Nurse H that her placement means she is not performing complex procedures. Nurse H responds by telling her that this is normal
practice. This is in contrast to the observations of a patient, Pastor
Messa, who tells Leesa that Nurse J has been performing complex procedures within the unit. Nurse H's assertion that Leesa's experience is
normal is contradicted by Pastor Messa's observations of Nurse J's
performance within the unit. This indicates that Nurse H is depriving
Leesa of training and giving preferential treatment to white graduate
nurses, who are allowed to conduct complex procedures.

Leesa subsequently brings her feelings of isolation and discrimination to the attention of the Head of Nursing, Nurse I, and the Education
Coordinator Jane, Mr. W, and Nurse K, the Clinical Nurse Consul-
tant. After listening to her complaint, no one investigates it; instead,
she is relegated to work within Aboriginal Health and allocated
menial tasks. The outcome of this meeting illustrates that it is Leesa
who is perceived again as being overly sensitive and incompetent. She
is removed and confined to carrying out menial tasks in an "Aboriginal identified domain" in the hope that she will be happier with her

people. No action is taken against the white nurses about whom she complained, and Leesa continues to be deprived of training in complex procedures, while other white graduate nurses acquire more skills.

On or about August 27, Nurse L speaks to Leesa in a demeaning and loud manner. According to Leesa, Nurse L's speech is witnessed by Linda, the Indigenous liaison officer, who comments on Nurse L's manner, stating to Leesa that "she speaks to you like a little girl." Nurse L's display of condescension illustrates that she thought Leesa was inferior to her and treated her accordingly. Nurse L's ability to speak openly to Leesa in this manner, in the presence of another Indigenous person, is expressive of a racial arrogance that is sanctioned by a culturally safe environment that tolerates such behavior.

On or about August 29, Leesa, on behalf of another Indigenous patient, informs Nurse L that the patient's son has not attended the unit for dialysis treatment and his mother wants Leesa to contact him. Nurse L does not discuss the matter with Leesa. Instead, Nurse L consults Nurse H and they move to another room to deal with the matter. While it can be acknowledged on one level that Nurse L and Nurse H, as senior nurses, are entitled to discuss the matter independently of Leesa, two questions arise: Why did they move away from Leesa to discuss it, and why did they not inform her subsequently of their discussions given that it was a simple request to make contact with an Indigenous patient? On another level, considered in the broader context of the pattern of behavior displayed by Nurse L, Nurse H, and other nursing staff, this event is consistent with a desire to marginalize Leesa for reasons other than professional or procedural considerations and demonstrates the possessive nature of the control of space by white staff.

On or about September 26, Nurse E requested that Leesa assist her with the connection of intravenous lines. Leesa seeks clarification on a preliminary procedure and is instructed by Nurse E to simply insert the syringe. Leesa complies and then is blamed by Nurse E, over a period of minutes in the presence of the patient, for the resulting mishap. Nurse E then leaves Leesa to deal with the distressed patient. Nurse E did not take responsibility for her incorrect instruction; instead, she openly criticizes Leesa's competency in an unfair manner in the presence of a patient. While Nurse E may act in this manner toward all her junior staff, every time Nurse E makes a mistake there is a consistency in her negative treatment of Leesa, which reflects the pattern of behavior of other white staff. This collective behavior indicates that Leesa's "Aboriginality" is a problem for the white nurses because it is "their" space.

On or about September 30, Leesa experiences exclusion by other members of staff in the renal unit. Leesa is not included in their social conversations and is ignored when Nurse D extends her courtesy to all staff to purchase items from the café. If all the staff are white, and none of them is excluded in this context, and Leesa is excluded as the only Aboriginal person in the room, then consistent with the behavioral trend, race must play a part in the act of exclusion.

On or about September 30, Leesa received notice that she was rostered on a shift on October 3 for peritoneal dialysis. However, she had requested to attend computer training on that date. Leesa approached Nurse H about attending the training, only to be told that the training had been cancelled on that date. Leesa responded to Nurse H by stating that she had that morning received confirmation of her attendance. Nurse H then replied that she could not attend because of staff shortages. The shift in explanation by Nurse H appears to have changed because the first excuse was exposed as a fabrication.

On or about October 8, Leesa requested time to attend a peritoneal course that would be conducted over five days. Nurse H told Lisa that she could attend for only one day. She would have to attend the remainder of the training on her own time. Leesa was aware that Nurse J and another white graduate nurse were permitted to attend the training. Nurse H's patently discriminatory denial of training opportunities appears to be tied to an assumption that she knows what is best for Leesa and she will determine who is worth investing in. This is consistent with Nurse H's previous behavior of not taking Leesa's complaints seriously. Nurse H does not value Leesa's concerns or her application to be trained, which indicates that she perceives Leesa as someone who does not belong within the hospital as a qualified nurse.

Open Remarks about Aboriginal People

On or about September 13, Leesa hears Nurse M openly remarking that Palm Island Hospital was dirty because the domestic staff were Indigenous—making the claim that her footprint remained on the floor from one day to the next. The existence of a footprint could be accounted for by any one of a number of explanations. The footprint may not have been Nurse M's, but for her it served as evidence of the uncleanliness of Aboriginal people. It reinforces the commonly held view that Aborigines contaminate the hospital space, which should be clean, pure, and white.

On or about September 24, Nurse E, from whom Leesa previously experienced discriminatory behavior, made comments to the effect that Aboriginal youth do not want to work and become responsible and that Aboriginal people lack knowledge about managing land. What underpins Nurse E's comments is the pathologizing of Aborigines as lazy, irresponsible, and incompetent.

The fact that both Nurse M and Nurse E could openly express these views in the presence of Leesa goes beyond mere insensitivity and illustrates the degree to which racialized power relations operated within the hospital. Both nurses demonstrated their indifference to Leesa's presence or causing her offense because it was safe to do so. Safety is predicated on certainty, which comes from repetition, and is one of the ways by which normalizing processes work. Thus their remarks would not be challenged because they would not be considered racist. They are not challenging the dominant view within the institution.

On or about September 13, Leesa observed that Indigenous patients were treated less favorably than white patients. Nurse G and Nurse M both made loud statements about Indigenous patients. Nurse G responded to an Indigenous hearing-impaired patient's lack of response to her by stating, "I may as well speak to the wall." Nurse G's statement illustrates that she had little or no compassion for the patient's disability, reducing him to being the equivalent of a wall, an inanimate object that lacks humanity.

On or about September 16, 2002, Nurse M, who had previously made comments about Indigenous cleaners at the Palm Island Hospital, when informed that an indigenous patient did not turn up for his appointment in Brisbane, stated that "it was a waste of tax payers' dollars." Nurse M's comment implies that it is only white people who pay taxes and taxpayers' money should not be wasted on an Indigenous person. Nurse G's and Nurse M's statements are consistent with racial stereotypes that position Indigenous people as inferior, less than human, and unworthy of the same treatment as white people. The fact that they felt they could make such statements aloud indicates that they felt safe in the institutional context to air such views. Their sense of safety signals that such comments are considered normal within the white space of the hospital.

Conclusion

The consistency of racially discriminatory individual behaviors and attitudes operating independently in different contexts, which Leesa experienced over a period of approximately six months, demonstrates that they cannot be reduced to individualized personality traits. These shared behaviors and attitudes display a pattern that forms part of the white culture and ownership of the hospital. It is a culture that supports management's refusal to deal with Leesa's grievances in a serious and professional way and lacks disciplinary processes for the staff involved, which, by omission and commission, reinforces the tolerance and perpetuation of racism. As Goldberg argues, "Where there is a recognizable, institutionally governed pattern of racially predicated discrimination or exclusion, ongoing because unrectified, the presumption must be that the continuing exclusions are considered permissible by those institutionally able to do something about them."[20]

The use of "overly sensitive" as an individual personality trait that was ascribed to Leesa was strategically deployed as a race-blind technique to mask the racism that underpins it. The staff operationalized a race-blind discourse to construct Leesa as the problem. Simultaneously, the possessiveness demonstrated by the white staff's actions signaled to Leesa that she had no proprietary claims on the space in which she worked, or to being a nurse, and she could be moved around at their discretion. The possessiveness of their white race privilege was exercised within the events that unfolded to exclude and inferiorize Leesa. Yet "race" was denied by all the white staff as having anything to do with the events, which is an example of how a race-blind and power-evasive discourse enables racism to flourish. When white people say that "race does not matter" and that "there are only small pockets of racism" within Australian society, they are speaking from a position whereby the possessive nature of their race privilege remains invisible to them. Indigenous people witness on a daily basis the luxury of being race-blind and possessive in institutions such as hospitals, universities, schools, bureaucracies, and the law. This raises the question of whether race-discrimination legislation can address the racism that Indigenous people experience if it serves to function discursively, informing white common-sense understandings of Australia's tolerance instead of our reality of white possession. As Gaze argues:

> The law's limited ability to deal with discrimination as a systemic practice is confirmed by the lack of provision for systemic remedies that can reach beyond the scope of a particular case and address problematic practices that extend beyond that case. Where discrimination results from weaknesses in personnel practices that may well occur in other cases, there should be power to require an employer to change its employment practices generally. However, Australian anti-discrimination laws do not allow such remedies. The remedial powers of the federal courts, for example in s 46PO(4) of the HREOC Act, are limited to actions and orders concerned with redressing the situations of complainant in the particular case—there is no power to make a broader order. This is an area in need of reform if systemic discrimination is to be addressed.[21]

Most Indigenous cases involving racial discrimination that are brought before the law are for the lack of customer service provision, such as the refusal of service within a department store.[22] Leesa's case was one of the few concerning racial discrimination within the workplace. For Leesa, it took a great deal of strength and courage to take action. She could have chosen silence, and thus self-denial, as the only way to survive. Instead, she chose to stand on her sovereign ground. As in other cases where Indigenous people have taken legal action, there is great personal cost. Leesa no longer practices as a nurse.

8   THE LEGACY OF COOK'S CHOICE

CAPTAIN JAMES COOK looms large as an iconic figure in the Australian imaginary. His name is synonymous with "discovering" Australia, and his reputation has grown over time as the West's greatest seafarer. As an enduring icon, his face is displayed on water bottles, plates, and other paraphernalia in Australian popular culture. As a historical figure, he is placed at the beginning of Australian history.[1] Within the academy, there is an impressive array of literature about Captain Cook, but perhaps the most controversial is the debate between Marshall Sahlins and Gananath Obeyesekere. Sahlins argued in *How "Natives" Think: About Captain Cook, for Example*, that Captain Cook's death at the hands of the Hawaiians in 1779 was not premeditated; rather, it was a ritual sequel to the Makahiki because Cook was perceived as being Lono: a god in Hawaiian mythology who must be killed when he returns from his journey.[2] Obeyesekere, responding to Sahlins's earlier work, questioned whether the Hawaiians did perceive Cook to be their returning God; instead, he argues that the apotheosis of Cook has more to do with Western mythmaking than with Hawaiian mythology.[3] This debate culminated in a special forum on theory in anthropology led by Robert Borofsky in the journal *Current Anthropology*.[4] It is an interesting debate about who possesses the most knowledge, the most legitimacy, and the most evidence about Cook's death. In responding to the debate, Hawaiian scholar Herb Kawainui Kane argues that the one cultural fact overlooked is that within Polynesian languages there is no language equivalent for "western religious terms such as 'divine,' 'god,' 'adoration,' 'holy,' 'sacrifice,' and 'religion'. . . . [He notes that] Cooks' men may be excused for their religious vocabulary, but social anthropologists may not be excused for perpetuating it as a scientific lexicon."[5]

This leads me to ask: If there is no Hawaiian language equivalent in relation to the concepts deployed by those who recorded the events of Cook's death, and these concepts are used as evidence for representing how the natives think, is it not reasonable to assume that it is not Hawaiian epistemology informing the debate? The "evidence" for how native Hawaiians thought about Cook's death illustrates how the "native" is an epistemological possession who is already known first by the white sailors and now academics. This chapter is not primarily concerned with the events surrounding Cook's death. Instead, it considers the epistemology and ontology informing Cook's choice to take possession of Australia in the name of King George III of Britain without the consent of, or treaty with, the "natives." His decision raises a question: What does the nonrecognition of Indigenous sovereignty impart about the constitution, currency, and circulation of white possession? In this chapter, I argue that possessiveness functions socio-discursively to inform and shape white subjectivity and the law.

White possession operates discursively within knowledge production through universals, dominant norms, values, and beliefs. Racialized knowledge was already operating as a discourse before Cook left England. In the sixteenth century, modernity gave rise to the construction of "blackness" as skin color,[6] which arose primarily because the contact between Englishmen and Africans was in West Africa and the Congo, "where men were not merely dark but almost literally black."[7] However, the meaning of "black" had currency before the trade in Africa. In the sixteenth century, it was identified in the *Oxford English Dictionary* as being "deeply stained with dirt; . . . Foul, iniquitous, atrocious, horrible, wicked. . . . Indicating disgrace, censure, liability or punishment, etc."[8] Over the next century the meanings attached to "blackness" as a color became transposed ephemerally to represent the black body as the signifier of inferiority. By the time Cook "discovered" Australia, the black/white binary had become a part of the English language and the inferiority of black people was entrenched in discourse.

The Constitutive Elements of White Possessiveness

James Cook came from a lower-class white family. His father worked on a farm near Whitby, where the young James attended school. He later worked as a haberdasher before taking up an apprenticeship in the coal trade, where under the tutelage of Quaker John Walker he studied mathematics and navigation. By the time he was twenty-eight years old, he had been offered the job of commander of a collier but chose instead to join the Royal Navy.[9] Beaglehole states that Cook

> volunteered just as the Seven Years' War was breaking out. He saw Channel service. In a few months he was promoted master's mate, and then master; he crossed the Atlantic and was one of the men responsible for sounding and charting the St. Lawrence river before the fleet went up with Wolfe's men for the assault on Quebec; and on the American station he had a period of wintering at Halifax that gave him a chance to read more deeply in mathematics and in astronomy, the foundations of the higher navigation. More, he met a military engineer famous in his day, Samuel Holland, who introduced him to the theory and practice of surveying. . . . His charts became known; the commodores and admirals began to take notice, and shortly after the war Cook had his first independent command.[10]

Beaglehole argues that it is difficult to ascertain Cook's character from his letters, but exploring the letters of those who worked for, or with him, provides insights. Cook was a meticulous planner, followed instructions, believed in taking calculated risks, was patient and observant, incorporated new technology, acquired new knowledge, and was passionate about exploring new horizons and creating new charts of new lands. He ran his ship on the basis of equity and fairness. He was concerned about the welfare of his crew and the maintenance of his ship. Cook took care of the things and people within his control and possession.[11] He was a disciplined subject who possessed the necessary skills, knowledge, and abilities to fulfill his goals in the service of the Crown, as he stated on his trip south to the Antarctic on January 30, 1774: "I whose ambition leads me not only farther than any other man has been before me, but as far as I think it possible for man to go."[12] Cook's words reveal a man who knew his achievements were great and his place in history secured.

History tells us that taking possession of Indigenous people's lands was a quintessential act of colonization. After crossing the Atlantic to chart the shores of Newfoundland in the schooner *Grenville*, James Cook was promoted to lieutenant and commissioned by the Royal Society in 1768 to travel to the south sea with two astronomers on board to observe the transit of Venus in 1769. While the commission was originally from the Royal Society, the Admiralty decided to extend the mission to include charting Tahiti and New Zealand and finding the great southern continent.[13] Cook's instructions from the Royal Society were clear should he encounter any "natives." James Douglas, president of the Royal Society, stated: "They are the natural, and in the strictest sense of the word, the legal possessors of the several regions they inhabit. . . . No European Nation has a right to occupy any part of their country, or settle among them without their voluntary consent. Conquest over such people can give no just title."[14] The Admiralty's secret instructions were, if Cook found the great southern continent and encountered "natives," to "endeavour by all proper means to cultivate a friendship and alliance with them. . . . You are also with the consent of the natives to take possession of convenient situations in the country in the name of the King of Great Britain, or, if you find the country uninhabited take possession for his Majesty."[15]

Both sets of instructions acknowledge that the "natives" had existing proprietary rights, but should they wish to forgo them by consent, then their lands could be possessed in the name of the king. Underpinning both sets of instructions is an assumption that the "natives" would agree to give up their sovereignty, which suggests, in turn, that the "natives" are already known in a particular way. As Cook made his way up the east coast of Australia, he wrote that the Indigenous people were small in number and were less technologically advanced than other Indigenous groups he had encountered elsewhere. They did not cultivate the land, were unwarlike, and were not interested in trade. He believed that they existed in a state of nature, noting that "we never were able to form any connections with them. . . . They had not so much as touch'd the things we had left in their hutts on purpose for them to take away. . . . [They] set no value upon any thing we gave them, nor would they ever part with anything of their own for any one article we could offer them."[16]

Cook's statement provides an insight into his decision to take possession in the name of King George III on August 22, 1770. Following Cook's logic, if Indigenous people did not value the possessions he offered and were not interested in trade, then they did not have an understanding of the exchange value of goods. Thus he could deduce that they must be living in a state of nature with a sense of property that did not go beyond satisfying their immediate needs. Thus, taking possession did not require their consent. Cook proclaimed possession of the whole of the eastern coast from the thirty-eighth-degree parallel in the name of the king after he landed on an island he named Possession situated off the tip of Cape York Peninsula. Taking possession involved the firing of guns, the raising of a flag, the crew bearing witness, and Cook's written record of the events. Although symbolic in nature, this performative act of sovereignty on Possession Island existed epistemologically and materially only for Cook and his crew, not for Indigenous people. It did not require the consent of the natives because Cook had already determined their willingness to forgo their sovereignty because of his perception that they did not display the kind of possessiveness that he knew and demonstrated.

Cook's subjectivity was the product of the transition from feudalism to modernity, which precipitated the emergence of a new white subject into history in Britain. Major social, legal, economic, and political reforms had taken place, changing the character of the persons and property relationship. "These changes centered upon the rise of 'possessive individualism,' that is, upon an increasing consciousness of the distinctness of each self-owning human entity as the primary social and political value."[17] Private ownership of property, both tangible and intangible, operated through mechanisms of the new nation-state in its regulation of the population and especially through the law. By the late 1700s, people in Britain could legally enter into different kinds of contractual arrangements whereby they could own land, sell their labor, and possess their identities, all of which were formed through their relationship to capital and the state. A new white property-owning subject emerged and became embedded in everyday discourse as "a firm belief that the best in life was the expansion of self through property and property began and ended with possession of one's body."[18]

Thus, within the realm of intrasubjectivity, possession can mean control over one's being, one's ideas, one's mind, one's feelings, and one's body, or within intersubjectivity it can mean the act or fact of possessing something that is beyond the subject, and in other contexts it can refer to a state of being possessed by another. Within the law, possession can refer to holding or occupying territory with or without actual ownership, or a thing possessed, such as property or wealth, and it can also refer to territorial domination of a state. Thus white possession functioned socio-discursively as a regime within Britain, enabling Cook's voyages and the spread of empire.

White possession operated through a socio-discursive regime that ontologically shaped the formation of white subjectivity regulated through various discourses, such as the law. Within modernity, subjectivity became constituted by two particularities: the substantive and the abstract. Substantive subjectivity is characterized by gender, race, sexuality, and nationality, but these characteristics are secondary to how we are constituted through the abstract formal particularity of being, which is institutionally embedded and invoked "when we function as citizens, as legal subjects or as participants in the market economy."[19] At an ontological level, the structure of subjective possession occurs through the imposition of one's will-to-be on the thing that is perceived to lack will; thus it is open to being possessed. This enables the formally free subject to make the thing its own. Ascribing one's own subjective will onto the thing is required to make it one's property, as "willful possession of what was previously a will-less thing constitutes our primary form of embodiment; it is invoked whenever we assert: this is mine."[20] To be able to assert "this is mine" requires a subject to internalize the idea that one has proprietary rights that are part of normative behavior, rules of interaction, and social engagement. Thus possession, which constitutes part of the ontological structure of white subjectivity, is also constituted socio-discursively. For Cook to be able to take possession of the east coast of Australia without the consent of the "natives" means that he had to position Aboriginal people as will-less things in order to take their land in the name of the king. Thus Cook's white possessiveness operated ontologically and epistemologically by willing away Indigenous people's sovereignty in order to make them appear will-less.

Cook described Indigenous people in terms of their range of color, from dark chocolate to soot, the further north he traveled. Cook's racialization of the Indigenous "other" is simultaneously a white proprietary exercise. When Cook deployed racialized discourse to mark the Indigenous "other" as will-less and black, he is producing through knowledge a subject of his own making, one that he interprets for himself. This process violates the subjectivity of Indigenous people by obliterating any trace of our ontological and epistemological existence. In other words, the Indigenous "others" are represented and constituted in discourse as white epistemological possessions. This epistemological possessiveness operated as an inhibitor to reduce the capacity for Indigenous people to be recognized as having a will, as property-owning sovereign subjects possessing different knowledges, which is why Cook perceived us as living in a "state of nature," where our possession was recognized only as satisfying our immediate needs.

Possessing Cook

Possessiveness as a constitutive element of white subjectivity is evidenced within Indigenous oral history, whether it relates specifically to Cook and his voyage or to subsequent acts of dispossession, suppression, and oppression. In July 1770, Cook spent time on the Endeavour River undertaking repairs to his ship *Endeavour*. During his stay, he ordered some of his men to catch fish and turtles in order to feed the crew. Over a number of days, the "natives" visit the *Endeavour* and on July 18, after returning from shore to the ship, Cook notes that they seemed curious, taking more notice of the twelve turtles on deck than anything else. On July 19, when a number of "natives" came on board the ship, he wrote:

> Those that came on board were very desirous of having some of our turtle and took the liberty to haul two to the gang way to put over the side but being disapointed in it this they grew a little troublesome, and was were for throwing every thing overboard they could lay their hands upon; as we had no victuals dress'd at this time I offer'd them some bread to eat, which they rejected with scorn as I believe they would have done any thing else excepting turtle—soon after they all went a shore Mr Banks my self and five or six more of our people being a shore at the same time, emmediatly upon their landing one of them took a handful of dry grass and lighted it at a fire we had a shore and before we well know'd what he was going about he made a large circuit round about us and set fire to the grass on the ground in this way which and in an instant burst like wild fire the whole place was in flames, luckily at this time we had hardly any thing ashire besides the forge and a sow with a Litter of young pigs one of which was scorched to death in the fire—as soon as they had done this they all went to a place where some of our people were washing and where all our nets and a good deal of linnen were laid out to dry, here with the greatest obstinacy they again set fire to the grass which I and some others who were present could to prevent until I was obliged to fire a musquet load with small shott at one of the rig leaders which sent them off. as we were apprised of this last attempt of theirs we got the fire out before it got head, but the first spread like wild fire in the woods and grass. Notwithstanding my fireing in which one must have been hurt because we saw some a few drops of blood on some of the linnen he had cross'd gone over, they did not go far from us for we soon after heard their voices in the woods upon which Mr Banks and I and 3 or 4 more went to look for them and very soon met them comeing [*sic*] toward us as they had each 4 or 5 darts a piece and not knowing their intentions we seized upon six or seven of the first darts we met with, this alarmed them so much that they all made off and we followd them for near half a mile and then set down and call'd to them and they stop'd also; after some little unintelligible conversation had

pass' between us they law down their darts and came to us in a very friendly
manner we now return'd them the darts we had taken from them which
reconciled every thing. We now found there were 4 strangers among them
that we had not seen before and these were interduce'd to us by name by
the others: the man which we suppos'd to have been wounded struck with
small shott was gone off, but he could not be much hurt as he was at a great
distance when I fired. They all came along with us abreast of the ship where
they stay'd a short time and then went away and soon after set the woods on
fire about a mile and a half and two miles from us.[21]

Cook's version of events takes place in Guugu Yimithirr's country.
More specifically, it is the land of the Bubu Gujin clan, and it is the only
place on Cook's voyage up the east coast of Australia where he spends
a number of days on dry land. Gerhardt Pearson from Hopevale explained to Peter Botsman that within Guugu Yimithirr's oral history
the incident on the Endeavour River is remembered in the following
way: "It was the taking of a dozen turtles by the desperate sailors that
precipitated the only violent conflict in the brief sojourn on what is now
the Endeavour River at Cooktown. Why? Wantonly killing a person's
totem was akin to murder of the person itself. No permission was
granted to take so many from the guardians of the turtle or its clan."[22]
According to their law, the Bubu Gujin were exercising their proprietary rights over the turtles that lay on the deck of the Endeavour. The
sailors did not have permission to take what was not theirs and the
Bubu Gujin retaliated. They consciously set fire to the area where
Cook's possessions lay on land in order to destroy them. They understood that what was important to Cook and his men were the things
that Cook and his men possessed. In order to protect his possessions,
Cook responds by firing and wounding one of the Bubu Gujin, who
then leave and subsequently return armed to do battle to defend their
territory. After Cook calls out to the Bubu Gujin, they stop and begin
to discuss the dispute, agreeing to end the conflict. Cook returns their
spears. For the Bubu Gujin, the return of their possessions was taken
as a reconciliatory act. However, they later set fire to the land as an act
of purging and purifying the country of their unwanted guests who
broke the law. Cook does not explain in his journal why this event happened; he only records that it did. He acknowledges the Bubu Gujin's
interest in the turtles but appears to regard that interest only in terms
of curiosity and the desire for food. In so doing, he misperceives the
Bubu Gujin's surveillance of his crew's actions over a number of days;

they were watching what was being taken without their consent. Cook and his men did not understand the Bubu Gujin's sovereign proprietary rights in the turtles. Instead, Cook's idea of possession was informed by the logic of capital, according to which possessions are those things having an exchange value when they are sold or otherwise traded, usually man-made material objects or things occurring naturally and taken without constraint. This logic underpins Cook's perception of Indigenous people as being propertyless and living in a state of nature where possessions do not go beyond satisfying their immediate needs. Being perceived as living in a state of nature relegates one's existence to being an inseparable part of nature and therefore incapable of possessing it.

Cook's inability to understand the complexity of Indigenous sovereign law and the ontological possessiveness of his subjectivity is also expressed in the cultural logic of the Yarralin people of the Victoria River district in the Northern Territory. As Bird Rose argues, the origins of injustices committed against Indigenous people are perceived to be embodied within the persona of Captain Cook.[23] In several discussions with Rose, an old man named Hobbles speaks about Captain Cook:

> And right up to Gurindji now we remember for you. . . . Captain Cook. I know. We're going to get a lot of people now. All over Australia, its belong to Aboriginal. But you made little mistake. Why didn't you look after London and big England? It's bigger than Australia. That's your country. Why didn't you stop your government, Captain Cook? You're the one bring it out now, all your government from big England. You brought that law.[24]
>
> You been bring that law. My Law only one. Your law keep changing. I know you keep changing now lotta law. You and Gilruth. That's another headquarters longa Darwin. That's the Gilruth. You, Captain Cook, you the one been bringing in now lotta man. Why didn't you give me fair go for my people. Why didn't you give it me fair go for my people? Should have asked them about the story. Same thing, I might go on another place, I must askem. I might stay for couple of days, you know. That's for the mefellow, Aboriginal people. But you the Captain Cook. I know you been stealing country belong to mefellow. Australia. What we call Australia, that's for Aboriginal people. But him been take it away. You been take that land, you been take the mineral, take the gold, everything. Take it up to this big England. And make all that thing, and make your big Parliament too.
>
> Nother thing. Captain Cook coming back big boss now. Bringing nother lot government belong you. Still you been bring your book, and follow your book, Captain Cook. We know you government. When you been bring it over to Sydney, there people been work it up. Government been work it up. You reckon: "white man's country." No. This not the white man's country. This Aboriginal country.[25]

Bird Rose argues that Hobbles provides many different stories of Cook, but that they are "all are based in the fundamental problematic of invasion and Law; all rest on the proposition that Captain Cook is an outlaw, morally speaking. . . . Many of the stories detail a process whereby conquest led to control which allowed the means for conquest to be continually reproduced."[26] The discursive turn in Hobbles's stories about Cook illuminate a white possessiveness that is synonymous with those who descended on this land claiming it as their own, establishing the Australian nation in the form of parliament and law. The past and the present become blurred by the repetition of injustice enabled by government control of Indigenous lands and people that is an outcome of their willful possession beginning with Cook. Hobbles's way of knowing and being comes from a different law that informs his sense of the injustice committed against his people in the name of white law. Although he recognizes the theft of Indigenous land, he is adamant that Australia was and continues to be owned by Indigenous people. Indigenous sovereignty continues because only Indigenous people have the proper law for the country. Within Hobbles's narrative, the possessive nature of white people is evidenced by their continual "taking" of resources and land sanctioned by their own law, which illuminates how white possession operates ontologically and epistemologically within white subjectivity and nationhood driven by the logic of capital.

Indigenous Possessions

Hobbles, like other Indigenous people, shares a history of colonization whereby we became the legal possessions of the Crown. Under the legal fiction of *terra nullius*, the law of the colonizer prevailed and Indigenous people were placed under British jurisdiction as subjects of the Crown who were entitled formally to the rights associated with this status. Equality of status did not prevent Indigenous people from being murdered, nor did it ensure their legal protection. Few punitive measures were taken against European offenders who killed them, yet Indigenous people who took the lives of colonists were charged under British law and dealt with accordingly.[27] The actions of the British military and colonists were more akin to a state of war, in which combatants do not have equal rights. The legal status of Indigenous people as subjects of the Crown was not sanctioned by the normative expectations of colonists who treated, constructed, and represented Indigenous people as less than human with no proprietary rights.

The diminished status of Indigenous people as subjects of the Crown was legally enhanced in the 1850s. New South Wales's Legislative Council denied Indigenous people civil rights even though the British House of Commons specifically legislated granting this right.[28] Within the racialized social contract between subjects and the Crown, it is civil rights that confer subjects with the right to own property and land as well as the right to representation within courts. The legislative council, in accordance with the colony's constitution and judiciary, revoked the British legislation because it was argued that Indigenous people were perceived as having no conception of the state and did not adhere to Christian beliefs. Indigenous people's proprietary rights became willed away through the deployment of white morality and the law. Effectively, Indigenous people were, in the absence of being subjects of the Crown, relegated to little or no more than living in a state of nature and thus, by definition, uncivilized. The prevention of Indigenous people from taking an oath also meant that white possession and title to land could not be legally contested. The actions of the legislative council had a powerful influence on the subsequent development of policy in other states and should be considered within the context of the appropriation of Indigenous lands. Transportation had ceased in 1840 and a colonial mode of production had been established that saw the rapid expansion of the wool industry from the 1820s.[29] Land grants until now had been in the hands of the governor, who acted on behalf of Britain. The British state had granted the formation of legislative councils in the colonies, appointing members who were largely landholders and whose primary concern was land ownership and the integration of the colony as a supplier of raw materials to Britain. These landholders began to push for the commodification of land by requiring that squatters purchase the land they leased from Britain. The outcome of this action was the Selection Acts of 1861.[30]

It was not until the 1880s that a formal policy of intervention was developed to control Indigenous people in the colony of New South Wales. The establishment of the office of the Protector by the Colonial Government meant the further erosion of civil rights for Indigenous people. Through this legal mechanism, Indigenous people became possessions of the Crown as wards of the state. Indigenous people's lives were controlled by the Protector; they received rations and clothes and had to reside on reserve land controlled by managers who worked for the state. For Indigenous people, the status of being a subject of the Crown became qualified through the assumption of legal guardianship by the state, the denial of civil rights, and vicarious assignment of their social rights. The rights of Indigenous people were vicarious in the sense that the government as guardian legally vested the rights in others who could exercise them on their behalf. The actions of the New South Wales colonial government toward Indigenous people set the precedent for other states. Indigenous people were the legal possessions of state and territory governments and were denied economic, civil, and political rights until the 1960s.

The eruption of the rights discourse in the 1970s was due to influences that were both global and national in character, influenced by events in the 1960s that challenged established norms, values, and social conventions. The antagonisms, confrontations, and struggles of the 1960s became represented strategically and tactically through a discourse of rights in the 1970s. In Australia, the effects were twofold: the formal assertion of Australia as an independent sovereign nation, and the rights claims of subjects within its borders. Australia's formal separation from British judicial review meant that the High Court of Australia was the final court of appeal. Discriminatory legislation affecting Indigenous people was revoked and our human rights were brought into a broader public discourse that encompassed racial and sexual discrimination. At the same time, what it meant to be an Australian was being redefined. The White Australia policy was formally abolished in 1972 and multiculturalism was promoted as Australia's new national policy.[31]

Since the 1970s, the national, territory, and state governments have implemented land rights regimes in one form or another, and in the 1990s native title became an aspect of Australian property law. The land rights and native title regimes currently in place hold that Indigenous title exists primarily in the form of traditional laws and customs or historical association and claims are restricted to vacant Crown land. While some mineral rights are acknowledged, as in the New South Wales Land Rights Act, the majority of land rights and native title regimes do "not come with commercially significant and legally recognised resource rights."[32] The current form of land tenures is either inalienable freehold title or native title, neither of which constitutes an

asset or equity for purposes of capital development. The right to negotiate under native title and the right to consent under land rights regimes
are nothing more than the right to a process. In the absence of equal
proprietary rights and bargaining power, they cannot deliver economic
development, locking Indigenous people into welfare. In their current
form, the right to negotiate and the right to consent and receive royal-
ties are insufficient to generate wealth, and the Crown reserves the right
to determine if its interests or those of private enterprise prevail. The
legislative and administrative arrangements that circumscribe Indigenous "ownership" in its current forms effectively reduce it to hunting-
and-gathering rights and some rights of residence. This resonates with
Cook's assumption that Indigenous people continue to live in a state of
nature with a sense of property that is confined to our immediate needs.
Nowhere is this more evident than in the findings of the United Nations
Committee on the Elimination of Racial Discrimination (CERD) in
March 1999, when the government led by then Prime Minister John
Howard amended the Native Title Act.

The United Nation's CERD found that Australian common law is
racially discriminatory because Native Title is a vulnerable property
right that is less protected from interference and forced alienation than
other land titles.[33] The main aims of the original Native Title Act, the
protection and recognition of Native Title, have been diminished to the
extent that the new provisions impair or extinguish Native Title rights
and interests. The increased criteria for registration under the amended
act reduce the ability of Native Title claimants to assert their native
title rights. With regard to the validation of certain past invalid acts,
the new amended act is discriminatory because it only provides for
extinguishment of Native Title and no other titles. In effect, the Native
Title Amendment Act 1998 discriminates against Indigenous native
titleholders by validating past acts, extinguishing native title, upgrading
non-Indigenous title, and restricting the Indigenous right to negotiate.
The CERD decision has not been attended to by the federal government, which illustrates the degree to which white possession will be
protected and reinforced as an attribute of white subjectivity and nationhood within Australia. Indigenous communal property rights are never
accorded equal value because ontologically white possession requires
that Indigenous people are not perceived as being out of a state of nature.
White possession can only recognize Indigenous people as being out
of nature through private property rights via the prism of citizenship.

Indigenous people can own property in this sense, but not a different epistemological and ontological embodiment of possession that is outside the logic of capital.

Conclusion

Since Captain Cook's original choice not to gain our consent, the legacy of white possession continues to function socio-discursively within Australian society. As a means of controlling differently racialized populations enclosed within its borders, white subjects are disciplined (though to different degrees) as citizens to invest in the nation as a white possession. As citizens of this white nation, they are contracted into, and imbued with, a sense of belonging and ownership. It is a sense of belonging derived from ownership, understood within the logic of capital, and, in its self-legitimation, it mobilizes the legend of Cook's discovery of an unpossessed land.

The current form of recognizing Indigenous communal property rights reinforces white possession because advantages continue to be accorded to "those who have profited most from present and post racial discrimination . . . especially through intergenerational transfers of inherited wealth that pass on the spoils of discrimination to succeeding generations."[34] The legacy of Cook's choice is the continual denial of Indigenous sovereignty rights and the creation of forms of communal title that continue to place Indigenous people within a state of nature attendant only to our immediate needs, such as hunting-and-gathering rights. Against this stands the continued willfulness of Indigenous people who have never ceded our sovereignty.

III. Being Property

9 TOWARD A NEW RESEARCH AGENDA

Foucault, Whiteness, and Sovereignty

Now post-*Mabo* and the "death" of *terra nullius*, questions lay
at the feet of the Australian state. What legitimises your entry?
Do you still require the consent of the natives? And if we give it
to you now what meaning will you or I give to that agreement?
For who will hold the colonising state and its growing globalised
identity to honour and respect our laws, territories and right to
life? No one has in the past.

—Irene Watson, *Aboriginal and the Sovereignty of Terra Nullius*

IN THE EPIGRAPH ABOVE, Indigenous scholar Irene Watson poses
questions that are almost unimaginable in the context of Australian
sociology where the discussion of "sovereignty" in modernity does not
include Indigenous subjects. The "sociological imagination" has not
been applied to investigate the existence of Indigenous sovereignty
within both structure and agency, yet this is surely what sociology
requires. C. Wright Mills coined this popular phrase, which is used as
an epistemic tool to distinguish the "sociological" from the social.
Developing a sociological imagination means one should be able to
think beyond the temple of one's familiar to examine the social world
in new and unfamiliar ways. My enthusiasm for Foucault's *Society
Must Be Defended* is predicated on the way in which the "unfamiliar"
in his work stimulates the sociological imagination.[1]

This chapter is also influenced by the work of Indigenous scholars
such as Irene Watson and Taiaiake Alfred, who advocate abandoning
the concept of Indigenous sovereignty as it is configured in debates about
Indigenous rights.[2] Raymond Williams and Patricia Monture-Angus,
whose scholarship questions the epistemological basis of Western law

and its application to Indigenous sovereignty struggles, also inform this piece.[3] The influence of their work has led me to consider the usefulness of Foucault's conceptual framework, as developed in *Society Must Be Defended*, for analyzing how white possession, as a mode of rationality, functions within disciplinary knowledges and regulatory mechanisms defining and circumscribing Indigenous sovereignty in particular ways.[4] This chapter considers recent work in whiteness studies in Australia and abroad as well as literature using Foucault's idea of the relationship between race, sovereignty, and war. I offer it as a work in progress to stimulate thinking about Indigenous sovereignty in a different way. The chapter begins with a discussion of the current literature on Indigenous rights followed by an overview of Foucault's central ideas in *Society Must Be Defended*. I then outline Australian critical whiteness literature concerning Indigenous sovereignty and, together with Foucault's ideas about race, war, and sovereignty, pose certain questions for future research. In the conclusion, I suggest that such a research agenda would contribute to the scope and depth of existing work on Indigenous sovereignty.

The Judicio-political Framework

In the past three decades, questions about the status and rights of Indigenous peoples within "settler" nation-states has led to the development of a new literature within the academy across a number of disciplines, such as Australian studies and Aboriginal studies, changes in domestic policy, and discussion of rights in public discourse and international law. Since the 1990s in particular, there has been a proliferation of literature on Indigenous sovereignty and rights. This literature is often international in scope, drawing on disciplines such as law, politics, history, anthropology, and philosophy to explore issues regarding Indigenous peoples' status and rights. It has raised fundamental questions about the complexion of the democratic state and has challenged the philosophical premises of concepts such as democracy and sovereignty. First, several scholars have addressed the limitations of liberalism as it applies to Indigenous sovereignty. Ivison, Patton, and Sanders argue that a new political theory should include the acknowledgment of Indigenous difference as the essential condition of the legitimacy of the institutions and practices within which rights and resources are to be distributed.[5] Second, the universalism of liberalism and the particularism of Indigenous rights should not be perceived as mutually exclusive but rather as reference points to begin a new form of negotiation. Other work offers a range of perspectives on the political, moral, and legal rights associated with Indigenous sovereignty and agreement making.[6] Several key legal texts have been published examining the status of Indigenous people in international law.[7]

In the Australian context the most cited work, *Aboriginal Sovereignty* by Henry Reynolds, charts the history of Indigenous sovereignty claims and their treatment by both law and government.[8] Bain Attwood critically extends Reynolds work by offering a history of campaigns for Indigenous rights between the 1870s and the 1970s.[9] Larissa Behrendt challenges the logic of formal equality by providing a clear and coherent articulation of Indigenous rights claims and the need for social justice.[10] This important and valuable literature offers detailed analyses of the racism embedded in the historical, political, and legal treatment of Indigenous sovereignty within the framework of sovereignty, rights, and law. It illustrates how Indigenous sovereignty claims have challenged conceptualizations of state sovereignty and, in a few instances, how it has worked to modify state rights through domestic and international law. The analysis of several case studies from Canada, the United States, New Zealand, and Australia provides insight into the pragmatics of exercising Indigenous sovereignty outside the realm of formal rights. In this body of scholarship, rights are perceived as being productive, enabling, and constraining, and the analysis of Indigenous rights is located within a judicio-political framework of law, right, and sovereignty. The limitation of this literature lies in the reliance on "rights" as the cipher for analyzing Indigenous sovereignty. It does not reorient our conceptualization of power outside of a law, right, and sovereignty paradigm to think about Indigenous sovereignty and power in different ways. Nor does this literature analyze race beyond "Indigeneity." However, it is my contention that using the work of Foucault and critical whiteness theorists to analyze the relationship between Indigenous sovereignty and state sovereignty promises to extend the scope of the existing literature.

Beyond the Judicio-political Framework

In *Society Must Be Defended*, Foucault offers an explanation of the development of racism and provides important insights into the mythology embedded in the history of the divine right of kings, the emergence of the theory of rights during modernity, and the establishment of what he conceptualizes as "biopower" through disciplinary and regulatory mechanisms. In these lectures, Foucault offers a genealogy of war from the seventeenth century to the present, arguing that war has been central to the development of the judicial edifice of right in democratic as well as socialist countries. He explains how the history of the divine right of kings, which worked in the interests of sovereign absolutism, was challenged through the work of Boulainvilliers, who produced a counterhistory to that of the king of France, effectively introducing the subject of rights into history. Refuting the myth of the inherited right to rule, Boulainvilliers's history of the nobility advanced the idea that because of war, they too had rights. Having become legitimate and normalized, Foucault argues, the nobility's assertion of rights was used by the commoners as an impetus to the French Revolution; in this way, a "partisan and strategic" truth became a weapon of war.[11] For Foucault, antagonisms, struggles, and conflict are processes of war that should be analyzed according to a grid of strategies and tactics. The relationship between the nobility, the third estate, and the king produced a form of society that became the basis of the modern nation, and war continues on within new mechanisms of power. Thus politics is war by other means. The ensuing conflicts between rulers and ruled increasingly involve a relation between a superior race and an inferior race. As Foucault argues, "The State is no longer an instrument that one race uses against another: the State is, and must be, the protector of the integrity, the superiority, and the purity of the race. . . . Racism is born at the point when the theme of racial purity replaces that of race struggle, and when counterhistory begins to be converted into biological racism."[12] The importance of Foucault's genealogical account of rights is that it provides a new framework through which to consider how sovereignty and rights come into being through different forms of war and, more specifically, how the Indigenous subject comes into history contesting the legitimacy of sovereign right in Australia during the 1970s.

Foucault defines "race" as a linguistic and religious marker that precedes the modern nation-state. While Foucault offers a genealogy of "race" tied to war, he does not make explicit how this conceptualization of race is tied to knowledge embedded in tactics or strategies of war. How did race play a part in the decision to go to war? How was it tied to the right to invade? These questions identify a gap in Foucault's notion of race that this chapter will seek to address. Foucault argues that race surfaces as a biological construct in the late eighteenth century because disciplinary knowledges came into being and regulatory mechanisms were developed to control the population. He describes this form of power as biopower, arguing that race became a means of regulating and defending society from itself. That is, war continues in modernity in different forms, while sovereignty shifts from a concern with society defending itself from external attacks to focus on its internal enemies. Race became the means through which the state's exercise of power is extended from one of "to let live or die" to one of "to let live and to make live." While Foucault acknowledges a relationship between biopower and colonization in *Society Must Be Defended*,[13] he does not extend his analysis of sovereignty to the colonial context. And while the limitations of Foucault's work on colonization have been addressed by a number of postcolonial theorists,[14] most fail to pursue the specific ramifications of these limitations on our understanding of the issue of Indigenous sovereignty. In contrast, I believe the use of Foucault's idea of biopower to explicitly address the context of a "postcolonizing" nation will produce a new understanding of how whiteness operates through the racialized application of disciplinary knowledges and regulatory mechanisms, which function together to preclude recognition of Indigenous sovereignty.[15]

At present, there is little work that engages with power relations at the intersection of biopower, Indigenous sovereignty, whiteness, and race. Critical engagement with some of the lectures in *Society Must Be Defended* is offered in the work of Anne Laura Stoler in *Race and the Education of Desire*.[16] Stoler takes up Foucault's idea of biopower to provide an understanding of the making of the European colonial bourgeois order in the nineteenth and twentieth centuries. While Stoler explores the role of biopower in constructing white subjectivity, she does not engage with Foucault's concern with sovereignty and war. Following Stoler, a small number of scholars have engaged specifically with *Society Must Be Defended* since its publication in English. While Brad Elliott Stone's review essay does address the role of inferior races constituting the abnormal in contemporary race war, he does not pursue the implications of biopower's normalizing regime for Indigenous sovereignty struggles.[17] Similarly, John Marks provides an excellent overview of the philosophical and historical contexts for Foucault's text, relating it to race through a discussion of Dominique Franche's account of the Rwandan genocide in 1994.[18] However, he does not extend the connotations to engage with whiteness and Indigenous sovereignty. Eduardo Mendieta elaborates on the implications of Foucault's work on the biopolitical state for our understanding of political rationality.[19] He examines the relationship between letting live and making live through several historical and contemporary examples, including the death penalty, lynching, and the human genome project. What his work does not address, however, is the relationship between Indigenous sovereignty and the biopolitical state. Race is discussed in this literature, but whiteness remains invisible as a significant racial characteristic of the biopolitical state. There is also a considerable body of Australian work applying Foucault's theory of governmentality to cultural and policy texts. However, this important literature rarely engages specific issues of whiteness and Indigenous sovereignty claims.[20] For this reason, it is productive to bring Foucault's concept of biopower into relationship with the critical whiteness literature.

This literature identifies whiteness as the invisible norm against which other races are judged in the construction of identity, representation, decision making, subjectivity, nationalism, knowledge production, and the law.[21] Montag argues that during modernity whiteness became an invisible norm through the universalization of humanness, which simultaneously erased its racial character and made it a universal.[22] This raises two questions: How does biopower work to produce whiteness as an invisible norm, and does it function as a tactic and strategy of race war?

Contributing to this growing literature is the work of Australian scholars who are establishing a field of whiteness studies that engages in a variety of ways with colonization and Indigenous sovereignty.[23] In particular, the work of Ravenscroft, Nicoll, and Vassilacopoulos and Nicolacopoulos considers the relationship between Indigenous sovereignty and the psychosocial and ontological realms of subjectivity, while others, such as Kate Foord, illustrate that the white fantasy of *terra nullius* and the disavowal of Indigenous sovereignty are fundamental to the narration of Australian identity and nation building.[24]

Toward a Research Agenda

The critical whiteness literature on Indigenous sovereignty in conjunction with Foucault's genealogy of race leads me to ask the following questions. If sovereignty is predicated on a fiction that arises through war, how does biopower enable sovereignty to deny war through a legal fiction of *terra nullius*? And is the refusal to declare war itself a tactic of war? What would be useful is to consider the representation of power within the law-rights-sovereignty paradigm by approaching the relationship between Indigenous sovereignty and state sovereignty as relations of force located within a matrix of biopower. This is to identify and explicate the coexistence and mutual imbrications of a universal discourse of individual human rights and the prerogative of collective white possession that underpins the Australian national project. The specific aims of such a challenge are: (1) To provide an extensive study of the emergence of Indigenous people into history as subjects of rights in the 1970s through political activism, legislative and policy change, the emergence of Australian nationalism, and media representations. (2) To trace how white possession manifests as a mode of rationality in a variety of disciplines, such as law, history, Australian studies, anthropology, Aboriginal studies, and political science, from the rights activism of the 1970s to the present. (3) To extend an understanding of the terrain of sovereignty in Australia as relations of force in a war of races normalized through biopower, contributing to an understanding of how Indigenous sovereignty and its disavowal have shaped Australian nationalism. This would facilitate an exploration of the proposition that white possession is more than a right and consider how it functions to reproduce procedures of subjugation that are tied to racialized and racializing knowledges produced by disciplines dedicated to the sciences of "man."[25] In particular, we could examine how academic disciplines such as history, political science, Aboriginal studies, Australian studies, and anthropology have operated as normalizing modes of rationality that facilitate procedures of Indigenous subjugation and mask non-Indigenous investments in relations of patriarchal white sovereignty.

This is to ask: To what extent does white possession circulate as a regime of truth that simultaneously constitutes white subjectivity and circumscribes the political possibilities of Indigenous sovereignty? How does it manifest as part of common-sense knowledge, decision making, and socially produced conventions and signs? This issue poses a series of further questions:

In what sense do rights function as tactics and strategies of race war? How do "rights" contribute to creating bodies of knowledge and multiple fields of "Aboriginal" expertise?

What was and is the role of the human sciences (anthropology, political science, Australian studies, and Aboriginal studies, etc.) in disciplining the rights claims of Indigenous people?

How does white possession of the nation function normatively within disciplines and their discourse of rights?

What are these disciplines and what truths do they produce about rights?

How and where do these truths circulate as rights claims and counterclaims?

What are their multiple forms?

Central to these questions is the question of how are we to define white possession as a concept? According to the judicio-philosophical tradition, possession is the foundation of property; it requires physical occupation and the will and desire to possess. Possession of lands is imagined to be held by the king, and in modernity it is the nation-state (the Crown) that holds possession on behalf of its subjects. Therefore, possession is tied to right and power. Foucault argues that right is both an instrument of, and vehicle for, the exercising of the multiplicity of dominations in society and the relations that enable their implementation. He notes that these relations are not relations of sovereignty and argues that the system of right and the judicial field are enduring channels for relations of domination and the many forms of techniques of subjugation. For this reason, right should not be understood as the establishment of legitimacy, but rather the methods by which subjugation is carried out.[26] The limitations of Foucault's definition of right is that he does not account for the whiteness of sovereignty, without which biopower could not function. As Stoler's work shows, racial thinking and notions of whiteness were powerfully determinative of imperial maps that were broader than Foucault's genealogy of bourgeois identity and its biopolitics.[27]

In *Society Must Be Defended*, Foucault defines a historico-political field as a shift from a history, "whose function was to establish right by recounting the exploits of heroes or kings, their battles and wars . . . to a history that continues war by deciphering the war and the struggles that are going on within all institutions of rights and peace. History thus becomes a knowledge of struggles that is deployed and that functions within a field of struggles; there is now a link between the political fight and historical knowledge."[28] A historico-political field is

constituted by certain elements: a myth of sovereignty, a counternarrative, and the emergence of a new subject in history. The 1970s in
Australia can be identified as a historico-political field in this sense because a new Indigenous subject emerged in history to challenge the
myth of patriarchal white sovereignty through a counternarrative.
This is not to say that Indigenous sovereignty and resistance did not
exist before the 1970s; they always have. However, what marks this
period for investigation is the eruption of the discourse of rights and the
Australian nation's exposure to Indigenous sovereignty claims through
mass media and Indigenous demonstrations. Before the 1970s, the implicit subject of the rights discourse was the white subject, who represented the universal in human rights. This did not take account of the
specificities of the rights of subjects with different embodiments, histories, and sexual orientations. The eruption of rights claims by subjects under the banner of women's and gay and lesbian liberation, as
well as the fight to recognize the contribution of non-Anglo migrants,
has recently been refracted through the lens of a socially conservative
neoliberalism as a fractious form of identity politics. However, because
these claims are made within the judicio-political framework, they paradoxically assume the legitimacy of patriarchal white sovereignty. This
is in contrast to Indigenous sovereignty claims, which contested the very
premise of white sovereignty. *Talkin' Up to the White Woman* argues
that this distinction between non-Indigenous claims for recognition and
equality within the nation-state and claims to ontological precedence
and belonging is why Indigenous women's rights are not commensu-
rable with those of white women.[29]

The eruption of the rights discourse in the 1970s was due to influences
that were both global and national in character, influenced by events
in the 1960s that challenged established norms, values, and social conventions. In Foucaultian terms, this represents a phase of war whereby
the antagonisms, confrontations, and struggles of the 1960s became
represented strategically and tactically through a discourse of rights in
the 1970s. In Australia, the effects were twofold: the formal assertion
of Australia as an independent sovereign nation, and the rights claims
of subjects within its borders. Australia's formal separation from British judicial review meant that the High Court of Australia was the final
court of appeal. Discriminatory legislation affecting Aborigines was
revoked and our human rights were brought into a broader public discourse that encompassed racial and sexual discrimination. At the same

time, what it meant to be an Australian was being redefined. The white Australia policy was formally abolished in 1972 and multiculturalism was promoted as Australia's new national policy.[30] Within the academy, Australian studies centers were funded here and abroad to explore, examine, and define Australian national identity, and Indigenous studies emerged as a field of study in its own right. This raises the following questions: Did the eruption of "rights," in its many forms, produce new procedures of Indigenous subjugation? Do these procedures continue today in the remaking of Australian national identity evident in neoconservative politics, the history wars, and the High Court decisions on *Mabo* and Indigenous native title?

My concern is not with how Indigenous sovereignty can be accommodated or included within the discourse of rights or how it is located within an identity politics framework. Rather, it is to propose that we need to investigate how white possession functions through a discourse of rights within the disciplines of law, political science, history, and anthropology, on which Australian studies and Indigenous studies have relied since their formation, and examine how white possession manifests in regulatory mechanisms, including legal decisions, government policy, and legislation. Critical analysis of the role of these disciplines and regulatory mechanisms in reinforcing the prerogatives of white possession should provide a significant new perspective on the politics of sovereignty in Australia.

Foucault's work on rights, race, war, and sovereignty lends itself to the analysis of legislation and legal decision making about Indigenous sovereignty, land rights, and native title. In substantive terms, this could entail:

Examination of anthropological models of Indigenous land tenure and their representation in legislation and court decisions.

Textual analysis of media representations of Indigenous sovereignty claims and decisions, such as land rights, native title, and reparations.

An explication of the emergence of "Aboriginal" history and associated debates about Indigenous sovereignty.

Analysis of government policy concerning Indigenous sovereignty, land rights, and native title.

Critical evaluation of representations of national identity and Indigenous sovereignty within Australian studies, political science, and Aboriginal studies.

This would be an innovative approach in bringing to bear upon Indigenous sovereignty in a sustained and analytic way the kinds of questions that have emerged in recent years from the rich and suggestive body of theoretical work in whiteness and race studies in the new and interdisciplinary humanities. As the United State pursues an imperial project of delivering democratic rights and freedoms throughout the world, a growing body of whiteness theory in the United States has provided a counternarrative of a nation-state that continues to privilege the collective interests of white people in spite of the civil rights gains of the 1960s and 1970s. Underlying this approach is the theoretical problem central to whiteness studies of understanding how racialized knowledge works in power relations. Understanding the complexity of power as both productive and repressive involves not only exploring disciplinary knowledges but also their regulative mechanisms and techniques of subjugation.

Conclusion

Applying the sociological imagination to bring together Foucault's ideas about race, war, and sovereignty, critical whiteness studies and Indigenous sovereignty has produced unfamiliar questions that are being raised for future research. This chapter offers a challenge to Australian sociology to consider researching Indigenous sovereignty, exploring the way racialization works by extending the concept of "race" to denote more than just the bodies of the nonwhite "other." A new research agenda could extend the scope and the depth of existing work on Indigenous sovereignty, whiteness, and race by producing analytical insights at the national level and making the Australian case central to international developments in the field. This may require Australian sociology to be more flexible with its imagination if it is to develop conceptual models that do not obscure fundamental problems with contemporary understandings of society and politics in Western countries where Indigenous sovereignty continues to exist.

10 WRITING OFF SOVEREIGNTY

The Discourse of Security and Patriarchal
White Sovereignty

RACE HAS BEEN CENTRAL to Australian politics and the transition
from colony to nation, yet its significance as a concept has often been
overlooked in Australian political theory, with the exception of its application to those who are not white. Since the election of the Liberal Party
to government in March 1996, several scholars have written about how
"race" plays a role in conservative politics. Judith Brett's *Australian
Liberals and the Moral Middle Class* foregrounds how under Prime
Minister John Howard's leadership the Liberal Party was reconfigured
to represent the nation.[1] Brett argues that his stand on multiculturalism, immigration, and Indigenous issues "are not the result of his racism but of his liberal individualism" and commitment to nationalism.[2]
She notes that Howard has continually stated that he is opposed to
"any form of discrimination . . . based on ethnic background, nationality, race, colour of skin, religious or political conviction and to bigotry
and intolerance" because we are all equal citizens of the one nation.[3]
Andrew Markus in his book *Race: John Howard and the Remaking of
Australia*, argues that "Howard has been instrumental in determining
the role of race politics within the unfolding Liberal agenda."[4] For
Markus, race politics are based on making race central to nation building and national identity through either exclusion or assimilation.[5] In
Against Paranoid Nationalism, Ghassan Hage argues that John Howard has given birth to a particular kind of fundamentalism in Australian politics that is predicated on having an idealist notion of national
core values, which are perceived to be coherent and normative.[6] As a
political ideology, fundamentalism operates by assuming that these core
values are good and that they have been eroded, which is why they need

to be recuperated and restored.[7] For Hage, this fundamentalism is tied to white colonial paranoia, a perception of white injury and an obsession "with border politics where 'worrying' becomes the dominant mode of expressing one's attachment to the nation."[8] Brett, Markus, and Hage offer compelling arguments in their analysis of Howard's politics, but they overlook or understate the role that Indigenous sovereignty plays in shaping the body politic through its relationship to patriarchal white sovereignty. This chapter begins to consider this proposition.

In former British colonies such as Australia, "race" indelibly marks the formation of nation-states and the development of national identity. As such, it was instrumental in the assertion and assumption of patriarchal white sovereignty and its manifestation in this place as the Australian nation-state. The intersection between race and property played a definitive role in international common law through the legal fiction of *terra nullius*, which enabled the assumption of patriarchal white sovereignty in the name of the British Crown. Indigenous sovereignty has never been ceded. However, the theft of Indigenous lands and the death of Indigenous people are inextricably tied to the assumption of patriarchal white sovereignty in Australia. Indigenous sovereignty is perceived to be foreclosed by this assumption and its existence is both refused and acknowledged through an anxiety of dispossession, which rises to the surface when the nation as a white possession is perceived to be threatened.[9]

Patriarchal white sovereignty is a regime of power that in the Australian context derives from the illegal act of possession and is most acutely manifested in the form of the state and the judiciary. The development of sovereignty as we now know it came into being through wars carried out by kings and their knights.[10] The transition to modernity precipitated the transfer of the king's sovereignty to the state, which in the form of the Crown is the sovereign holder of land, and this transference also encompassed authority over a territorial area and the people within it. Thus social contract theorists, such as Locke and Rousseau, argued that the formation of the democratic state within modernity was enabled by a contract between men to decide to live together, govern, and make laws for such living. The Crown has been symbolically represented as the king, and feminists have thus argued that modern patriarchy is characterized by a contractual relationship between men, and part of that contract involves power over women.[11] However, Charles Mills argues that the social contract underpinning the development of the modern state is also racialized.[12] The racial contract originally stipulated who counts as full moral and political persons, setting the boundaries for who can "contract" into the freedom and equality that the social contract promises. The universal liberal individual, who is the agent of social contract theory, was the European white male, who collectively identified as white and fully human. This racial contract allowed white colonists to treat Indigenous people as subhuman, appropriating Indigenous lands in the name of patriarchal white sovereignty. Thus sovereignty within Australian modernity is both white and patriarchal, and as a regime of power it is constraining and enabling. That is, it is both productive and oppressive; for example, all citizens have equal rights, but not all citizens have the resources, capacities, and opportunities to exercise them equally. Race, class, gender, sexuality, and ableness are markers that circumscribe the privileges conferred by patriarchal white sovereignty within Australian society. As a regime of power, patriarchal white sovereignty operates ideologically, materially, and discursively to reproduce and maintain its investment in the nation as a white possession. One of the ways in which the possessive investment manifests itself is through a discourse of security, which supports the existence, protection, and maintenance of patriarchal white sovereignty.

The Discourse of Security

A discourse of security pervades speeches made by John Howard, who since being elected to government has presented approximately 464 speeches between June 1997 and October 2004. The majority of these speeches have been concerned with commerce and business, the Liberal Party, war memorials and defense issues, trade and international relations, sporting events, and issues and policy announcements. A disproportionately small number of speeches are on issues specific to women, Indigenous people, and "migrants." There appear to be no speeches presented to the gay and lesbian community over this period of time. Howard's speeches are peppered with liberal theory's premise that traditionally citizens are white heterosexual men, who as free persons forfeited "certain individual rights to [patriarchal white sovereignty] to ensure their collective security."[13] Howard continually reiterates that there are core values to which Australians are committed and these values unite us despite our differences.

External National Security

The discourse of security involves prioritizing economic, military, and cultural protection, which are central elements of Howard's investment in patriarchal white sovereignty. This discourse is deployed in response to a perceived threat of invasion and dispossession from Indigenous people and others who are deemed not to belong for a variety of reasons. For Howard, the most important countries that contribute to the well-being and security of Australian patriarchal white sovereignty are Britain and the United States, two white Western nation-states. As Howard specifies, "Australia faces no choices between her history and geography."[14] What Howard conveyed in this statement is that Australia may be geographically located in Asia, but its history has determined that the nation is culturally white and Western. Howard's representation of a distinction between history and geography is a way to avoid any discussion of race.

Apart from our shared history, Britain is also important to Australia's economy; it is our second largest investor, and our bilateral relationship cements defense and security ties in our respective regions. We are allies separated only by geography. For Howard, Australia and Britain's national identities have been shaped by what we share in common: "The enduring ties that will continue to bind peoples: the shared values and aspirations, the historical and institutional associations, the ties of family and community, and the links established by cultural, education and sporting exchanges."[15] For Howard, Britain, as a Western nation, is positioned as Australia's cultural equivalent, and he continually references this sameness. What is not recognized about this sameness is the birth of Australia through the British imperial project, which refused Indigenous sovereignty while it simultaneously appropriated Indigenous lands. Seemingly all traces of colonialism have disappeared from our shared history, yet it is the foundation of our current relationship by which both nations are formally committed to the defense of each other's sovereignty. Howard's refusal to acknowledge Indigenous dispossession is symptomatic of his anxiety of dispossession. One does not need to defend one's security unless one perceives it to be threatened. The preoccupation with security is to bring the possibility of dispossession into being, to know it is possible in a geographical context that does not share his history. It is the recognition of this possibility within the subliminal that makes Australia's relationship with Britain an important and possessive investment in the stability and maintenance of patriarchal white sovereignty. As such, this relationship operates to reaffirm white national identity and the nation as a white possession while being shaped by the unfinished business of Indigenous sovereignty.

The relationship between the United States and Australia is similarly portrayed. In a speech made in New York on June 23, 1997, Howard stated that the affiliation between the two countries was "amongst the most important of all of the bilateral relationships that Australia has around the world." An enduring relationship sustained by common values and aspirations.[16] Howard states, "We both share an unequivocal commitment to democracy, to free speech, the freedom of the press and the independence and the authority of the rule of law. We both believe in the right of every citizen, regardless of colour, race or creed, to equality of opportunity to dignity and to individual self-respect."[17] For Howard, Australia, like the United States, is a race-blind nation. He notes that our common experiences extend to war and the sacrifices made by individual men and women; this experience has shaped our shared commitment to peace and prosperity throughout the world. Since World War II, Australia and the United States have worked together to build new global and political institutions such as the United Nations, the World Trade Organization, and the ANZUS alliance. The United States is our largest investor and largest source of imports, both of which contribute to the stability of our economy. As Howard notes:

> The role of the United States has been crucial to the unprecedented stability and growth that the Asia Pacific region has achieved. I believe it would be an error of historic proportions for the United States to diminish the level of its engagement in the Asia Pacific region. It would profoundly affect events in the region for the worse. . . . The United States military presence has provided the security, which allows the countries of the region to focus on economic development. United States capital, technology and management skills will continue to be vital in sustaining the region's growth. Australia and the United States have fundamental interests and objectives in common. We will both always stand up for the values and principles on which our societies are based.[18]

Howard's anxiety about dispossession is evidenced in his appeal to the United States to retain its level of engagement within the Asia-Pacific region. The relationship between Australia and the United States is underpinned by the security offered both economically and militarily through such an alliance. The importance of U.S. support is articulated through stressing common values, objectives, aspirations, and a shared history of war. What is not stressed, as a common feature of both countries, is the history of colonization and war with Indigenous peoples, who fought to defend their respective sovereignties. Nor is the common history of racist treatment of Indigenous and nonwhite people by both nations acknowledged as part of each nation's shared values and aspirations. Howard refuses the shared history of Indigenous dispossession by valorizing each nation's virtue, which operates discursively to placate anxiety about dispossession.

For Howard, the United States is the dominant patriarchal white sovereign nation that will extend its protection to its smaller mirror images in the Asia-Pacific region. Australia's support for U.S. foreign policy in Afghanistan and Iraq can thus be perceived as a dividend paid in the nation's economic, political, and military interests. Howard's use of the United States' false justification for going to war—that Iraq had weapons of mass destruction, which could be inflicted on the white Western world—to rally support for our participation served a number of purposes. One of which was to reinforce our commitment to an alliance that binds the United States to the protection of Australia's patriarchal white sovereignty within the Asia-Pacific region. This relationship also operates in the interests of the United States, not necessarily by our economic and military contributions, but by the worth of our moral authority as a white Western nation: a member of the axis of good and the coalition of the willing. Nicoll argues that "by establishing a proprietary relationship to virtue [patriarchal white sovereignty] is . . . staking a possessive claim which effectively dispossesses [others] from the ground of moral value."[19] In this context, Howard's reliance on the United States can be seen as an investment to minimize anxiety about dispossession within a nation burdened by its origins and the persistence of Indigenous sovereignty.

Howard's perception of our role in the Asia-Pacific region does not reflect his views on Australia's moral and cultural commonalities with Britain and the United States. In a speech presented to the Menzies Research Centre on August 22, 2001, he reiterated that it is not necessary to choose between our history and our geography. The differentiation between these two categories simultaneously masks the racialized borders by which they are marked. For Howard, the Asia-Pacific region is "culturally different." It is characterized by change and unpredictability, but he notes that "these are not . . . tendencies to fear, so long as you have the credentials and institutions to deal with them."[20] He argues that it is therefore in Australia's interests to "work to ensure that our region, the part of the world that has the most direct bearing on our fortunes, is as stable and prosperous as we can make it. And we need to have an armed force that has the capacity to defend us if necessary and to act with others in support of regional stability."[21] Howard's anxiety about dispossession informs his strategy to ensure stability and predictability within the region through increasing Australia's defense capability while protecting and maximizing our economic prosperity.

Australia seeks to foster the development of democracy and economic growth within the region through various forms of aid. Howard states, "The nations of Asia matter because they are important political partners with whom we have worked for many years to build a more stable and secure region. They matter because of where they are. Their proximity inextricably links their future prosperity and security with ours. And they matter because of what they are—our largest export markets and the source of much of our investment and imports."[22] Despite the "cultural differences," it is Asia's geography and markets that are important to national security and prosperity. In addressing Australia's Pacific neighbors, Howard recognizes that they are underdeveloped and in need of our financial assistance. Invoking the authority of patriarchal white sovereignty, he states that "we now see ourselves as more active, more engaged, more willing to help, but reasonably seeking reforms and better governance as conditions of that assistance."[23] The norms, values, and ideas of reform and governance attached to patriarchal white sovereignty are to be adopted. Howard requires an adherence to sameness in exchange for aid, ensuring that white normalizing techniques discipline small nation-states within the region to conform and maintain stability and security.

In a speech made to the Asia Society Luncheon in Manila in July 2003, Howard asserted that the greatest challenge facing the region is terrorism: "You cannot talk about the challenge of terrorism without recognising the need to address the fundamental challenge of poverty and economic development. And unless that is understood at the very beginning, all of us will find our efforts to deal in a day to day sense with the challenge of terrorism will fall short of the mark and will be undermined."[24] Howard's focus on economic reform is linked to issues of poverty and terrorism, hence the need for democratic reform in the

Asia-Pacific region to ensure Australia's security and minimize the threat of "attack." Australia's role is to guide Asia-Pacific nations toward the goals usually associated with modernity and progress.[25] There is an unconscious association that links developing nations with blackness and corresponding links of achievement and progress with white superiority. Development and aid are tied to achieving modernity and progress as well as white morals and values. The relationship between Australia and the Asia-Pacific region is based on maximizing an investment in patriarchal white sovereignty through economic prosperity, ensuring the continuation of the nation as a white possession. For Howard, economic prosperity and democratic reform within the Asia-Pacific region will minimize "instability" and "unpredictability," increase our export markets, and thus decrease the threat of invasion. Australia's future will be made secure because our credentials and institutions will be in place and our investments will work in the interests of patriarchal white sovereignty.

The Howard government's concern with security in the region is inextricably linked to an anxiety about dispossession, which is why it requires the continued presence of the United States in the region. This anxiety is evidenced by the slogan "We will decide who comes to this country and the circumstances under which they come," which was deployed by the Liberal government during the 2001 election in response to "illegal immigrants" entering Australia.[26] This assertion of sovereignty is made in the face of a perceived invasion by "illegal immigrants." As Ravenscroft argues, this anxiety is tied to the original dispossession of Indigenous people: "Indeed, under the logic of colonialism, if Australia were invaded by Asia, the European would be positioned as he has positioned the Indigenes and remade in the terms of the coloniser."[27] This anxiety about dispossession is not just tied to the possibility of an invasion in the present and divestment of patriarchal white sovereignty; its roots lie in history. Thus the unfinished business of Indigenous sovereignty continues to psychically disturb patriarchal white sovereignty and shape the possessiveness of its foreign policy.

National Security

Within the confines of its own borders, Australian patriarchal white sovereignty continues to invest in itself. Since 1997, Howard has sought to reproduce the nation as a white possession through various forms of security. Howard recentered heterosexual patriarchal whiteness by identifying the "mainstream" as his primary constituency, stipulating that the family unit was the foundation of the nation. For Howard, same-sex relationships do not constitute a family; instead, they are perceived as a threat to heterosexual marriage, where reproductive services are required to provide the labor to invest in patriarchal white sovereignty.[28] "Gay and Lesbian people" can be included within the "mainstream" as individuals on the basis that they deny their sexuality and do not want to marry. His conceptualization of the "mainstream" is reflected in a quote from Prime Minister Robert Menzies's speech entitled "The Forgotten People." Quoting Menzies, Howard states:

> "I do not believe that the real life of this nation is to be found either in the great luxury hotels and the petty gossip of so called fashionable suburbs, or in the officialdom of organised masses. It is to be found in the homes of people who are nameless and unadvertised and who, whatever their individual religious conviction or dogma, see in their children their greatest contribution to the immortality of their race." Those words are in substance as true today as they were then.[29]

When Menzies made this speech, Australia was demographically and culturally a white nation. Howard's reiteration of these sentiments, as being as true today as they were then, is to communicate the idea that the mainstream is the white race, which is reproduced through heterosexual marriage. As Stratton argues, "The 'mainstream' are perceived to be those people who are the remnants of a pre-existing unified society that can speak on its behalf. They welcome ethnic groups and others into the 'mainstream' but only as individuals." He notes that "Howard's deployment of the 'mainstream' coincides with a voting cohort who support a move back to assimilationism and a more racialised basis to the migration program."[30]

Howard's main concern is for "mainstream" Australia, the people who were feeling disenfranchised and disadvantaged under the previous Keating government, because of their perception of its capitulation to special-interest groups and promotion of a multicultural Australia. Howard's vision to repair the nation, informed by a lower-middle-class ethos, was in response to this perceived white injury. The election of Pauline Hanson assisted his vision for the Australian nation, a vision shaped by Howard's experiences of the Australia he knew and knows.[31] Howard is symbolically the white patriarch, the mirror of national identity; thus it is white men who represent the nation. This is evidenced in his speeches valorizing Australian characteristics and values with reference to sporting and war heroes like "Weary" Dunlop and Don Bradman, who embody mateship, tolerance, and fairness.[32] Howard constantly identifies the Battle of Gallipoli as the defining moment of national identity and character, using war to remind the Australian public of the need to value the freedom fought for and won by white men.[33] Gallipoli has given us "so much of the inspiration of our sense of independence, our sense of our place as a nation in the world, of our separate identity from others—those qualities that we like to believe lie at the heart of the Australian spirit and the Australian character."[34] Howard's emphasis on core Australian values and characteristics, born of defending patriarchal white sovereignties in a far-off country that posed no immediate threat to our shores, offers security and pride to a nation anxious about its dispossession.

For Howard, a secure national identity is also linked to economic security. Howard's promise to establish programs aimed at the social concerns of mainstream Australia has been tied to his financial deregulation of the economy: "The floating of the Australian dollar, the admission of foreign banks . . . the abolition of exchange controls . . . tariff reform . . . deregulation of the labour market" and the introduction of the goods and services tax.[35] He believes his economic reforms have seen the Australian economy prosper and the mainstream benefit through lower interest rates and higher levels of home ownership and investment properties. The mainstream as property-owning subjects can possess the nation through their ontological relationship to capital. Their possessive investment in patriarchal white sovereignty is enhanced through private property ownership. This security produces an effect that is encapsulated in a sense of home and place, mobilizing an affirmation of a white national identity that has surfaced as the result of the heroic deeds of white men. This sense of belonging is derived from ownership, as understood within the logic of capital, but it continues to be tormented by its pathological relationship to Indigenous sovereignty.

Similarly, in addressing migrant communities, it is their contributions to the economy that are emphasized and applauded.[36] The contribution of migrants to the nation is primarily through their industry and business, although Howard does acknowledge the cultural enrichment they offer Australia. As he notes in his speech at the launch of the National Multicultural Advisory Council report in May 1999, Australia's multiculturalism is special:

> We've always found a particular Australian way of doing things. And one
> of the elements, one of the genius elements of the Australian story is the way
> in which we have been able to retain the good bits that have been contrib-
> uted to Australian society by the various tributaries, cultural tributaries,
> that make up our nation and reject the bad bits. . . . We have been very suc-
> cessful and the reason we have been very successful is that within the indi-
> vidual commitment and affection people have to the culture and the land of
> their birth they have developed, and all of us together, acquired a common
> overriding commitment to the values of the Australian nation.[37]

Howard's use of the term "tributaries" here to distinguish "cultural"
others from the river itself illustrates that his use of the term "mainstream" does represent white Australia. Thus the tolerance extended to
migrants is tied to their commitment to the economic and social values
of the nation, not their cultural difference. And it is only the "good bits"
from the tributaries that he wishes to retain, the ones that benefit patriarchal white sovereignty. As Nicolacopoulos and Vassilacopoulos argue,
the migrant is positioned as the perpetual foreigner, who is allocated
a position within whiteness that is off white. "Dominant white Australia posits a suitable 'other' through whom whiteness marks rightful
control of Australian territory. A certain category of (im)migrant is positioned to give and receive the necessary form of mutual recognition
whilst remaining readily visible as a foreigner."[38] Certain migrants function within the logic of possession, to legitimize patriarchal white sovereignty through their presence and subscription to national core values
tied to capital. Their legitimizing presence is linked to patriarchal white
sovereignty's disavowal of Indigenous sovereignty. Thus, the omnipresence of Indigenous sovereignty is part of the ontological condition that
shapes patriarchal white sovereignty's investment in itself and its anxiety about dispossession.

   In a different way the idea of the "illegal immigrant" serves to ideologically affirm the possessiveness of patriarchal white sovereignty
through its border-protection policy. In August 2001, Howard's response
to what became known as the "Tampa incident" was to define the mainly
Muslim Afghan refugees as queue jumpers, who resorted to extreme
measures to gain asylum in Australia.[39] His response to Captain Rinn
of the movement of the cargo ship *MV Tampa* into Australian waters,
which was legal under international law, was to order the Navy to intervene to prevent it from happening. In a speech made to the Federal
Liberal Party, he stated: "I want to place on record my gratitude . . . to

the men and women of the Royal Australian Navy who have not only been protecting our borders but saving lives in the process of doing it. Now that's the face of Australia to the world. We will be compassionate, will save lives, will care for people but we will decide and nobody else who comes to this country."[40]

Events of September 11 also contributed to cementing the idea that "the Muslim" invaded and terrorized. Howard used these events to muster support for his border-protection policy and detention centers here and in the island nation of Nauru in Micronesia. These two events served to position the Muslim as the invading "other," thus enabling Howard to demarcate, secure, and protect the territorial integrity of patriarchal white sovereignty within Australian and international law. Howard's possessive investment in patriarchal white sovereignty was further expressed after the bombings in Bali in 2002, when he proclaimed that he would take preemptive action in the Asia-Pacific region should it be perceived that Australia was threatened by terrorists. Howard fed the fear attached to Australia's anxiety about dispossession, a fear that is embedded in the nation's denial of the continuing existence of Indigenous sovereignty. This denial of Indigenous ownership ensures the legitimacy of patriarchal white sovereignty and its right to exert border protection against others. In this way Indigenous sovereignty subliminally shapes Australia's border-protection policy.

Between June 1997 and October 2004, Howard made fewer than ten speeches concerning Indigenous issues in which he consistently positioned Indigenous people's rights and interests as adverse to the nation. When the *Wik* decision was handed down in 1997, he made an address to the nation in which "he displayed a map claiming that Indigenous people could veto development over 79% of Australia's land mass. Later in the same week in Parliament, he stated that it was possible for native title claims to be made of 79% of Australia."[41] Howard traded on the fear and insecurity attached to Australia's anxiety about dispossession by bringing to the surface the possibility of dispossession by the Indigenous "other." In November, he addressed the nation, reiterating that the sooner the whole debate about native title was over, the better it was for all of us.[42] He did make it better for "us" in September 1998, when his amendments to the Native Title Act 1993, which diminished the rights of Indigenous people, were implemented. Despite the success in reducing Indigenous interests, in addressing the National Farmers Federation conference in May 1999 he stated that "this native title thing has gone on for too long. . . . I mean this native title thing is hurting Western Australia, it's hurting the country. We should have resolved it."[43] Native title is positioned as adverse to the nation's interests; as such, it is separated from the nation, which is perceived to be a white possession. This possessiveness is illustrated by Howard's appointment to the High Court of two conservative judges, who formed part of the majority decision reaffirming patriarchal white sovereignty's security of tenure in the *Yorta Yorta* decision on December 12, 2001. This decision effectively determined that no native title claims will be successful unless Indigenous people can prove that their native title is consistent with that which existed at the time of the original assumption of patriarchal white sovereignty.[44]

The refusal of Indigenous sovereignty is also evident in the way in which Howard has responded to the recommendations of the Council for Aboriginal Reconciliation, most notably the recommendation for a treaty. In his address to Corroboree 2000, he disingenuously acknowledged the traditional lands of the Eora people.[45] This is an acknowledgment he only performs when addressing Indigenous people, because the protocol of recognizing Indigenous "traditional lands" is simultaneously a reminder and a denial of the existence of Indigenous sovereignty. The reminder is evidenced by the presence of Indigenous bodies, but its denial is contained in the words "traditional lands," which transports ownership back into the past, not the continuing present. Howard stated that Corroboree was an occasion "to honour the contribution of the Indigenous people of Australia . . . the special character of their cultures . . . to thank them for the generosity of spirit [and] the richness that their cultures bring to modern Australian life."[46] Howard positions Indigenous people within multiculturalism: we are reduced to being one culture among many, another "cultural tributary." Like migrants, we contribute to the nation through our cultures, but our presence cannot serve the legitimacy of patriarchal white sovereignty because we are the source of its insecurity.

Howard refuses to recognize how the exploitation of Indigenous land, resources, and labor contributed to the making of the nation, just as he does not recognize that Indigenous people have any of the core Australian values that he cherishes. Instead, Indigenous people are "the most profoundly disadvantaged . . . and part of the process of reconciliation is to adopt practical measures to address that disadvantage."[47] Howard's idea of addressing Indigenous disadvantage is to offer the same opportunities that are available to other citizens through mainstream programs. However, our citizenship is not predicated on the same basis as everyone else. Our sovereignty has never been ceded and our rights as Indigenous people have yet to be formally recognized. Our rights are not the same as the rights of other citizens. Yet Howard believes that "true reconciliation can never be said to have occurred until Indigenous Australians enjoy standards of opportunity and treatment the equal of their countrymen and women."[48] Howard wants to include Indigenous people in the nation through the provision of welfare measures that do not provide for the control and ownership of our lands and resources, which is what is required to address our poverty. Howard totally rejected the council's call for a treaty, saying that it would be divisive and that his government could only make treaties with other nation-states. Our economic interests, which would be protected by a treaty, are denied in favor of the interests of patriarchal white sovereignty. Howard's refusal of the Council for Aboriginal Reconciliation's recommendation of a treaty is a disavowal of Indigenous sovereignty and the history of colonization. As Nicolacopoulos and Vassilacopoulos argue, a condition of the ontological pathology of Australian whiteness is that Indigenous people must not be recognized as property-owning subjects whose sovereignty is different.[49] The premise of *terra nullius* prevails as a possessive investment in patriarchal white sovereignty and its required security.

Howard's refusal of Indigenous sovereignty is tied to the "history wars" and his recuperation of the virtue of white national identity.[50] It is no coincidence that we have seen the eruption of the history wars during his time in government. In fact, he regularly reads the journal *Quadrant*, which fostered the work of Keith Windschuttle, a right-wing historian. The history wars are a recuperative act of possession whereby people like Windschuttle want to restore the virtue of the white nation and secure national identity through claims that massacres are a fiction and that Indigenous people had no word in their language for "property." Following Windschuttle's logic, Indigenous people did not have a concept of ownership, which means that we had no sovereignty to defend. Thus there was no theft, no war, and no need to have a treaty. What underpins his work is the belief that the assumption of patriarchal white sovereignty is morally right and legally correct. The disadvantage that Indigenous people suffered is not perceived as an effect of this assumption, but rather the implication is that Indigenous people lack the core values required to contribute to the development of the nation. The perception that we lack core values is evidenced by the recent proposal that we may be required to carry a "smart card," which will be tied to behavioral outcomes to ensure that the nation's welfare dollars are well spent. The rights of citizenship are not the same for all. The differential treatment of Indigenous people by patriarchal white sovereignty has always been in its best interests, which is why it gave rise to policies allowing Indigenous children to be removed and trained as domestic servants for white homes. Indigenous people were placed on reserves and missions and their labor used to service the pastoral and cattle industries. The low wages paid to Indigenous people were appropriated by state governments to supplement reserve and mission infrastructure. The current relationship of Indigenous people to capital is primarily as consumers; our unemployment rate is approximately 48 percent when the number of people working for the dole and those registered as unemployed are combined.[51] The Indigenous industry is an income-generating service for predominantly white professionals, tradespeople, and public servants. Our welfare dependency has been structured by and in the interests of patriarchal white sovereignty; it is the investment that we have been offered. Howard's denial of Indigenous sovereignty masks the continuing effects of dispossession and the benefits of colonial theft reaped by the white Australian nation.

Howard's disavowal of Indigenous sovereignty is also evident in the dismantling of the Aboriginal and Torres Strait Islander Commission (ATSIC). After Geoff Clarke became chairperson of ATSIC, the policy direction shifted to Indigenous rights advocacy. ATSIC's funding contributed to exposing the racism within the amendments of the Native Title Act at the United Nations and Indigenous participation in the draft declaration of Indigenous rights, both of which emphasized the need for a treaty in Australia. This advocacy embarrassed Howard's government and differed from its practical reconciliation process. Media reports supported Howard's agenda to dismantle ATSIC by attacking the character of two ATSIC Indigenous patriarchs, who were represented as rapists, thugs, and thieves, coupled with the appalling conditions of Indigenous health and education, two policy areas controlled and delivered by mainstream departments, not ATSIC. The representation of Indigenous pathology provided Howard with the moral authority to silence Indigenous advocacy for our sovereignty within and outside the nation. Howard's practical reconciliation, which includes the

mainstreaming of Indigenous programs, is a strategy designed to protect the cultural and territorial integrity of the nation, thereby securing
a possessive investment in patriarchal white sovereignty.

Conclusion

Race indelibly marks the politics of possessive investments in patriarchal white sovereignty, which are often invisible and unnamed in
everyday discourse and academic analyses. This is because Indigenous sovereignty is never positioned as central to shaping the terms
and conditions of the very making of the nation; nor is its continuing
refusal understood as shaping a politics based on white anxiety of dispossession. Brett's explanation, that it is Howard's commitment to individual liberalism and nationalism that informs his policies, can only
be sustained if race in the form of patriarchal white sovereignty is
perceived not to function discursively within the epistemology that constructs and supports such political ideologies. As I have argued, Howard's deployment of the discourse of security is inextricably linked to
an anxiety about dispossession shaped by a refusal of Indigenous sovereignty with clear roots in white supremacy.

I concur with Markus that race operates through strategies of exclusion and assimilation by groups to resolve racial problems, but Marcus
does not address the way in which they are marked by the exercising
of patriarchal white sovereignty. The roots of strategies of exclusion
and assimilation do not just lie in the conservative mobilization orchestrated by Howard and his government. They are epistemologically
and ontologically buried in the assumption of patriarchal white sovereignty, where they function as tools of white possession. I agree with
Hage's thesis that Howard's fundamentalism is tied to white colonial
paranoia, perceived white injury, and an obsession "with border politics where worrying becomes the dominant mode of expressing one's
attachment to the nation."[52] However, white colonial paranoia, injury,
and worrying are inextricably tied to an anxiety about dispossession
that is harnessed to instill hope through possessive investments in
patriarchal white sovereignty. This is how the unfinished business of
Indigenous sovereignty continues to shape and disturb the security of
patriarchal white sovereignty.

11 IMAGINING THE GOOD INDIGENOUS CITIZEN

Race War and the Pathology of
White Sovereignty

IN JUNE 2007, the federal government sent military and police into
Indigenous communities of the Northern Territory on the premise that
the sexual abuse of children was rampant and a national crisis. This
"crisis" was constructed as something extraordinary and aberrant, requiring new governmental measures. Giorgio Agamben argues that this
"state of exception" is now the normal form of governance within democracies, which "establishes a hidden but fundamental relationship between
law and the absence of law. It is a void, a blank and this empty space
is constitutive of the legal system."[1] Guantánamo Bay has become the
public face of the deployment of this state of exception where law and
lawlessness exist in dealing with detainees as a response to the events
of 9/11. But it is not exceptional. Other detainees are held in various
prison camps, such as Abu Ghraib, Camp Bucca, and Camp Cropper
in Iraq. In these camps, the United States determined its own rules,
rules that are outside the law. In this sense, exceptionalism is dispersed
and not unified; instead, it is a discursive formation that can only be
partially known.[2]

While the state-of-exception thesis provides a way of explaining how
sovereign states responded to terrorism through security measures,
which requires disciplining detainees and citizens, the historical conditions of its possibility can be linked to colonization. Australia, New
Zealand, Canada, and the United States have a long history of detain-
ing Indigenous people, denying their rights, and controlling behavior
through and beyond the law. From the late nineteenth century, reserves,
privately owned pastoral stations, and missions were the places where
the majority of Indigenous people in Australia lived under the control of
white managers and missionaries appointed by government. Indigenous

people, while living in poverty, were treated differently than white Australian citizens and were subject to "special" laws, regulations, and policies that were racist. Knowledge of the impoverished conditions under which Indigenous people lived was shared by those who controlled their lives. They acted disingenuously, and their silence about Indigenous poverty operated repressively as "an injunction to silence, an affirmation of nonexistence, and, by implication, an admission that there was nothing to say about such things, nothing to see, and nothing to know."[3] During the campaign for citizenship rights in the 1960s, Indigenous poverty was first brought into the public consciousness of white Australia through the advocacy of Indigenous people and their white supporters. This occurred during the time that the white Australia policy was incrementally being phased out. The impoverished conditions under which Indigenous people lived were televised and beamed into the living rooms of white middle-class Australia and represented within the print media. White Australians voted in overwhelming numbers to endorse the 1967 referendum, believing they were casting a vote for Indigenous people to be included in the nation by being granted full citizenship rights. Within the white imaginary, citizenship represented equality, and it was assumed that this status would enable Indigenous people to overcome their poverty and become equal to other Australians.

The 1967 referendum did not confer citizenship rights on Indigenous people. Instead, the Constitution was changed to give the federal government the power to make laws on behalf of any race, and Indigenous people could be counted in the census.[4] The federal government of the day was well aware that these were the changes being made. The rhetoric of citizenship became a strategy by which Indigenous people could now come under federal government control instead of being primarily the responsibility of state governments. These changes to the Constitution did not emerge publicly until the 1990s, after academics revealed that Indigenous people had been accorded civil, industrial, social, and political rights incrementally from the 1960s through the removal of explicitly racially discriminatory legislation and policies.[5] Irrespective of this research, the idea that Aborigines were granted citizenship rights in 1967 continues to circulate discursively. As a consequence, the lack of citizenship rights is no longer linked causally to Indigenous poverty within the White Australian imaginary; instead, their social rights in the form of welfare payments have contributed to this outcome.

Since 1967, Indigenous people have continued to live in poverty regardless of the level of economic prosperity of the nation or whether there are Labor or Liberal Federal and State governments in power, implementing their "different" Indigenous affairs policies. There are still large gaps in outcomes between Indigenous people and other Australian citizens on all social indicators. Our life expectancy rates are seventeen years less than the rest of the population, our health is the worst in the country, we live in overcrowded houses, we have the highest unemployment rates, are overrepresented in the criminal justice system, and our education outcomes are well below the Australian average.[6] These differential outcomes and their history raise a question: Do citizenship rights enable or constrain Indigenous people within society? In this chapter, I will address this question by focusing on the Northern Territory intervention. I argue that patriarchal white sovereignty as a regime of power deploys a discourse of pathology as a means to subjugate and discipline Indigenous people to be good citizens, and that the tactics and strategies deployed within this race war reveal its own pathology.[7]

Social Contract and Rights Theory

Social contract theorists, such as Locke and Rousseau, argued that the formation of the state was enabled by a contract between men to decide to live together, govern, and make laws for such living. It is a contract that secures the right of the sovereign in the form of the state to govern and the right of citizens to partake in that governance and to live in society through the rights and responsibilities conferred on them. The problem with most social contract theories is that the moral egalitarianism that underpins it is predicated on the theory that the transition from a state of nature to civil society "founds government on the popular consent of individuals taken as equals."[8] The white patriarchs who theorized about the social contract were primarily concerned with it being a means of agreement between white men to live together, make laws, and govern, incorporating white women into the polity as their subordinates through the marriage contract.[9]

In contrast to social contract theorists, Michel Foucault offers a genealogy of rights from the seventeenth century to the present, arguing that war has been central to the development of the judicial edifice of right in democratic as well as socialist countries.[10] He explains how in

France the history of the divine right of kings, which worked in the interests of sovereign absolutism, was challenged through the work of Henri di Boulainvilliers, who produced a counterhistory to that of the king, effectively introducing the new subject of rights into history. Refuting the myth of the inherited right to rule, Boulainvilliers's history of the nobility advanced the idea that because of their investments in participating in war, they too had rights. Having become legitimate and normalized, Foucault argues, the commoners used the nobility's assertion of rights as an impetus to the French Revolution; in this way a "partisan and strategic" truth became a weapon of war.[11] The commoners' assertion of rights as subjects of the Crown became the rationality for war against the monarch. It is only by repressing the founding violence of sovereignty's emergence through war that equality can circulate as a truth constitutive of citizenship and its relationship to state sovereignty. While it is a truth that is challenged by theorists of citizenship within modernity, the right of state sovereignty functions discursively as not being born of conflict and war but rather of agreement between citizens.[12]

For Foucault, antagonisms, struggles, and conflict are processes of war that should be analyzed according to a grid of strategies and tactics because war continues within modern mechanisms of power such as government. The ensuing conflicts from the late eighteenth century between rulers and ruled increasingly involve a relation between a superior race and an inferior race. Foucault argues that "the State is no longer an instrument that one race uses against another: the State is, and must be, the protector of the integrity, the superiority, and the purity of the race. . . . Racism is born at the point when the theme of racial purity replaces that of race struggle, and when counterhistory begins to be converted into biological racism."[13] He defines "race" as a linguistic and religious marker that precedes the modern nation-state. Race surfaces as a biological construct in the late eighteenth century because disciplinary knowledges came into being and regulatory mechanisms were developed to control the population. He describes this form of power as "biopower," arguing that race became a means of regulating and defending society from itself. That is, race war continues in modernity in different forms, while sovereignty shifts from a concern with society defending itself from external attacks to focus on its internal enemies, though sovereign right continues to protect its boundaries from external attacks. Politics becomes war by other means. Race became the means through which the state's exercise of power is extended from one of "to let live or die" to one of "to let live and to make live." What is important about Foucault's work is how race and war are tied to sovereign right. It offers us a different understanding of how colonization operates through sovereign right as a race war whose power effect on the Indigenous population was one of "to let live or die," and after occupation it becomes one of "to let live and to make live." The origins of sovereignty in Australia are predicated on a myth of *terra nullius* (the imagination of an unpossessed continent), which functioned as a truth within a race war of coercion, murder, and appropriation that white men carried out in the service of the British Crown. The military secured sovereignty on Australian soil in the name of the white king of England; in this way sovereignty was both gendered and racialized upon its assumption. Patriarchal white sovereignty is a regime of power that enabled the "seizing, delimiting, and asserting control over a physical geographic area—of writing on the ground a new set of social and spatial relations" underpinned by the rule of death.[14]

As I have argued elsewhere, patriarchal white sovereignty in the Australian context derives from the illegal act of possession and is most acutely manifest in the state and its regulatory mechanisms, such as the law.[15] Therefore possession is tied to right and power in ways that are already racialized. Foucault argues that "right" is both an instrument of and vehicle for exercising the multiplicity of dominations in society and the relations that enable their implementation. He argues that the system of right and the judicial field are enduring channels for relations of domination and the many forms of techniques of subjugation. For this reason, "right" should not be understood as the establishment of legitimacy but rather the methods by which subjugation is carried out.[16] In this sense citizenship rights are a means by which subjugation operates as a weapon of race war that can be used strategically to circumscribe and enable the biopower of patriarchal white sovereignty. Thus rights can be enabling and constraining.

Rights and Race War

Disciplinary knowledges that developed and deployed "race" as a biological concept in the eighteenth century in Australia did so through a prevailing racist discourse. Indigenous people were considered a primitive people, nomadic, sexually promiscuous, illogical, superstitious, irrational, emotive, deceitful, simpleminded, violent, and uncivilized. We were perceived as living in a state of nature that was in opposition to the discourse of white civility. This racist discourse enabled patriarchal white sovereignty to deny Indigenous people their sovereign rights while regulating and disciplining their behavior through legislative and political mechanisms and physical and social measures. After the 1967 referendum, which gave the federal government the power to make laws on behalf of any race, it became increasingly difficult to continue to deny citizenship rights to Indigenous people. "Race" had become the means to let live and to make live.

After World War II, the Allies agreed to establish an international regulatory mechanism to preserve human rights and justice while upholding state sovereignty in their respective countries. The United Nations was established in 1942, and in 1948 member countries agreed to be bound to the Declaration of Human Rights. Two important covenants were also ratified in 1966 by the United Nations, which gave all people the right to self-determination, and by virtue of that right they were free to pursue their political, cultural, social, and economic rights within society. They were the Covenant on Political and Civil Rights and the Covenant on Economic, Social, and Cultural Rights. These covenants supplied moral and political strategies for the emergence of decolonization and civil rights movements, which soon spread globally. The eruption of the rights discourse in the 1960s was due to influences that were both global and national in character and influenced by events that challenged established norms, values, and social conventions. In Foucaultian terms, this represents a phase of war whereby the antagonisms, confrontations, and struggles of the 1960s became represented strategically and tactically through a discourse of Indigenous rights in the 1970s. In Australia, the effects were the advocacy of civil, women's, gay, and Indigenous rights claims of subjects within its borders. Discriminatory legislation specifically designed for Indigenous people was revoked and the Racial and Sexual Discrimination Acts 1975 were enacted to protect against racial and gender discrimination. And an Indigenous land rights discourse encompassing Indigenous sovereignty claims was placed on the public agenda, which saw the Aboriginal Land Rights (Northern Territory) Act 1976 established for the application and granting of land claims in the Northern Territory. The white Australia policy was formally abolished in 1972 and multiculturalism was promoted as Australia's new national policy.[17]

Just as human rights were becoming an effective political weapon, Australia strengthened its internal sovereignty by formally separating from British judicial review, which meant that the High Court of Australia was the final court of appeal. The impact of this separation is that the nation-state's management of the rights claims of its citizens is no longer subject to the scrutiny of an external sovereign.

Race War and the Discourse of Indigenous Pathology

A new mechanism of government regulation of Indigenous people began through the bureaucratic infrastructure of the Federal Department of Aboriginal Affairs. Since the 1970s, government policy has oscillated between self-management and self-determination. The former was concerned with administration and management of communities and organizations, while the latter "implied control over policy and decision making, especially the determination of structures, processes and priorities."[18] While it is often argued that self-determination has been the dominant policy framework since the early 1970s, a closer analysis of government processes and practices would reveal that self-management has occupied center stage, despite the establishment of the Aboriginal and Torres Strait Islander Commission (ATSIC) in 1989. ATSIC was represented to the world as the epitome of Indigenous self-determination by the Keating-led Labor government. However, regional councils did not have autonomous control over expenditure in their regions, and ATSIC's budget was controlled and monitored in the same way as other government departments. The federal government determined what policy areas it would allow ATSIC to administer. ATSIC commissioners were "developing" policy prepared by bureaucrats who worked within the confines of the government's overall policy on Indigenous affairs. When the ATSIC commissioners did change the policy agenda, under the stewardship of Geoff Clarke, from one of self-determination involving decision making to a self-determination model that advocated Indigenous rights, the newly elected Howard government in concert with the media represented the commission as being mismanaged, misguided, and corrupt. Howard strategically deployed a discourse of pathology to win electoral support, which was aided by the mainstream media. Chairperson Geoff Clarke and Deputy Chair "Sugar" Ray Robinson were represented as being criminal and violent and ATSIC was blamed for the underperformance in Indigenous health and education; both policy and program areas were administered by mainstream departments. Howard had made an electoral promise that he would cut funding for Indigenous affairs, review ATSIC, and ensure that Indigenous rights claims would be controlled because the pendulum had swung too far in the direction of Indigenous people's rights. He amended the Native Title Act 1993, reducing even further than the Keating government had the property rights Indigenous people had won in the High Court's *Mabo* decision. Through the use of the law, the Howard government reconfigured Indigenous affairs by containing, reducing, and controlling the rights claims of Indigenous people, positioning us as having received more than our entitlements as citizens and not taking responsibility for our "dysfunctional" behavior. Rights of citizenship were deployed as weapons within the race war serviced by a discourse of Indigenous pathology. Within this discourse, social problems are considered to be any forms of behavior that violate the norms of white civility.

Since the year 2000, Howard's Indigenous affairs policy agenda was concerned with "practical reconciliation" involving mutual obligation contracts with Indigenous communities. The government's closure of ATSIC and amendments to the Native Title Act 1993 signaled the end of an Indigenous rights-based policy consistent with international human rights covenants and the beginning of a focus on "practical measures" to alleviate Indigenous disadvantage. Significantly, the Howard government rejected the Aboriginal Reconciliation Council's *Declaration Towards Reconciliation* and the *Roadmap for Reconciliation* at Corroboree 2000, which recommended a treaty. The former Indigenous Social Justice Commissioner, Mick Dodson, states:

> Howard responded with his own version of the Declaration. While there is considerable similarity between the two documents, there are more subtle differences in wording. The Howard government said that it is unable to endorse the approach to customary law in the Council's Declaration, believing that all Australians are equally subject to a common set of laws. It refused to endorse the term "self-determination," claiming that it implies the possibility of a separate Indigenous state or states. More significantly, the Howard government refused to support a formal apology to Indigenous people for past injustices, claiming that such an apology could imply that present generations are in some way responsible and accountable for the actions of earlier generations.[19]

Howard's tactics in the race war were to contain Indigenous rights and protect the state against compensation claims by recognizing only those rights that were available to other citizens. One of the social rights of citizenship (the right to welfare support) became the means of disciplining Indigenous subjects containing their human right to be self-determining, using the regulatory mechanism of the government's bureaucratic infrastructure. This regulation was rationalized within a neoliberal discourse that privileged individualized rights and the democratic process while advocating that the market should manage and direct the fate of all human beings as free agents. Neoliberal discourse promotes formal equality of individuals through citizenship, allowing government to implement economic and social policies that reinforce structural inequalities between Indigenous people and the rest of Australian society. The individualism of neoliberalism informs the discourse of pathology within the race war, enabling the impoverished conditions under which Indigenous people live to be rationalized as a product of dysfunctional cultural traditions and individual bad behavior. In this context, Indigenous pathology, not the strategies and tactics of patriarchal white sovereignty, is presented as inhibiting the realization of the state's earlier policy of self-determination. Citizenship becomes a weapon of race war, deployed to advance the idea that because citizens have "rights" the king no longer rules, despite his "Crown" remaining intact as the holder of radical title to all land. As the holder of the radical title of all land, patriarchal white sovereignty can invade land occupied or owned by citizens when it wishes to do so. This was clear when the federal government sent the army and police into seventy-three Indigenous communities in the Northern Territory in response to the "Little Children Are Sacred" report, which identified sexual abuse and child neglect as issues of urgent national significance.[20] The government's use of the term "emergency response" signified that it was a life-or-death situation, requiring a response out of necessity; it was a state of exception. In effect, patriarchal white sovereign right was exercised using the report as evidence to further regulate and manage the subjugation of Indigenous communities. The discourse of Indigenous pathology provided the rationale for the containment of people within specific regulated areas, and the Northern Territory became the new laboratory for an experiment in Indigenous civility.

The federal government passed five bills enabling the "emergency response" and suspended the Racial Discrimination Act 1975 to protect the state from litigation on the basis that the intervention was racist. The suspension of law was used as a weapon of race war to enable and regulate the intervention. The media had prepared the white Australian imaginary by using a discourse of pathology that involved constantly reporting negative stories of Indigenous dysfunction, corruption, neglect, and sexual abuse to elicit white virtue and possessive investments in citizenship. This discourse was deployed by Noel Pearson, an Aborigine from Cape York, who was later appointed as Howard's adviser on welfare reform. Pearson's collusion with the media resulted in his being the first "Aboriginal leader" to have a regular column in the *Australian* newspaper. In August 2000, in his address entitled "The Light on the Hill," which he presented as the Ben Chifley Memorial Lecture, he stated:

> In my consideration of the breakdown of values and relationships in our society—I have come to the view that there has been a significant change in the scale and nature of our problems over the past thirty years. Our social life has declined even as our material circumstances have improved greatly since we gained *citizenship*. I have also come to the view that we suffered a particular social deterioration once we became dependent on passive welfare. So my thinking has led me to the view that our descent into passive welfare dependency has taken a decisive toll on our people, and the social problems which it has precipitated in our families and communities have had a cancerous effect on our relationships and values. Combined with our outrageous grog addiction and the large and growing drug problem amongst our youth, the effects of passive welfare have not yet steadied. Our social problems have grown worse over the course of the past thirty years. The violence in our society is of phenomenal proportion and of course there is inter-generational transmission of the debilitating effects of the social passivity which our passive economy has induced.[21]

Pearson strategically uses citizenship rights to welfare as the enabler of Indigenous "dysfunction" by arguing that these rights have given Indigenous people entitlements but no responsibilities. Between 2000 and 2004, Pearson produced twenty-five papers elaborating on his thesis on welfare reform and Indigenous pathology while also acknowledging that communities require service provision and resources to enable a change in behavior.[22] His argument is that citizenship rights should be tied to behavioral outcomes for Indigenous people as a means to let live and make live. Focusing on individualist explanations for Indigenous poverty, Pearson promoted welfare reform within Indigenous affairs by mimicking the U.S. neoliberal conservative position of the early 1990s, which advocated that "a) The receipt of welfare should be predicated on reciprocal responsibilities whereby society is obliged to provide assistance to welfare applicants who, in turn, are obligated to behave in socially approved ways; and b) able-bodied adult welfare recipients should be required to prepare themselves for work, to search for employment and to accept jobs when they are offered."[23]

Pearson's thesis that the right to welfare facilitates Indigenous addiction and dysfunction circulates as a truth in the race war while masking the strategies of patriarchal white sovereignty that perpetuate Indigenous welfare dependency. Pearson indigenizes welfare dependency through a discourse of pathology that effectively silences talk about the behavior of millions of non-Indigenous people who receive welfare in one form or another to enable them to live within society. In 2007, he wrote in the *Australian* a response to Indigenous people who were advocating an Indigenous rights agenda, stating:

> Let me conclude by pointing out three problems with the indigenous rights agenda as it is now presented. First, it is just not credible on too many questions. Ordinary Australians are simply not convinced that land rights and culture alone will solve social problems. Ordinary Australians can see through the fact social order is an urgent imperative. . . . Ordinary Australians are not like old progressive converts. They can no longer be sold slogans. The evidence of social and economic disrepair is too obvious for them to accept the old solutions. Those seeking indigenous rights must come up with more compelling justifications for the policies they propose. Second, the advocacy must be more sophisticated and have more of an impact. . . . Instead of retreating into righteous impotence, the rights advocates must become a lot more competent than they have been. Third, those concerned about rights must understand that most rights—the right to better health and education and safe and healthy children—cannot be delivered by rights alone. They require behavioural responsibility on behalf of our people. And this is why the recent launch by Aboriginal and Torres Strait Islander Social Justice Commissioner Tom Calma of Closing the Gap . . . is only partly convincing. . . . The gap will not close unless we have a plan that is as forthright about these responsibilities as it is about rights.[24]

Pearson's pathologizing of Indigenous people works discursively. He positions Indigenous rights advocates as being unsophisticated, righteously impotent, incompetent, and naive. He stipulates that good citizenship requires both rights and responsibilities, which appeals to and elicits the virtue of "ordinary Australians," who are already assumed to be "good citizens." He strategically uses the term "ordinary Australians," as did Howard and Pauline Hanson, a right-wing member of parliament, in their anti-Indigenous rights politics, to seduce his white middle-class audience and affirm the characteristics of white civility.

Pearson's explanation for the existence of poverty and inequality is the "problematic" characteristics of Indigenous people, not patriarchal white sovereignty's right to disavow Indigenous sovereign resource rights. Indigenous people are perceived and talked about as the undeserving poor, who lack initiative, proper money management skills, a sense of morality, the ability to remain sober and to resist drugs, and a work ethic. Pearson has staked a possessive claim to patriarchal white sovereignty in his welfare reform agenda, which seeks to discipline and produce the good Indigenous citizen who is perceived as having no inherent sovereign right to their resources, which were illegally appropriated by the Crown. The media and government have conferred on Pearson a leadership role in Indigenous welfare reform, one that services the legitimacy of patriarchal white sovereignty through a discourse of Indigenous pathology by denying the effects of colonization in producing economic dependency. This serves, in turn, to make invisible the ongoing race war against Indigenous people.

Race War and Tactics of Intervention

The print media's representation of Indigenous pathology in the race war was actively promoted by the national magazine *The Bulletin* in the late 1880s, and cartoons of drunken and destitute Aborigines were a regular feature during the twentieth century in its promotion of the White Australia Policy.[25] This pathologizing took a different form in the negative headlines and stories that circulated and began building in the 1970s after land rights were granted in the Northern Territory, and in the 1980s, when traditional owners in Noonkanbah protested mining on their sacred site in the Kimberleys. In its investigation into media representation, the National Inquiry into Racist Violence in 1991 concluded that the Australian media was responsible for the "perpetuation and promotion of negative and racial stereotypes, a tendency towards conflictual and sensationalist reporting on race matters."[26] Over the next fifteen years, it became the norm for negative stories about Indigenous people's "demands" and "dysfunctional behaviour" to circulate in the popular press. On May 5, 2006, the feature story on the Australian Broadcasting Commission's (ABC) program *Lateline* was on Indigenous sexual abuse in Central Australia. The main interview was with Dr. Nanette Rogers, Crown Prosecutor in Alice Springs.[27] Rogers provided information on cases that had come before her involving children as young as two years of age who had been raped. She explained that the silence around sexual abuse in Indigenous communities can be attributed to the entrenched violence, failure to take "responsibility for their own actions," and the punitive nature of Indigenous society where reporting an incident could lead to "harassment, intimidation and sometimes physical assault." What Rogers did not disclose is the way in which sexual abuse operates through repression and how silence operates as part of the cycle of sexual abuse in white communities, whether they are remote, rural, or suburban. Child sexual abuse is not openly discussed, easily reported, or prosecuted. The government deals with child sexual abuse in white homes as though it is something aberrant that requires intervention only on a case-by-case basis. There is no intervention into the whole community where the perpetrators reside; instead, the civil rights of perpetrators are respected. In contrast, child sexual abuse is treated as being normative within Indigenous communities, requiring everyone to be placed under surveillance, scrutinized, and punished. In this way, the receipt of welfare payments, which is a social right, allows the government to discipline Indigenous people at the margins of Australian society.

There was a flurry of media activity pathologizing Indigenous communities after Rogers's interview on national television. This was in stark contrast to the media's lack of response to Indigenous women's recommendations about the violence and alcohol, substance, and sexual abuse in communities, which were being made as early as 1980. Recommendations from Aboriginal women and the need for increased service provision and resources were made at the Australian and New Zealand Association of the Advancement of Science (ANZAAS) 50th conference in Adelaide in 1980, the Federation of Aboriginal Women's conference in Canberra in 1982, the National Aboriginal Women's Taskforce in 1986, the First Indigenous Women's Conference in Adelaide in 1989, the Remote Area Aboriginal and Torres Strait Islander Women's meeting in Laura in July 1991, and the ATSIC national Women's Conference in Canberra in 1992.[28] Governments and the media did not respond to any of these recommendations. As a white woman and a lawyer, Rogers was already conferred with authority, legitimacy, and virtue within the white imaginary. The media and political institutions strategically deployed her revelations to confirm Indigenous pathology and feed moral outrage within the race war. The decades of silence and inaction by government and media on these issues confirms that politics is race war by other means; during the year of an election, the media and government strategically deployed the discourse of Indigenous pathology as a weapon by making child sexual abuse a central issue for voters.

In response to Rogers's national disclosure, on August 8, 2006, the Northern Territory Labor government commissioned the Board of Inquiry into the Protection of Aboriginal Children from Sexual Abuse, led by Rex Wild QC [Queen's Counsel] and Dr. Patricia Anderson, signaling that Labor, not the federal liberal national coalition government, was concerned about Indigenous child sexual abuse. In this way the Labor Party, which was in opposition federally, could stake a possessive claim to morality and virtue, attributes of white civility. Wilson and Anderson tabled their report entitled *Ampe Akelyernemane Meke Mekarle* ("Little Children Are Sacred") to the Northern Territory government in April 2007. They found that there was sufficient "anecdotal and forensic and clinical information available to establish that there is a significant problem in Northern Territory communities in relation to the sexual abuse of children."[29] The report acknowledged that alcohol and drug abuse, poverty, housing shortages, poor health, and poor education were contributing factors to its prevalence. The inquiry recommended that the government consult with Indigenous communities on the implementation of their recommendations concerning service provision and resources in key areas such as health, education, housing, employment, and policing. The majority of recommendations reveals the years and the level of government neglect in service provision to its Indigenous citizens, who have the highest levels of mortality and morbidity rates in the Western world. This illustrates that within the race war, the exercising of patriarchal white sovereignty's right to let live or make live produces an early death for Indigenous people.

The recommendations in the "Little Children Are Sacred" report echo the reports of the Aboriginal and Torres Strait Islander Social Justice Commissioner and the Human Rights and Equal Opportunity Commission of Social Justice from 1993 to 2007.[30] In a speech made to the Committee for Economic Development in Australia, the chairman of the Australian Productivity Commission, Gary Banks, presented an overview of the commission's "Overcoming Indigenous Disadvantage: Key Indicators 2005" report to the government, which identified strategic areas for government action, including: "Early child development and growth (prenatal to age 3); Early school engagement and performance (preschool to year 3); Positive childhood and transition to adulthood; substance use and misuse; functional and resilient families and communities; effective environmental health systems and economic participation and development."[31] Similar recommendations were made in the Senate's Legal and Constitutional References Committee report in 2003 entitled "Reconciliation: Off Track."[32] Despite the advice and recommendations of its own regulatory mechanisms, the federal government failed to take responsibility for its policies. The exercise of sovereign right by patriarchal white sovereignty has continuously denied Indigenous sovereign rights by containing Indigenous people through social rights to welfare. Indigenous people have limited social capital and resources, independent of welfare, to engage in economic development.

Since colonization began, patriarchal white sovereignty has deployed punitive action as a technique of subjugation in its relations with Indigenous people. And it has been cunning and deceitful in masking its subjugation. In 1996, for example, Prime Minister Howard removed $470 million from ATSIC's budget; and in 2007, $39 million was cut from Abstudy, which had a direct impact on Indigenous peoples' participation in the education system. Between 2000 and 2007, the federal government increased its Indigenous budget to $3 billion. However, $360 million of those funds, which were identified for family violence programs, health, child care, business, education, housing, and schooling, was not spent in 2007. And $136 million of the Indigenous budget was used as substitute funding on programs that benefit all Australians. These funds were spent by the Northern Authority Quarantine Strategy, the Bureau of Meteorology, Reconciliation Australia, the National Museum, public phones, the Tax Office, and Centrelink's administrative costs in delivering its mainstream services to Indigenous clients.[33] A similar picture has emerged from the Northern Territory, where large spending shortfalls in Indigenous affairs have occurred in the areas of child and family services, with $177 million allocated by the federal government, but only $43 million had been spent. Professor Rolf Gerritsen stated that federal funds are channeled into wealthy electorates for political purposes and that over 50 percent of Indigenous funding "ends up in white hands."[34] The lack of resources and underspending of funds in the provision of government services to Indigenous communities are not perceived to be linked to the impoverished conditions under which Indigenous people live. Instead, the discourse of pathology

prevails as the government's explanation for not fulfilling its responsibilities in providing services to Indigenous citizens. "Knowledge"
about Indigenous pathology circulates as strategic truth in the race
war to rationalize the continuing subjugation of the Indigenous population and encourage non-Indigenous investment in patriarchal white
sovereignty.

In his speech to the National Press Club, which was televised nationally on July 15, 2007, Mal Brough, the minister for Families, Community Services, and Indigenous Affairs, took the opportunity to discuss
the Howard government's welfare reform agenda.[35] Brough began his
speech with a list of welfare reforms in mainstream areas where further funding was needed because of state government neglect. In his
pledge of $1.8 billion for older carers of disabled children, he stated
that "the Howard government has now said to older carers that we will
ensure that you have a place and that you will have the services that
you need as you grow older and frailer and that you have given your
love and your life to your child who's disabled, we'll guarantee that.
No state government has done it in the past."[36] In the speech, Brough
makes a discursive shift between the deserving poor and the undeserving poor. The deserving poor are white citizens and the undeserving
poor are Indigenous people, who are rarely represented in the white
national imaginary as carers or as disabled in spite of the well-known
health statistics. When discussing Indigenous housing needs, he stated:
"We've faced up to the fact that over years, ATSIC and successive
federal governments have gifted over $3 to $4 billion worth of housing, lost control of it, don't know who's in the houses, whether they're
appropriate people, whether rents are being paid, whether maintenance
has been undertaken. We said, no, that's got to stop. Put away the
political correctness, let's stop that and let's do something that actually will provide more housing and better housing."[37] Brough accuses
ATSIC and Labor governments of mismanaging government funds by
gifting houses to Indigenous people, who may be inappropriate tenants,
who behave irresponsibly by not valuing or maintaining their assets.
By implication, inappropriate Indigenous people should be homeless
or in prison, which speaks to the punitive nature of the government's
approach to Indigenous people. This statement is patently disingenuous, as federal assets cannot be gifted to individual citizens without the
consent of parliament. The discourse of pathology is used to vilify Indigenous people while promising them more and better housing only if

they behave like good white citizens. Throughout his speech, Brough gave highly emotive individualized anecdotal evidence of the violence, substance and sexual abuse, and neglect in Indigenous communities in order to substantiate the measures the government took to intervene in the Northern Territory. Brough deployed the discourse of pathology to mask the government's neglect in service provision to Indigenous communities and justify increasing surveillance and subjugation.

The imposition of martial law and the emergency measures were outlined in a press release from Mal Brough's office on July 6, 2007. Brough stated that the legislative package would allow the federal government to restrict alcohol, audit computers to detect pornographic material, lease Indigenous land and change land tenure to allow for private purchase, remove customary law as a mitigating factor for bail and sentencing, put in place business managers in remote communities, quarantine income support payments for basic necessities (such as food, clothing, and shelter), impose compulsory health checks for Indigenous children, change the permit system for access to Indigenous lands, and abolish the Community Development Employment Program, which is a work-for-unemployment-benefits scheme. The law enables patriarchal white sovereignty's regulation of Indigenous behavior through their social rights entitlements. Brough said: "The Little Children Are Sacred Report highlighted horrific abuse of children in remote communities. . . . I was astounded that the report's authors provided *no recommendations* designed to immediately secure communities and protect children from abuse. The legislative measures being introduced tomorrow will achieve that."[38] In order to shift responsibility back onto Indigenous people for their poverty, Brough negates the recommendations of the "Little Children Are Sacred" report, which clearly outlines substantial government neglect. Neglect, denial, blame, abdication of responsibility, and violence are attributes of the dysfunctional behavior of patriarchal white sovereignty that service Indigenous economic dependency and the negation of Indigenous sovereign rights.

In the conflict over the intervention, the response to government from rights advocates was framed within both citizenship and human rights, seeking to deploy them as a strategic truth to make claims and repatriation against patriarchal white sovereignty. The Human Rights and Equal Opportunity Commission welcomed the government's announcements but argued that they should be delivered within a human rights framework.[39] Approximately 175 representatives of church, social service, and civil rights organizations wrote an open letter to Brough arguing that the services provided to other Australians are rarely delivered to Indigenous communities.[40] In response to the emergency measures, they argued that "in their present form the proposals miss the mark and are unlikely to be effective. There is an over-reliance on top-down and punitive measures, and insufficient indication that additional resources will be mobilized where they are urgently needed; to improve housing, child protection and domestic violence supports, schools, health services, alcohol and drug rehab programs." In a briefing paper for Oxfam, Jon Altman argued that there is no evidence to show the relationship between child sexual abuse and changes to the permit system and compulsory acquisition of five-year leases over township land owned by Aboriginal people under inalienable freehold title: "In particular both measures will lessen the property rights, and associated political and economic power, of an already marginalized Indigenous minority."[41]

Several months after the intervention, the Central Land Council consulted with traditional owners from across Central Australia. They found that overall most Indigenous people supported steps to address child abuse, housing shortages, and increased policing, but they were opposed to "five year lease, changes to the permit system, welfare reform measures and the current changes to the operation of Community Development Employment Program Scheme (CDEP)."[42] The Aboriginal Rights Coalition's research into experiences and attitudes toward compulsory welfare management revealed that "85 percent of respondents do not like the intervention and see the overall changes as negative. 90 percent of respondents experience serious problems with income management. The changes have caused problems within families for 74 percent and made no change for 23 percent."[43] Rallies were held in June 2008 demanding "the repeal of the NT Emergency Response legislation, the restoration of the Racial Discrimination Act (1975), increased funding for infrastructure and community controlled services and the implementation of the UN Declaration on the Rights of Indigenous Peoples." The dissenting citizens sought to make social and human rights the enabler of justice and provision of resources that would improve the mortality rates of Indigenous people. However, patriarchal white sovereignty continued its welfare reforms to regulate and defend society from itself and external sources by actively rejecting counter-rights claims. The Australian government did not ratify the UN Declaration on the Rights of Indigenous Peoples, which was passed by the

UN General Assembly on September 13, 2007. The Declaration recognizes the inherent sovereign rights of Indigenous peoples to their lands, but such rights cannot be exercised if they infringe on the rights of the nation-state.

The successful election of the Rudd Labor government in November 2007 did not signal a radical shift in policy. Rudd committed to Howard's measures but agreed not to abolish the Community Development Employment Program and allowed the permit system to stay in place. The community development employment program allows Indigenous people to work for their unemployment benefits in areas where virtually no labor markets exist. The 2006 census of the Bureau of Statistics revealed that in remote communities in the Northern Territory, 80 percent of the 22,055 Indigenous people of working age were unemployed and 20 percent were on CDEP.[44] At the time, national statistics for unemployment were at 6 percent. Keeping Indigenous people on CDEP hides the real levels of unemployment and exclusion from the economy. If the state of Indigenous economic disadvantage were reflected within the broader Australian citizenry, there would be outrage and government would seek to intervene in the market, providing industry and workers with financial incentives to stimulate employment and economic development.

The government's agreement to retain the permit system was influenced by police, the Northern Territory government, and Indigenous people, who advocated that it assisted in regulating the unwanted activities of outsiders concerning running drugs and alcohol and exploiting Indigenous artists. In its first budget, the new federal government committed a further $1.2 billion to Indigenous expenditure over the next five years. The majority of these funds were committed to the Northern Territory Intervention with only $554 million allocated to the majority of the Indigenous population who live in other states and territories but share the same socioeconomic position in Australian society. The Rudd government called for a review of the intervention measures and sought to establish an independent Indigenous body that would advise on Indigenous policy and programs, but it would have no fiscal responsibility for them. The Federal Department of Health's analysis of the mandatory child health checks revealed that out of the 7,433 mandatory health checks of Indigenous children in the Northern Territory, only 39 were considered at risk of neglect or abuse, and only 4 children were identified as being sexually abused.[45]

Conclusion

The discourse of pathology is a powerful weapon that the patriarchal white sovereignty deploys to gain support from its white citizens. Race and rights are the means by which patriarchal white sovereignty exercises its power to let live and make live where the granting of life is conditional on the perceived appropriateness of the individual, the measure of which is the good white citizen. As a regime of power capillarizing through rights and possession, patriarchal white sovereignty allows the law and government to intervene in the lives of Indigenous people to let them live and to make them live as welfare-dependent citizens, not as property-owning subjects with sovereign resource rights. In this way, citizenship rights are methods of subjugation because in their relations with sovereign right they can be both enabling and constraining.

In the race war with Indigenous people, patriarchal white sovereignty pathologizes itself through the tactics and strategies it deploys to maintain subjugation. Deceit, neglect, blame, abuse, violence, and denial become tactics and strategies of war to subjugate the Indigenous enemies and their counterclaims of sovereign rights, which are perceived to threaten the integrity of patriarchal white sovereignty's inherited right to rule. The pathological behavior of patriarchal white sovereignty has been produced by the contradictions and imbalances in its fundamental constitution originating in Australia through theft and violence. Patriarchal white sovereignty refuses the unfinished business of Indigenous sovereignty because Indigenous entitlements to inherent resources would allow Indigenous people to engage in the economy as self-determining property-owning subjects, which would alter the current state of exception. Within the race war, Indigenous sovereign counter-rights claims pose a threat to the possessiveness of patriarchal white sovereignty, requiring it to deploy a discourse of Indigenous pathology as a weapon to circulate a strategic truth: if Indigenous people behaved properly as good citizens, then their poverty would disappear.

12 VIRTUOUS RACIAL STATES

White Sovereignty and the UN Declaration on
the Rights of Indigenous Peoples

> For, indeed, in a society in which the machinations of racism are
> everywhere, white people are *the* problem. Said differently, racism
> is a *white* problem. People who are white created white supremacy
> and people who are white sustain it. Our actions, attitudes, and
> ways of being subvert justice, cross-racial solidarity, and
> reconciliation. More insidiously, we benefit profusely from the
> prevalence of racial injustice, even as we are spiritually,
> psychologically, and morally malformed by it.
>
> —Jennifer Harvey, *Whiteness and Morality: Pursuing Racial
> Justice through Reparations and Sovereignty*

THE CONTENTIONS IN THE EPIGRAPH ABOVE by white American
scholar Jennifer Harvey are not new to Indigenous people. We experience and tolerate racism on a daily basis, and its perpetration is usually invisible to those who practice it, particularly when it is exercised
with a reliable self-calibrated moral compass. It would be a mistake,
however, to place total responsibility on individual white subjects for
their attitudes and behavior when relations of force shape and produce
the conditions under which racism flourishes. Governments were responsible for facilitating and appropriating Indigenous lands, and
through the use of the law enabled the death of Indigenous peoples, who
impeded progress. Governments dehumanized Indigenous peoples in
order to legitimize their actions and then sought to make us fully human
by exercising benevolence and virtue in its many forms.[1] As Brickman
argues, "Through the legal structures that were the legacy of the Cru-
sades, the necessity of converting [Indigenous] peoples to Christianity
would provide the mandate for the conquest of their lands and the

appropriation of their wealth and labour."[2] In the twenty-first century, colonization remains unfinished business in countries such as Australia, New Zealand, Canada, and the United States, as evidenced by the very existence of the Declaration on the Rights of Indigenous Peoples.

After more than two decades of deliberations, the Declaration on the Rights of Indigenous Peoples was tabled at the United Nations' General Assembly for its consideration on September 13, 2007. The political roots of this declaration lie with Haudenosaunee Chief Deskaheh[3] and Māori T. W. Ratana, who, in 1923 and 1925 respectively, sought access to the League of Nations to bring to the attention of the international community Canada's and New Zealand's violations of treaty agreements and rights.[4] They were both denied access to the League of Nation's assembly after successful lobbying by Britain, Canada, and New Zealand, which argued that the issues raised were domestic rather than international matters and should be treated accordingly. Chief Deskaheh and T. W. Ratana, though unsuccessful in their advocacy, provided a pathway for the contemporary global Indigenous rights movement. Some eighty-six years later, Indigenous peoples continue to express the same concerns at the United Nations. The United Nations is primarily a statist organization as is evidenced in Article 2 of its charter, which "consecrates the doctrine of equal sovereignty, territorial integrity, and non-intervention."[5] Australia, Canada, New Zealand, and the United States are founding members and were instrumental in its development.

The UN Declaration on the Rights of Indigenous Peoples was the outcome of the accumulated efforts of Indigenous nongovernmental organizations (NGOs), activists, and transnational networks. In the 1970s they began to develop an international Indigenous rights document to protect the rights of Indigenous peoples.[6] Indigenous people from Australia, New Zealand, Canada, and the United States played key roles in the deliberations. They advocated for the declaration to be a major objective of the UN International Decade of the World's Indigenous Peoples, which was from 1995 to 2004. However, its fruition did not occur until the UN's second Decade of the World's Indigenous Peoples, which started in 2005 and ends in 2015. The delay in finalizing the declaration was due in large part to the opposition and debates generated by several states as it moved through UN processes. In particular, Canada, New Zealand, Australia, and the United States were persistent objectors on "provisions relating to the right to self-determination and lands, territories and resources."[7] The United States, Canada, New Zealand, and Australia were the only states to vote against the declaration, which was endorsed by 144 member states, constituting the majority of the UN General Assembly. Almost half of the Indigenous population of the world lives within the borders of these four countries.

Anaya and Wiessner argue that there were very few changes made to the draft declaration after its endorsement by the Human Rights Council and transition to the General Assembly:

> Beyond recognition of the right to self-determination, the Council's text formulated an array of tailor-made collective rights, such as the right to maintain and develop their distinct political, economic, social and cultural identities and characteristics as well as their legal systems and to participate fully, "if they so choose," in the political, economic, social and cultural life of the state. [Indigenous peoples] were guaranteed the right not to be subjected to genocide or ethnocide, i.e., action aimed at or affecting their integrity as distinct peoples, their cultural values and identities, including the dispossession of land, forced relocation, assimilation or integration, the imposition of foreign lifestyles and propaganda. The stated rights guaranteed . . . include the right to observe, teach and practice tribal spiritual and religious traditions; the right to maintain and protect manifestations of their cultures, archaeological-historical sites and artifacts; the right to restitution of spiritual property taken without their free and informed consent, including the right to repatriate [Indigenous] human remains; and the right to protection of sacred places and burial sites . . . the rights to maintain and use tribal languages, to transmit their oral histories and traditions, to education in their language and to control over their own educational systems . . . the right to maintain and develop their political, economic and social systems, and to determine and develop priorities and strategies for exercising their right to development. Their treaties with states should be recognised, observed and enforced. The Declaration supports the right of indigenous people to own, develop, control, and use the lands and territories which they have traditionally owned or otherwise occupied and used, including the right to restitution of lands confiscated, occupied or otherwise taken without their free and informed consent, with the option of providing just and fair compensation wherever such return is not possible.[8]

Since the adoption of the declaration, several legal scholars have examined the history of its development and the scope of its influence on international law.[9] Others have argued that the declaration "declares a set of rights and morally obligates all declaring states to implement and enforce those rights."[10] It "lays a foundation for the creation of future binding international law, expressed primarily through multilateral treaties based on the [declarations] principles and secondarily through the development of customary international law."[11] However, state violation of Indigenous rights is not judicially enforceable within international courts. This body of literature responds implicitly or explicitly to two of the key assertions made by the States that voted against the declaration. The first assertion is that the declaration is a moral and political document, but not a legally binding one, and the second is that the internal laws of the state will prevail. These assertions were made by the dissenting states even though Article 46 (1) of the declaration qualifies the Indigenous rights encapsulated in the document. It does so by precluding the right to take any action by state, people, group, or person contrary to the Charter of the United Nations or any that would "dismember or impair, totally or in part, the territorial integrity or political unity of sovereign and independent States."[12] Article 46 (2) states that the exercising of the rights enshrined in the document are limited by law and human rights obligations.

The limitations imposed on Indigenous rights and the protection afforded state sovereignty by the declaration raises a question: If, as Canada, New Zealand, the United States, and Australia assert, the declaration is a moral and political document that is not legally binding, what is operating discursively to affect their opposition and subsequent endorsement of it? In this chapter, I am not concerned with the function of the declaration within international law. Instead, my focus is on the ways in which morality and politics were deployed by nation-states. I will demonstrate this by analyzing four key rights areas that were contested by Canada, Australia, the United States, and New Zealand, and will then examine the core elements of their subsequent endorsement of the declaration.

Patriarchal White Sovereignty

In this chapter, I argue that the possessive logic of patriarchal white sovereignty operates discursively, deploying virtue as a strategic device to oppose and subsequently endorse the declaration. As an attribute of patriarchal white sovereignty, virtue functions as a usable property to dispossess Indigenous peoples from the ground of moral value.[13] My concept of patriarchal white sovereignty draws on the work of Foucault, who argued that sovereignty is born of war enabled by a mythology of the divine right of kings. Sovereign absolutism was marked by gender and race in the seventeenth century, though race was considered a linguistic marker. Patriarchal white sovereign absolutism, though internally fractured, waged war to appropriate land and resources. Thus, the foundations of modern sovereignty have a gendered and racial ontology; that is, sovereignty's divine being as a regime of power is constituted by and through gender and race. The transition from sovereign absolutism to its modern form was produced through a counterdiscourse of rights through the challenge to the king's power by his knights. Foucault argues that having become legitimate and normalized, commoners rebelled against the nobility's assertion of rights, which led to the French Revolution; in this way, a "partisan and strategic" truth became a weapon of war.[14] In modernity, sovereignty shifts from being concerned with society defending itself against external threats to focusing on its internal enemies. Race becomes the means through which the state's exercise of power is extended from one of "to let live or die" to one of "to let live and to make live."[15] For Foucault, race and sovereignty are symbiotic. Goldberg further develops this point when he argues that sovereignty is the defining and refining condition of modern state formation and the law is deeply embedded in intensifying and cementing "lines of power in state formation."[16] In discussing states of racial being, he argues that "it is important to recognise that the racial state trades on gendered determinations, reproducing its racial configurations in gendered terms and its gendered forms racially. Bodies are governed colonially and postcolonially, through their constitutive positioning as racially engendered and in the gendering of their racial configuration.[17]

Australia, Canada, the United States, and New Zealand are racial states whereby patriarchal white sovereignty as a regime of power is the defining and refining condition of their formations, ordaining them ontologically with a sense of divinity. When Foucault argued metaphorically that sovereignty in its modern form is represented as a headless king whose body is still intact, he is talking about the manifestation of sovereign power within the modern state.[18] However, he leaves unexamined the trace metaphysical connection between head and body. Unlike Foucault, Derrida recognized this in his construction of sovereignty as a metaphysical category that encroaches on life, insofar as it nominates a power, potency, or capability that is found in the very "I can"; thus "there is no liberty without selfhood and no selfhood without liberty."[19] Derrida's notion of "I can" requires will as much as it requires freedom in his concept of popular sovereignty. However, there is a fundamental distinction between the sovereignty of the individual and the sovereignty of the state, though both require the prevention of outside intervention. This protection from the intervention of others has its ontological roots in Christianity. Kahn argues:

> Historically it emerges directly from the wars of the reformation and represents the same kind of prudential response to diversity within the Christian faith that liberalism more generally represents. The prudential, however, rests on a deeper principle of Christian belief: The truth, and the true virtue of the individual, is located in the interior working of the will, in the way in which the subject brings himself into a relationship with God. Politically, this point supports a conception of truth of the [state] as a manifestation of interior self-realization, rather than outward power.[20]

In this way sovereign power is a state's internal self-realization of its truth and virtue whereby will and possession operate discursively. Virtue functioned as useble property within the legal doctrine of discovery, which provided the rationale for sovereign wills to take possession of Indigenous peoples' lands from the sixteenth century onward. This doctrine was developed in the fifteenth and sixteenth centuries by Spain, Portugal, England, France, and the Church to enable the theft of Indigenous peoples' lands.[21] It was their divinely ordained destiny to redeem the lesser humans of the world through the application of their unique moral virtues. In this way virtue functions within the ontology of possession that occurs through the imposition of sovereign will-to-be on Indigenous lands and peoples, which are perceived to lack will; thus they are open to being possessed. This enables sovereignty to lay claim to own Indigenous lands and peoples because "wilful possession of what was previously a will-less thing" is constitutive of its ontology.[22] It is invoked whenever the state proclaims its ownership. The state's assertion that it owns the land becomes part of normative behavior, rules of interaction, and social engagement embodied by its citizens. It is most acutely manifested in the form of the state and the judiciary. Thus, possession and virtue form part of the ontological structure of patriarchal white sovereignty that is reinforced by its socio-discursive functioning within society enabled by the body of the state.

As part of state formation and regulation, patriarchal white sovereignty is mobilized through a possessive logic that operates ideologically and socio-discursively. Here I use the concept of "possessive logic" to denote a mode of rationalization, rather than a set of positions that produce a more or less inevitable answer, that is underpinned by an excessive desire to invest in reproducing and reaffirming the state's ownership, control, and domination. The possessive logic of patriarchal white sovereignty is compelled to deny and refuse what it cannot own—the sovereignty of the Indigenous other. This ontological disturbance/fracture is one of the reasons why the state deploys virtue when working hard at racial and gendered maintenance and domination in the guise of good government. Virtue functions through reason within sets of meanings about patriarchal white ownership of the nation within the law, as part of commonsense knowledge, decision making, and socially produced conventions by which societies live and govern behavior. The possessive logic of patriarchal white sovereignty has served to define the attributes of personhood and property through the law. As Harris argues, the theft of Indigenous lands was ratified by bestowing and "acknowledging the property rights of whites in [Indigenous lands]. Only white possession and occupation of land was validated and therefore privileged as a basis for property rights."[23] The possessive logic of patriarchal white sovereignty was deployed in defining who was, and who was not, white, conferring privilege by identifying what legal entitlements accrued to those categorized as white. At the beginning of the twentieth century, this same logic was operative, making whiteness itself a visible form of property, particularly through immigration laws and those affecting Indigenous peoples, and at the beginning of the twenty-first century it continues to function invisibly to inform the legal exclusion and regulation of those who transgress within and outside its borders. For example, after the 9/11 attacks on domestic soil, the U.S. government increased domestic security measures through the law, which enabled the hyper-regulation and surveillance of citizens and visitors within its borders. It is no coincidence that Canada, Australia, and New Zealand followed the United States and implemented a similar domestic security regime. I will now turn to examine their collaborative efforts against the Declaration of Indigenous rights.

Dis/senting States: Possessing the Moral High Ground

The endorsement of the declaration by majority vote within the UN General Assembly produced an existential crisis for Australia, Canada, New Zealand, and the United States, which responded to this overwhelming support as if their sovereignty had been transgressed. They operationalized their possessive logic by mobilizing virtue as a strategic device to explain their dissent. Australia stated that it "has actively worked to ensure the adoption of a meaningful declaration,"[24] Canada noted that "it has been an active participant in its development" (12) and New Zealand said it had "worked hard to the very end to narrow our concerns and to be able to support this text" (14), while the United States stated that "we worked hard for 11 years in Geneva for a consensus Declaration" (15). In deploying the notion of "working hard" as a virtue, these states are implicitly positioning the rest of the participants as not sharing their commitment and values, which is evidenced by their criticism of the process for the final drafting of the declaration. Australia said it had engaged constructively in the elaboration of the text but was not given "a chance to participate in the negotiations on the current text of the declaration" to achieve consensus (11). Canada believed that "had there been an appropriate process in place to address these concerns, and the concerns of other States, a stronger Declaration would have emerged" (12), while the United States asserted that "the document before us is a text that was prepared and submitted after the negotiations had concluded. States were given no opportunity to discuss it collectively. It is disappointing that the Human Rights Council did not respond to calls we made, in partnership with Council members, for States to undertake further work to generate a consensus text" (15).

These assertions of constructive participation in the development of the declaration belie their consistent objections during the twenty years of its formation. In a discursive turn, they operationalize virtue by positioning themselves as willing and constructive participants, implying that Indigenous participants were destructive and unwilling. This is why the process was inappropriate and their concerns were not addressed. The process is positioned as being flawed to the extent of the lack of prioritization and inclusion of their concerns in the final text. Their assumed sovereign right to possess and control the process is asserted, notwithstanding their minority representation as dissenting states. This is evidenced by the way they exaggerate the degree of support from other states in order to amplify their opposition. The appeal to reaching consensus on the document, which they assert would have been made stronger by their involvement, is a disingenuous strategy aimed at recuperating virtue to mask how they actively worked against any consensual outcome.

In their opening remarks, Canada, New Zealand, and the United States stated that they hoped the document would promote harmonious relations between states and Indigenous peoples. Canada noted that "we have sought for many years, along with others, an aspirational document that would advance indigenous rights and promote harmonious arrangements between indigenous peoples and the states in which they live" (12). New Zealand said that "in our experience, the promotion and protection of indigenous rights requires a partnership between the State and Indigenous peoples that is constructive and harmonious" (14). While the United States stated that "the declaration on the rights of indigenous peoples, if it were to encourage harmonious and constructive relations, should have been written in terms that are transparent and capable of implementation" (15). Australia did not mention that harmonious relations were an aspiration of the document, and all four states reiterated that they would continue to work to promote Indigenous rights nationally and internationally. By raising or ignoring the concern that the declaration should have promoted harmonious relations between Indigenous peoples and states, these states are implicitly blaming it for promoting disharmony. By bringing the need for harmony to the surface, they are unconsciously acting out that which is repressed: their disharmonious relations with Indigenous peoples. If harmony existed between Indigenous peoples and states, there would be no need to raise it as an issue to be promoted. They discursively deploy virtue through reiteratively stating that they are working to protect Indigenous rights while displacing the cause of their respective internal Indigenous/state conflict onto the document and, by default, Indigenous peoples. They take possession of the moral high ground by blaming Indigenous peoples for not wanting to work in harmony, a strategy they deployed in their opposition to core provisions of the declaration.

Aspirations

In particular, the nature of the declaration was a core shared concern. Australia stated that "it is the clear intention of all States that it be an aspirational document with political and moral force but not legal force. It is not intended itself to be legally binding or reflective of international law" (12). Canada noted that "for clarity, we also underline our understanding that this Declaration is not a legally binding instrument. It has no legal effect in Canada, and its provisions do not represent customary international law" (13). In contrast, New Zealand stated that the declaration is explained as being aspirational, "intended to inspire rather than to have legal effect. . . . It is unable to support a text that includes provisions that are so fundamentally incompatible with our democratic processes, our legislation and our constitutional arrangements" (14). The United States said that "it was the clear intention of all States that it be an aspirational declaration with political and moral, rather than legal force. . . . The United States rejects any possibility that this document is or can become customary international law" (15). If states stipulate Indigenous rights are only aspirational, something desired to achieve, then why invoke the law, domestic or international, to refuse any legality. In doing so, they are staking a possessive claim to international law by defining its limits. They reduce the contents of the declaration to mere aspiration, albeit with moral and political force, to argue against the legality of Indigenous rights. In doing so they reveal a displaced desire to render the declaration legally void in order to refuse Indigenous rights claims. They recuperate virtue by negation: Indigenous rights should have no legal status within international law because states are the primary subjects of international law and possess the greatest range of rights and obligations. It is interesting that these four states express no real concern about the moral and political force of the declaration. This is because as members of the United Nations their sovereign independence is guaranteed. It is their sovereign right to subject Indigenous peoples to their law, morality, and politics without intervention.

Self-Determination

One of the core rights within the declaration, the right to self-determination, was opposed by Australia and the United States. Australia argued that the right of self-determination only applied to "situations of decolonization and the breakup of States into smaller states within clearly defined population groups. . . . It is not a right that attaches to an undefined subgroup of a population seeking to obtain political independence" (11). The Australian state, by referring to Indigenous peoples as an "undefined subgroup of a population," is clearly signifying what our status should be. The United States stipulated that the right to self-determination, which was extracted from Article 1 of the Covenant on Civil and Political Rights and the Covenant on Economic and

Social Rights, is ambiguous (15). However, it does not confer a right for Indigenous peoples to be independent or self-governing within nation-states, nor does it confer permanent sovereignty over resources. The United States argued that this was the clear intent of states during consultations, whereas the declaration implies a right that does not exist.

The United States appears not to have a problem with the ambiguity of self-determination as defined within the respective covenants that it endorsed, but the right to self-determination within the Declaration on Indigenous Rights is a problem. Both Australia and the United States argue that the Indigenous right to self-determination is a false rights claim and one that was not supported by other states. This is a spurious assertion given that the majority of states voted for the declaration. Invoking state homogeneity within the UN on this provision is a way of positioning the document as being falsely representative of state views. Self-determination has been primarily a right of states and is inextricably tied to exercising sovereignty. To deny this right to Indigenous peoples is a way of refusing and disavowing Indigenous sovereignty, which is consistent and all too evident in their respective treatment of Indigenous peoples. For example, the unresolved issues first brought to the League of Nations by Chief Deskaheh continue today between the Six Nations Haudenosaunee and the Canadian federal government.[25] Virtue operates discursively to question the legitimacy of this provision within the declaration by Australia and the United States, reiterating a possessive claim to the integrity of their sovereignty against Indigenous counterclaims.

Lands and Resources

The possessiveness of the four states was also exhibited in their response to the provisions on lands and resources contained with the declaration. Australia asserted that they "could be read to require recognition of Indigenous rights to lands without regard to other existing legal rights pertaining to land both Indigenous and non-Indigenous. . . . Any right to traditional lands must be subject to national laws."[26] Canada iterated that it had processes in place to deal with lands, territories, and resources through its treaty mechanisms and constitution. It argued that the broad and unclear provisions could be susceptible to a number of interpretations, "discounting the need to recognise a range of rights over land and possibly putting into question matters that have already been settled by treaty in Canada" (12). New Zealand stated that "the provisions on lands and resources simply cannot be implemented" (14). Article 26 "appears to require recognition of rights to lands now lawfully owned by other citizens" and the entire country "is potentially caught within the scope of the article" (ibid.). The United States asserted that "the provision on lands and resources are phrased in a manner that is particularly unworkable. The language is overly broad and inconsistent. . . . Article 26 appears to require recognition of indigenous rights to lands without regard to other legal rights existing in lands" (15). These states disavow the collective rights of Indigenous peoples by positioning themselves as virtuous states that govern in the interests of other legal rights in land. The discursive twist in the use of "other legal rights" to appeal implicitly to diversity is an attempt to deflect attention away from the protection of their sovereign rights. In effect, they are proclaiming that land already owned and occupied under state sovereignty will not be diminished or changed by Indigenous proprietary rights. With missionary zeal, these states have already determined what is best for "their" Indigenous peoples by defining what Indigenous rights are acceptable. In this way, they stake a possessive claim to us.

Prior Free and Informed Consent

The right to determine what constitutes Indigenous rights was also manifest in these states' opposition to the article on prior free and informed consent. Australia argued that "any right to free, prior and informed consent" goes too far. It would mean that states are obliged to consult with Indigenous peoples about every aspect of law that might affect them. That would not only be unworkable, but it applies a standard that others do not have.[27] Canada stated that this was unduly restrictive and that it had consultation processes in place supported by the law. It asserted that "a complete veto power of legislative and administrative action for a particular group would be fundamentally incompatible with Canada's parliamentary system" (11). New Zealand argued that it welcomed Māori involvement in its democratic process, but that "these articles in the Declaration text imply different classes of citizenship, where Indigenous people have a right of veto that other groups or individuals do not have" (ibid.). New Zealand cannot endorse a document that does not reflect state practice or can be recognized as general principles of law. The United States said that it supported Indigenous peoples' involvement in government decision making, "but [it] could not accept the notion of a sub-national group having a 'veto' power over the legislative process."[28] The assertion that Article 19 confers a right that other citizens do not have is disingenuous to the extent that it is qualified by Article 46 in the declaration. These four states rationalize their opposition on the grounds that all citizens should have the same rights and that prior, free, and informed consent is unworkable. They make a possessive claim that there is no space to negotiate the law's application. Yet they have created a distinct legal position for the Indigenous peoples who reside within their borders, one that is not shared by other citizens. The originary lack of prior, free, and informed consent by states created a status of Indigeneity and the matters pertaining to it are already prepossessed. States regulate and discipline Indigenous peoples on the basis of our different status and rights claims in ways that do not threaten their sovereignty. In negating a qualified Indigenous right to prior, free, and informed consent, these states turn equal rights for all citizens into a virtue of their own making as they claim to govern for the good of all.

Repossessing the Declaration

In spite of these strenuous objections, Australia endorsed the declaration on April 3, 2009, followed in 2010 by New Zealand on April 19, Canada on November 12, and the United States on December 16. In their statements of endorsement, these four states made a discursive shift from indignation to reconciliation. They mobilized virtue to stake a possessive claim to the declaration while affirming patriarchal white sovereignty. All four states acknowledged that injustices have been committed in the past. Canada and the United States referred to their formal apologies as evidence that they were sincere and now they are transcending their histories. Australia stated that the declaration offered "a new era of relations between states and Indigenous peoples grounded in good faith, goodwill and mutual respect."[29] The government would not forcibly remove Indigenous peoples from their lands or territories, nor will their culture be destroyed. There will be no repetition of past policies. Canada said the declaration was important to Indigenous peoples throughout the world.[30] Endorsing the declaration will reconcile and enable stronger relations between the Canadian state and Aboriginal peoples. Canada noted that it has a productive and active partnership

with Aboriginal peoples and has advanced Indigenous rights domesti-
cally and abroad. The principles of the declaration are consistent with
the government's approach to working with Aboriginal peoples. And
New Zealand noted that the principles of the declaration "are consistent with the duties and principles inherent in the Treaty, such as
operating in the spirit of partnership and mutual respect."[31] President
Barack Obama announced the endorsement of the United States at
the Tribal Nation's Conference and stated that the promises he made
on the campaign trail in 2007 would be kept.[32] This included Native
Americans having a voice at the White House. The appointment of
Native American advisers and convening the largest Native American conference to discuss the relationship between the government
and Native Americans are evidence of his commitment. The endorsement by these four states functions as both confession and absolution.
They have atoned for the past by apologizing and recognizing that
injustices occurred. They are moving toward a more just future based
on a new relationship of working together to bring about change.
Their virtue is now recuperated through faith and hope.

    All four states outlined either directly or indirectly how they have
acted to implement rights contained in the declaration. Australia advised
that it has returned large tracts of land and is committed to improving
the social, cultural, and economic lives of Indigenous people through
an Indigenous Land Fund.[33] It acknowledged that Indigenous people
do have the right to be free from discrimination and prejudice and will
reinstate the Racial Discrimination Act, which had been suspended to
allow the government to intervene into Indigenous communities. It further noted that vulnerable Indigenous people have the right to be free
from violence and to lead safe and healthy lives and that policies are
in place to achieve change. Australia stated that education is the key
to economic and social prosperity and respect for Indigenous culture
is part of this process. The government will interpret the issue of free,
prior, and informed consent in accordance with Article 46 of the declaration. Australia will ensure that Indigenous involvement in the democratic process is enabled by the establishment of a national Indigenous
representative body, public consultation on key policy decisions, support for Indigenous leadership, and constitutional recognition of Indigenous people. Canada argued that it is a leader in protecting Aboriginal
peoples' rights, which it says it has demonstrated in its initiatives in
amending the Canadian Human Rights Act and changing the Indian

Registration Act to enable gender equity concerning the matrimonial transfer of property.[34] Canada noted that its endorsement of the declaration adds scaffolding to the government's existing initiatives in the areas of "education, economic development, housing, child and family services, access to safe drinking water, and the extension of human rights protection and matrimonial real property protection to First Nations on reserve."[35] New Zealand reported that it has transferred land and resources back to Māori and has offered redress constrained by monetary circumstances.[36] The principles for involvement in decision making in the declaration will be accommodated within the existing frameworks for Māori participation, of which consent is a part. Recognition is given to Māori worldviews and their cultural heritage should be reflected in laws and policies. New Zealand will continue to work for the human rights of Indigenous peoples while understanding that there will be debate and dialogue about the meanings that may be given to the aspirations put forward by the declaration. The United States outlined how the government was working with Native American tribes to improve conditions on their lands.[37] It has committed funds for the Internet and physical infrastructure to improve economic growth on reservations, renovate schools, increase the size of tribal lands, improve health care, and continue to improve culturally relevant programs at tribal colleges. President Obama has also signed the Tribal Law and Order Act (to enable the reduction of substance abuse and crime), settled disputes between Native American farmers and the Department of Agriculture, and provided funds to settle outstanding lawsuits over water rights. Virtue circulates discursively through these good intentions. As benevolent states, they are working hard and consistently to improve the life chances of Indigenous peoples who live within their borders. They want to do the right thing to bring about change in accordance with the principles of the declaration. They are contributing to the fulfillment of these rights and thereby the good life for Indigenous peoples.

Despite the deployment of virtue and the reconciliatory tone of their statements of endorsement, Australia, Canada, New Zealand, and the United States repeated their core objection to the declaration in their endorsement of it. Australia reaffirmed its position that the document is not legally binding and does not affect Australian law, but recognizes that the principles of the declaration are already mirrored in international human rights to which it is committed.[38] The declaration cannot

be used in any way to impair Australia's territorial integrity or political unity, and current native title and land rights laws are not altered
by supporting the declaration. Canada asserted that the document is
aspirational, not legally binding, and does not change Canadian law
and is not reflective of international law, but its endorsement "is a significant step forward in strengthening relations with Aboriginal peoples."[39] Canada feels it can now "interpret the principles expressed in
the declaration in a manner that is consistent with [its] Constitution
and legal framework," though the concerns raised in 2007 remain:
"Aboriginal and treaty rights are protected in Canada through a unique
framework. These rights are enshrined in our Constitution, including
our Charter of Rights and Freedoms, and are complemented by practical policies that adapt to our evolving reality. This framework will
continue to be the cornerstone of our efforts to promote and protect
the rights of Aboriginal Canadians."[40] New Zealand concluded that it
has a "strong commitment to human rights and indigenous rights in
particular" and that the latter are enshrined in the Treaty of Waitangi.[41]
In supporting the rights in the declaration, the existing legal and constitutional arrangements remain. Though they will evolve, they are the
foundations that determine the boundaries of any engagement. These
existing legal and constitutional arrangements will be maintained.
The United States noted that the declaration is not legally binding or
a statement of current international law, but it has moral and political
force. "It expresses the aspirations of the United States, aspirations
that this country seeks to achieve within the structure of the U.S. Constitution, laws, and international obligations, while also seeking, where
appropriate, to improve our laws and policies."[42] The United States
believes that the concept of self-determination is not the same as in
international law and views it as being consistent with its recognition
of tribes to be self-governing, and it will act to extend this to Native
Hawaiians. The United States argued that the declaration did not
change or define the concept of self-determination under existing international law, stating that "article 46 . . . does not imply any right to
take action that would dismember or impair totally or in part the territorial integrity or political unity of sovereign and independent states."[43]
The United States qualified its acceptance of the right to prior, free,
and informed consent by noting that while it will consult, it does not
necessarily require the consent of tribal leaders to act. The message is
clear from all four states: Indigenous rights shall be reconciled to their

sovereignty. It is their divine right to demarcate the limits of what they are willing to do.

Conclusion

The declaration's qualifications on Indigenous rights provide fertile ground for the application of exclusionary practices by states that discriminate in their favor, ensuring that they protect and maintain their sovereign interests by the continuing denial of Indigenous sovereignty. Patriarchal white sovereignty's possessive logic determines what constitutes Indigenous peoples' rights and what they will be subjected to in accordance with its authority and law. These subjections are always exclusionary for Indigenous peoples because the divine right of patriarchal white sovereignty prevails and the definition and circumscription of rights become methods by which subjugation is carried out.[44]

The declaration ontologically disturbed patriarchal white sovereignty, which retaliated through political, legal, and moral force to disavow the virtue of Indigenous rights. The declaration was treated as an outside intervention that required the containment of the enemy within its borders: Indigenous peoples whose existence threatens the self-realization of patriarchal white sovereignty's interior truth. Canada, Australia, New Zealand, and the United States position themselves as enlightened, tolerant, and virtuous states. They want the United Nations to believe that deep in their hearts they have compassion for Indigenous peoples and are sorry about past injustices. They want the world to think highly of them, to admire their humanity, their sense of international responsibility, and their acceptance of all races and religions. This is how virtue functions discursively within the possessive logic of patriarchal white sovereignty to dispossess Indigenous peoples from the ground of moral value, enabling racism to be exercised with the best of intentions.

AFTERWORD

POSSESSION WORKS IN DIFFERENT WAYS. Throughout this book I have illustrated how the possessive logics of patriarchal white sovereignty discursively disavow and dispossess the Indigenous subject of an ontology that exists outside the logic of capital, by always demanding our inclusion within modernity on terms that it defines. Think of how we are overdetermined as Indigenous peoples, simultaneously relegated to the past while existing in the present, saturated with meanings operationalized within racialized discourses. The possessive logics of patriarchal white sovereignty require the constructions of Indigeneity to be validated and measured through different regulatory mechanisms and disciplinary knowledges within modernity. Regulatory measures of Indigeneity can take the form of criteria for becoming an enrolled citizen of a tribe or genealogical proof of biological descent or the enactment of practices and rituals that can be confirmed, contested, and denied, usually by trained experts such as anthropologists and lawyers. Through these and other means, the possessive logics of patriarchal white sovereignty restrict the availability of the modern world for Indigenous embodied ontologies. As Sara Ahmed so brilliantly argues:

> [A] body-at-home in its world, a body that extends into space through how it reaches toward objects that are already "in place." Being in place, or having a place, involves the intimacy of cohabiting spaces with other things. . . . For Fanon, racism "stops" [Indigenous] bodies inhabiting space by extending through objects and others; the familiarity of "the white world," as a world we know implicitly, "disorients" [Indigenous] bodies such that they cease to know where to find things—reduced as they are to things among things.[1]

As things that are possessed, Indigenous people must be emptied of our ways of being in order to come into existence as the homogenous Indigenous subject created through a racialized rights discourse, first in the form of treaties, then in the form of citizen and human rights. As a technique of subjectification, rights are exercised by Indigenous subjects who act upon and resist under contextual conditions while being determined by them. Thus the "rights" conferred in various forms and racial measures, such as blood quantum and skin color, contracted with and defined by the possessive logics of patriarchal white sovereignty, quantify what is recognizable as Indigeneity within modernity. In this sense, I am arguing that even where the recognition of political sovereignty exists through treaties, the constitution of rights is tied to recognition and configured through the possessive logics of patriarchal white sovereignty. For centuries, the logics of possession have treated the earth and its Indigenous peoples as something that is always predisposed to being possessed and exploited.

In the twenty-first century, the terms "Aborigine," "Native," and "Indian" continue to function as white epistemic possessions circulating as though their etymological roots are no longer connected to their function as homogenous racialized concepts discursively signifying our savagery, primitiveness, barbarianism, and overall lack. We claim and name ourselves Aborigines, Indians, and Natives even though these concepts do not hold only the meanings we ascribe to them. As homogenizing concepts, we operationalize them to form alliances in our political struggles and we redefine their meanings. Our ability to resist in this way is informed by our sovereign ontologies through which we know ourselves within our respective knowledge systems, as being, for example, Goenpul or Seneca or Kanaka Maoli.

Our capacity for self-definition lies within a counter-discourse informed by our sovereignty and ontologies, but the discursive nature of racialized discourse means we are never beyond it, even when we are resisting it; our lives are forged through struggle.[2] The struggle began to materialize with colonization. As Lumbee legal scholar Robert Williams Jr. has argued, there is an intimate relationship between the invention of Western civilization, the deployment of the "savage," and the appropriation of Indigenous lands.[3]

At the beginning of the second decade of the twenty-first century, the shape-shifting nature of colonization persists in the present and will remain unfinished business for Indigenous peoples in Canada, the United States, New Zealand, Australia, and Hawai'i. Racism is an important part of the way these nation-states operationalize their possessive logics to maintain ownership of our lands. Perhaps it is time in Critical Indigenous studies for Indigenous scholars to build on our work to develop theories of why, how, when, and where race matters. As I have tried to unmask in this book, the possessive logics of patriarchal white sovereignty and the disavowal of Indigenous sovereignty are inextricably linked, anchored, and regulated through race.

NOTES

Introduction

1. I acknowledge that there are thousands of Indigenous peoples around the world. I use the terms Indigenous and Aboriginal interchangeably within the Australian context. Otherwise, my use of the term Indigenous in this book is restricted to Native Americans, Kanaka Maoli, Māori, First Nations, Métis, Aborigines, and Torres Strait Islanders.

2. *Eatock v. Bolt* [2011] FCA 1103 (September 28, 2011), http://www.austlii.edu.au/cgi-bin/sinodisp/au/cases/cth/FCA/2011/1103.html?stem=0&synonyms=0&query=Bolt.

3. *Adoptive Couple v. Baby Girl*, 570 U.S. (2013), http://www.supremecourt.gov/opinions/12pdf/12–399_q86b.pdf.

4. Elizabeth Cook-Lynn, "Who Stole Native American Studies?" *Wicazo Sa Review* 12, no. 1 (Spring 1997): 9–28.

5. Mason Durie, "The Development of Māori Studies in New Zealand Universities," *He Pukenga Korero, Nghuru* 1, no. 2 (1996): 22–25.

6. Ibid., 24.

7. Audra Simpson, "On Ethnographic Refusal: Indigeneity, 'Voice,' and Colonial Citizenship," *Junctures*, no. 9 (December 2007): 67–80.

8. Chris Andersen, "Critical Indigenous Studies: From Difference to Density," *Cultural Studies Review* 15, no. 2 (September 2009): 80–100.

9. Martin Nakata, "Australian Indigenous Studies: A Question of Discipline," *Australian Journal of Anthropology* 17, no. 3 (2006): 265–75.

10. Andrea Smith, "Queer Theory and Native Studies: The Heteronormativity of Settler Colonialism," *GLQ* 16, nos. 1–2 (2010): 41–68.

11. Ibid., 41–42.

12. Ibid., 44.

13. Circe Sturm, *Blood Politics: Race, Culture, and Identity in the Cherokee Nation of Oklahoma* (Berkeley: University of California Press, 2002); Kim TallBear, *Native American DNA: Tribal Belonging and the False Promise of Genetic Science* (Minneapolis: University of Minnesota Press, 2013); Brendan Hokowhitu, "Indigenous

Existentialism and the Body," *Cultural Studies Review* 15, no. 2 (September 2009): 101–19.

14. Tiya Miles, *Ties That Bind: The Story of an Afro-Cherokee Family in Slavery and Freedom* (Berkeley: University of California Press, 2005); Miles, *The House on Diamond Hill: A Cherokee Plantation Story* (Chapel Hill: University of North Carolina Press, 2010).

15. Stephen P. Knadler, *The Fugitive Race: Minority Writers Resisting Whiteness* (Jackson: University of Mississippi Press, 2002), 204.

16. Cheryl Harris, "Whiteness as Property," *Harvard Law Review* 106, no. 8 (1993): 1701.

17. Theodore Allen, *The Invention of the White Race: Racial Oppression and Social Control*, vol. 1 (London: Verso, 1994); David Roediger, *The Wages of Whiteness: Race and the Making of the American Working Class* (London: Verso, 1991); Ruth Frankenberg, *White Women Race Matters: The Social Construction of "Whiteness"* (Minneapolis: University of Minnesota Press, 1993); George Lipsitz, *A Possessive Investment in Whiteness: How White People Profit from Identity Politics* (Philadelphia: Temple University Press, 1998); Karen Brodkin, *How Jews Became White Folks and What That Says about Race in America* (New Brunswick, N.J.: Rutgers University Press, 1998).

18. David Roediger, *How Race Survived U.S. History from Settlement and Slavery to the Obama Phenomenon* (New York: Verso, 2008); Sherrow O. Pinder, *Whiteness and Racialized Ethnic Groups in the United States* (New York: Lexington Books, 2012).

19. Jean M. O'Brien, *Firsting and Lasting: Writing Indians Out of Existence in New England* (Minneapolis: University of Minnesota Press, 2010).

20. David Theo Goldberg, *The Racial State* (Malden, Mass.: Blackwell, 2002); Steve Martinot, *The Machinery of Whiteness: Studies in the Structure of Racialization* (Philadelphia: Temple University Press, 2010).

21. Aileen Moreton-Robinson, "Race Matters: The 'Aborigine' as a White Possession," in *World of Indigenous North America*, ed. Robert Warrior (New York: Routledge, 2013).

22. David Theo Goldberg, *Racist Culture: Philosophy and the Politics of Meaning* (Oxford: Blackwell, 1996), 49.

1. I Still Call Australia Home

I am indebted to Jane Haggis, Alison Ravenscroft, and Fiona Nicoll for their invaluable comments on this chapter.

1. I use the verb "postcolonizing" to signify the active, the current, and the continuing nature of the colonizing relationship that positions us as belonging but not belonging.

2. Amanda Nettelbeck, "South Australian Settler Memoirs," *Journal of Australian Studies* 68 (2001): 100.

3. A. Markus, *Australian Race Relations, 1788–1993* (St. Leonards: Allen and Unwin, 1994).

4. G. Hogue, "Letter to the Editor," *Courier Mail*, February 17, 1998, 17.

5. A. James Hammerton and Catherine Coleborne, "Ten-Pound Poms Revisited: Battlers' Tales and British Migration to Australia," *Journal of Australian Studies* 68 (2001): 86–96; Alistair Thomson, "Recording British Migration: Place, Meaning, and Identity in Audio Letters from Australia, 1963–1965," *Journal of Australian Studies* 68 (2001): 105–16.

6. Peter Read, *Belonging: Australians, Place, and Aboriginal Ownership* (Cambridge: Cambridge University Press, 2000), 217.

7. Ibid., 223.

8. My point here is that the law shapes our behavior, but our consciousness of it usually occurs through breaking it. We do not walk around contemplating what piece of legislation governs our ability to function and perform in any context on a daily basis second by second, minute by minute, hour by hour.

9. Bill Ashcroft, Gareth Griffiths, and Helen Tiffin, *The Post-Colonial Studies Reader* (London: Routledge, 1995); Leela Gandhi, *Postcolonial Theory: A Critical Introduction* (St. Leonards: Allen and Unwin, 1998); Homi Bhabha, *The Location of Culture* (London: Routledge, 1994); Iain Chambers and Lidia Curti, *The Post-Colonial Question: Common Skies, Divided Horizons* (London: Routledge, 1996).

10. Stuart Hall and Paul du Gay, *Questions of Cultural Identity* (London: Sage, 1996), 249.

11. G. Huggan, "Unsettled Settlers, Postcolonialism, Travelling Theory, and the New Migrant Aesthetics," *Journal of Australian Studies* 68 (2001): 117–27, 119.

12. Homi Bhabha, "Unpacking my Library . . . Again," in Chambers and Curti, *The Post-colonial Question;* and Iain Chambers, *Border Dialogues: Journeys in Postmodernity* (London: Routledge, 1990).

13. Ken Gelder and Jane Jacobs, *Uncanny Australia: Sacredness and Identity in a Postcolonial Nation* (Melbourne: Melbourne University Press, 1998).

14. Susanne Schech and Jane Haggis, "Migrancy, Multiculturalism, and Whiteness: Re-charting Core Identities in Australia," *Communal Plural: Journal of Transnational and Crosscultural Studies* 9, no. 2 (October 2001): 145.

15. I used "whiteness" in accordance with Frankenberg's definition: a position from which white people view the world, as a privileged structural location and a set of cultural practices: Ruth Frankenberg, *White Women: Race Matters: The Social Construction of Whiteness* (London: Routledge, 1993).

16. Schech and Haggis, "Migrancy, Multiculturalism, and Whiteness," 148.

17. Paula Gunn Allen, *The Sacred Hoop: Recovering the Feminine in American Indian Traditions* (Boston: Beacon Press, 1992); Jackie Huggins, *Sister Girl* (St. Lucia: University of Queensland Press, 1998); Patricia Monture-Angus, *Journeying Forward: Dreaming Aboriginal Peoples' Independence* (Annandale: Pluto Press, 2000).

18. Aileen Moreton-Robinson, *Talkin' Up to the White Woman: Indigenous Women and Feminism* (St. Lucia: Queensland University Press, 2000).

19. Sally Morgan, *My Place* (South Freemantle: Freemantle Arts Centre Press, 1987).

20. Glenyse Ward, *Wandering Girl* (Broome: Magabala Books, 1988).

21. Alice Nannup, *When the Pelican Laughed* (South Freemantle: Freemantle Arts Centre Press, 1992).

22. Ruby Langford, *Don't Take Your Love to Town* (Ringwood: Penguin Books, 1988).

23. Barry Morris, *Domesticating Resistance: The Dhan-Gadi and the Australian State* (Oxford: Berg, 1989), 215.

24. Kent McNeil, "Native Title and Extinguishment," in *FAIRA Native Title Conference Papers* (Brisbane: Foundation for Aboriginal and Islander Research Action, 1995), 36.

25. Ibid., 39.

26. Ibid., 41.

27. Aileen Moreton-Robinson, "Witnessing Whiteness in the Wake of Wik," *Social Alternatives* 17, no. 2 (1998): 11–14.

28. Sara Ahmed, *Strange Encounters: Embodied Others in Post-Coloniality* (London: Routledge, 2000).

2. The House That Jack Built

1. Toni Morrison, "Black Matters," in *Race Critical Theories: Text and Context*, ed. Philomena Essed and David Theo Goldberg (Maldon, Mass.: Blackwell, 2002), 266.

2. Department of Immigration and Multicultural and Indigenous Affairs, *Fact Sheet 6*, 1.

3. John Howard, The 5th Annual Sir Edward "Weary" Dunlop Asialink Lecture, Melbourne, November 11, 1997, http://www.pm.gov.au/news/speeches/1997/waerydun.htm.

4. Ghassan Hage, *Against Paranoid Nationalism: Searching for Hope in a Shrinking Society* (Annandale: Pluto Press, 2003), 73.

5. Fiona Nicoll, *From Diggers to Drag Queens: Configurations of Australian National Identity* (Annandale: Pluto Press, 2001), 29.

6. Carol Johnson, "The Dilemmas of Ethnic Privilege: A Comparison of Constructions of 'British,' 'English' and 'Anglo Celtic' Identity in Contemporary British and Australian Political Discourse," *Ethnicities* 2, no. 2 (2002): 163–88.

7. *Weekend Australian,* February 26–27, 2005, 19.

8. Ghassan Hage, *White Nation: Fantasies of White Supremacy in a Multicultural Society* (Annandale: Pluto Press, 1998), 48 (my emphasis).

9. Ibid., 64.

10. Aileen Moreton-Robinson, "The Possessive Logic of Patriarchal Whiteness: The High Court and the *Yorta Yorta* Decision," *borderlands ejournal* (2005), http://www.borderlandsejournal.adelaide.edu.au/issues/vol3no2.html.

11. Cheryl Harris, "Whiteness as Property," in *Critical Race Theory: The Key Writings That Formed the Movement,* ed. Kimberlé Crenshaw, Neil Gotanda, Gary Peller, and Kendall Thomas (New York: New Press, 1995), 277–78.

12. Gerald Torres and Kathryn Milun, "Translating 'Yonnodio' by Precedent and Evidence: The Mashpee Indian Case," in *Critical Race Theory,* 186.

13. Hage, *Against Paranoid Nationalism,* 70–73.

14. T. Allen, *The Invention of the White Race: Racial Oppression and Social Control,* vol. 1 (London: Verso, 1994).

15. Stuart Ward, "Sentiment and Self-Interest: The Imperial Ideal in Anglo-Australian Commercial Culture," *Australian Historical Studies* 32, no. 116 (2001): 104; Neville Meaney, "Britishness and Australian Identity: The Problem of Nationalism in Australian History and Historiography," *Australian Historical Studies* 32, no. 116 (April 2001): 89.

16. Tara Brabazon, *Tracking the Jack: A Retracing of the Antipodes* (Sydney: University of New South Wales Press, 2000).

17. Amanda Nettelbeck, "South Australian Settler Memories," *Journal of Australian Studies* 25, no. 68 (2001): 97–104.

18. David Malouf, "Made in England: Australia's British Inheritance," *Quarterly Essay* 12 (2003): 39.

19. Ibid., 43.

20. Ibid., 47–48.

21. Nicoll, *From Diggers to Drag Queens.*

22. Miriam Dixson, *The Imaginary Australian: Anglo-Celts and Identity—1788 to the Present* (Sydney: University of New South Wales Press, 1999), 24.

23. Ibid., 30.

24. Alistair Thompson, "Recording British Migration: Place, Meaning, and Identity in Audio Letters from Australia, 1963–1965," *Scatterlings of Empire, Journal of Australian Studies* 32, no. 116 (2001): 106.

25. Ibid., 1114.

26. Jon Stratton, "'Not Just Another Multicultural Story': The English, from 'Fitting in' to Self-Ethnicisation," *Vision Splendid, Journal of Australian Studies* 24, no. 66 (2000): 47.

27. Ibid., 23.

28. Sara Wills and Kate Darian-Smith, "Beauty Contest for British Bulldogs? Negotiating (Trans)National Identities in Suburban Melbourne," *Cultural Studies Review* 9, no. 2 (November 2003): 67.

29. Susanne Schech and Jane Haggis, "Terrains of Migrancy and Whiteness: How British Migrants Locate Themselves in Australia," in *Whitening Race: Essays in Social and Cultural Criticism,* ed. Aileen Moreton-Robinson (Canberra: Aboriginal Studies Press, 2004), 6.

30. Ann Curthoys, "Expulsion, Exodus, and Exile," *Imaginary Homelands, Journal of Australian Studies* 23, no. 61 (1999): 2–3.

31. Ken Inglis, *Sacred Places: War Memorials in the Australian Landscape* (Carlton South: Melbourne University Press, 1998), 21.

32. Moreton-Robinson, "The Possessive Logic of Patriarchal Whiteness."

33. Harris, "Whiteness as Property," 277–78.

34. Andrew Markus, "Legislating White Australia, 1900–1970," in *Sex, Power, and Justice: Historical Perspectives on Law in Australia*, ed. Diane Kirkby (Melbourne: Oxford University Press, 1995), 238.

35. George Lipsitz, *The Possessive Investment in Whiteness: How White People Profit from Identity Politics* (Philadelphia: Temple University Press, 1998).

36. Markus, "Legislating White Australia, 1900–1970."

37. Harris, "Whiteness as Property," 104.

38. Jon Stratton, "Multiculturalism and the Whitening Machine; or, How Australians Become White," in *The Future of Australian Multiculturalism: Reflections on the Twentieth Anniversary of Jean Martin's "The Migrant Presence,"* ed. Ghassan Hage and Rowanne Couch (Sydney: Research Institute for Humanities and Social Sciences, University of Sydney, 1999), 177.

39. Harris, "Whiteness as Property," 283.

40. Lipsitz, *The Possessive Investment in Whiteness*, vii.

3. Bodies That Matter on the Beach

1. Regina Ganter, *Mixed Relations: Asian-Aboriginal Contact in North Australia* (Crawley: University of Western Australia Press, 2006).

2. Michael Taussig, "The Beach (A Fantasy)," *Critical Inquiry* 26 (Winter 2000): 249–77; 258.

3. Aileen Moreton-Robinson and Fiona Nicoll, "We Shall Fight Them on the Beaches: Protesting Cultures of White Possession," *Journal of Australian Studies* 30, no. 89 (December 2007): 151–62.

4. Judith Butler, *Bodies That Matter: On the Discursive Limits of "Sex"* (New York: Routledge, 1993).

5. Richard Dyer, *White* (London: Routledge, 1997).

6. Keith Vincent Smith, "Voices on the Beach," in *Lines in the Sand: Botany Bay Stories from 1770*, ed. Ace Bourke (Gymea: Hazelhurst Regional Gallery and Arts Centre, 2008), 13–22; 13.

7. Aileen Moreton-Robinson, "White Possession: The Legacy of Cook's Choice," in *Imagined Australia: Reflections Around the Reciprocal Construction of Identity Between Australia and Europe* (Bern: Peter Lang, 2009).

8. Butler, *Bodies That Matter*.

9. Damien Riggs and Martha Augoustinos, "The Psychic Life of Colonial Power: Racialised Subjectivities, Bodies, and Methods," *Journal of Community and Applied Social Psychology* 15, no. 6 (2005): 461–77; 471.

10. Caroline Ford, "Gazing, Strolling, Falling in Love: Culture and Nature on the Beach in Nineteenth-Century Sydney," *History Australia* 3, no. 1 (2006): 8.1–8.14; 8.3.

11. Ibid., 8.2.

12. Cameron White, "Representing the Nation: Australian Masculinity on the Beach at Cronulla," in *Everyday Multiculturalism, Conference Proceedings*, Macquarie University, September 28–29, 2006 (Centre for Research on Social Inclusion, Macquarie University, 2007), 2.

13. H. C. Coombs, *Aboriginal Autonomy: Issues and Strategies* (Cambridge: Cambridge University Press, 1994), 71.

14. Douglas Booth, "Ambiguities in Pleasure and Discipline: The Development of Competitive Surfing," *Journal of Sport History* 22, no. 3 (Fall 1995): 189–206; 190.

15. Sara Ahmed, *Differences That Matter: Feminist Theory and Postmodernism* (New York: Cambridge University Press, 1998), 116.

16. Farid Farid, "Terror at the Beach: Arab Bodies and the Somatic Violence of White Cartographic Anxiety in Australia and Palestine/Israel," *Social Semiotics* 19, no. 1 (2009): 59–78; 66.

17. "Yamba Call to Oars," *Daily Examiner*, January 16, 2010, http://www.daily examiner.com.au.

18. Fiona Nicoll, *From Diggers to Drag Queens: Reconfigurations of National Identity* (St. Leonards: Pluto Press, 2001).

19. White, "Representing the Nation," 5.

20. Ibid., 6.

21. Booth, "Ambiguities in Pleasure and Discipline," 190.

22. Ibid.

23. I. Helekunihi Walker, "Terrorism or Native Protest? The Hui 'O He'e Nalu and Hawaiian Resistance to Colonialism," *Pacific Historical Review* 74, no. 4 (2005): 575–601; 576.

24. http://www.absolutearts.com/artsnews/2003/03/03/30797.html.

25. Aileen Moreton-Robinson, *Talkin' Up to the White Woman: Indigenous Women and Feminism* (St. Lucia: University of Queensland Press, 2000).

26. Aileen Moreton-Robinson, "The House That Jack Built: Britishness and White Possession," *ACRAWSA ejournal* 1 (2005), http://www.acrawsa.org.au/files/ejournalfiles/97AileenMoretonRobinson.pdf.

27. Sue Ebury, *Weary: The Life of Sir Edward Dunlop* (Penguin Books, 1994).

28. Nicoll, *From Diggers to Drag Queens*, 29.

29. Moreton-Robinson, "The House That Jack Built."

30. *The Weekend Australian*, February 26–27, 2005, 19.

31. Moreton-Robinson and Nicoll, "We Shall Fight Them on the Beaches."

32. Cheryl Harris, "Whiteness as Property (1993)," in *Black on White: Black Writers on What It Means to Be White,* ed. David Roediger (New York: Shocken Books, 1998).

33. Moreton-Robinson and Nicoll, "We Shall Fight Them on the Beaches."

4. Writing Off Treaties

1. Mike Hill, *After Whiteness: Unmaking an American Majority* (New York: New York University Press, 2004), 16.

2. Robyn Wiegman, "Whiteness Studies and the Paradox of Particularity," *Boundary 2*, 28, no. 3 (1999): 121.

3. Peter Kolchin, "Whiteness Studies: The New History of Race in America," *Journal of American History* 89 no. 1, (June 2002): 154–73, par. 30.

4. Stephen. P. Knadler, *The Fugitive Race: Minority Writers Resisting Whiteness* (Jackson: University Press of Mississippi, 2002).

5. Mark Bay, "Becoming a Cosmopolitan: What It Means to Be a Human Being in the New Millennium," *Library Journal* 125, no. 5 (2000): 112.

6. Toni Morrison, *Playing in the Dark: Whiteness and the Literary Imagination* (Cambridge: Harvard University Press, 1992).

7. Ibid., 76.

8. Toni Morrison, "Black Matters," in *Race Critical Theories: Text and Context*, ed. Philomena Essed and David Theo Goldberg (Maldon, Mass.: Blackwell, 2002), 266.

9. R. Williams, *Like a Loaded Weapon: The Rehnquist Court, Indian Rights and the Legal History of Racism in America* (Minneapolis: University of Minnesota Press, 2005), 35–37.

10. Margaret Davies and Ngaire Naffine, *Are Persons Property? Legal Debates about Property and Personality* (Burlington, Vt.: Ashgate, 2001), 32–33.

11. Thomas K. Nakayama and Judith N. Martin, eds., *Whiteness: The Communication of Social Identity* (Thousand Oaks, Calif.: Sage, 1999), 16.

12. Toula Nicolacopoulos and George Vassilacopoulos, "Racism, Foreigner Communities, and the Onto-pathology of White Australian Subjectivity," in *Whitening Race: Essays in Social and Cultural Criticism*, ed. Aileen Moreton-Robinson (Canberra: Aboriginal Studies Press, 2004), 38.

13. Theodore Allen, *The Invention of the White Race, Volume One: Racial Oppression and Social Control* (London: Verso, 1994).

14. David Roediger, *Towards the Abolition of Whiteness* (London: Verso, 1994).

15. Karen Brodkin, *How the Jews Became White Folk* (New Brunswick, N.J.: Rutgers University Press, 1999).

16. M. F. Jacobson, *Whiteness of a Different Color: European Immigrants and the Alchemy of Race* (Cambridge: Harvard University Press, 1998).

17. Ruth Frankenberg, *Displacing Whiteness: Essays in Social and Cultural Criticism* (Durham: Duke University Press, 1997).

18. Ibid., 6.

19. Richard Dyer, *White* (London: Routledge, 1997).

20. Ruth Frankenberg, *White Woman Race Matters: The Social Construction of Whiteness* (London: Routledge, 1993).

21. Barbara Flagg, *Was Blind But Now I See: White Race Consciousness and the Law* (New York: New York University Press, 1998); Ian F. Haney Lopez, *White by Law: The Legal Construction of Race* (New York: New York University Press, 1996).

22. George Lipsitz, *The Possessive Investment in Whiteness: How White People Profit from Identity Politics* (Philadelphia: Temple University Press, 1998).

23. Nakayama and Martin, *Whiteness*.

24. Joe L. Kincheloe, Shirley R. Steinberg, Nelson M. Rodriguez, Ronald Chennault, eds., *White Reign: Deploying Whiteness in America* (New York: St. Martin's Griffin, 2000); Michelle Fine, Lois Weis, Linda C. Powell, and L. Mun Wong, eds., *Off White: Readings on Race, Power, and Society* (New York: Routledge, 1997).

25. Stephen P. Knadler, *The Fugitive Race* (Jackson: University Press of Mississippi, 2002), 204.

26. bell hooks, *Black Looks: Race and Representation* (Boston: South End Press, 1992), 166.

27. Charles W. Smith, "Racial Exploitation and the Wages of Whiteness," in *What White Looks Like*, ed. George Yancy (New York: Routledge, 2004), 32.

28. George Yancy, ed., *What White Looks Like: African American Philosophers on the Whiteness Question* (New York: Routledge, 2004), 1–7.

29. Valerie Babb, *Whiteness Visible: The Meaning of Whiteness in American Literature and Culture* (New York: New York University Press, 1998), 170.

30. Charles W. Mills, *The Racial Contract* (Ithaca: Cornell University Press, 1997).

31. Robert Williams, *Like a Loaded Weapon: The Rehnquist Court, Indian Rights, and the Legal History of Racism in America* (Minneapolis: University of Minnesota Press, 2005), xxxv.

32. http://www.multiracial.com/government/whitehouse-eo13050.html.

33. http://www.dickshovel.com/sonsham.html.

34. Kevin Bruynell, *The Third Space of Sovereignty: The Postcolonial Politics of U.S.-Indigenous Relations* (Minneapolis: University of Minnesota Press, 2007), 215.

35. http://aad.english.ucsb.edu/docs/PBS-july98.html.

36. Williams, *Like a Loaded Weapon*, 33.

37. Ibid.

38. Frances Reins, "Is the Benign Really Harmless? Deconstructing Some 'Benign' Manifestations of Operationalised White Privilege," in *White Reign*, 80.

39. Williams, *Like a Loaded Weapon*; Vine Deloria Jr., *Red Earth, White Lies: Native Americans and the Myth of Scientific Fact* (Golden, Colo.: Fulcrum Publishing, 1997); Philip Deloria, *Playing Indian* (New Haven: Yale University Press, 1988).

40. Devon A. Mihesuah, *American Indians: Stereotypes and Realities* (Atlanta: Clarity Press, 1996).

41. Vine Deloria Jr., and D. M. Lytle, *American Indians: American Justice* (Austin: University of Texas Press, 1983), 3.

42. R. A. Grounds, G. E. Tinker, and D. E. Wilkins, *Native Voices: American Indian Identity and Resistance* (Lawrence: University Press of Kansas, 2003); J. Barker, *Sovereignty Matters: Locations of Contestation and Possibility in Indigenous Struggles for Self-determination* (Lincoln: University of Nebraska Press, 2005).

43. Robert Warrior, *Tribal Secrets: Recovering American Indian Intellectual Traditions* (Minneapolis: University of Minnesota Press, 1995), 87.

44. Noenoe Silva, *Aloha Betrayed: Native Hawaiian Resistance to American Colonialism* (Durham: Duke University Press, 2006).

45. Philip Deloria, *Playing Indian*, 3.

46. Kehuani Kauanui, "Diasporic Deracination and 'Off-Island' Hawaiians," *Contemporary Pacific* 19, no. 1 (2007): 137–60; 140.

47. Warwick Anderson, *The Cultivation of Whiteness: Science, Health, and Racial Identity in Australia* (Melbourne: Melbourne University Press, 2002).

48. Ghassan Hage, *White Nation: Fantasies of White Supremacy in a Multi- cultural Society* (Annandale: Pluto Press, 2000).

49. Jon Stratton, *Race Daze: Australia in Identity Crisis* (Sydney: Pluto Press, 1998).

50. Belinda McKay, ed., *Unmasking Whiteness: Race and Reconciliation* (St. Lucia: University of Queensland Press, 1999); Anderson, *The Cultivation of Whiteness*; Aileen Moreton-Robinson, *Talkin' Up to the White Woman: Indigenous Women and Feminism* (St. Lucia: University of Queensland Press, 2000); Moreton-Robinson, "The Possessive Logic of Patriarchal White Sovereignty: The High Court and the Yorta Yorta Decision," *Borderlands* 3, no. 2 (2004), http://www .borderlandsejournal.adelaide.edu.au/vol3no2_2004/moreton_possessve.htm; Moreton-Robinson, ed., *Whitening Race: Essays in Social and Cultural Criticism* (Canberra: Aboriginal Studies Press, 2004); Fiona Nicoll, "Indigenous Sovereignty and the Violence of Perspective: A White Woman's Coming Out Story," *Australian Feminist Studies* 15, no. 33 (December 2000): 369–86; Nicoll, "Reconciliation in and out of Perspective: White Knowing, Seeing, Curating, and Being at Home in and against Indigenous Sovereignty," in *Whitening Race*, ed. Moreton-Robinson; Ghassan Hage, *Against Paranoid Nationalism* (Sydney: Pluto Press, 2003).

51. Alison Ravenscroft, "Anxieties of Dispossession: Whiteness, History, and Australia's War in Viet Nam," in *Whitening Race*, ed. Moreton-Robinson; Nicoll, "Reconciliation in and out of Perspective"; Nicolacopoulos and Vassilacopoulos, "Racism, Foreigner Communities, and the Onto-pathology of White Australian Subjectivity"; Kate Foord, "Frontier Theory: Displacement and Disavowal in the Writing of White Nations," in *Whitening Race*, ed. Moreton-Robinson.

5. Nullifying Native Title

1. Aileen Moreton-Robinson, "Witnessing Whiteness in the Wake of Wik," *Social Alternatives* 17, no. 2 (April 1998): 11.

2. George Lipsitz, *The Possessive Investment in Whiteness: How White People Profit from Identity Politics* (Philadelphia: Temple University Press, 1998).

3. Catharine MacKinnon, "Reflections on Sex Equality under Law," in *American Feminist Thought at Century's End: A Reader*, ed. Linda S. Kauffmann (Cambridge: Blackwell, 1993), 367.

4. H. Jones, *In Her Own Name: A History of Women in South Australia from 1836, including the Story of Women's Suffrage* (Adelaide: Wakefield Press, 1994), 10.

5. Cheryl Harris, "Whiteness as Property," in *Black on White: Black Writers on What It Means to Be White* (New York: Schocken Books, 1998), 104.

6. Kent McNeil, "Native Title and Extinguishment," in *FAIRA Native Title Conference Proceedings* (Brisbane: Foundation for Aboriginal and Islander Research Action [FAIRA], 1995), 36.

7. (1879) 4 AC 294.

8. Ibid., 40–41.

9. Ibid.

10. Aileen Moreton-Robertson, "Native Title: Social Justice," in *Indigenous Rights National Conference Proceedings* (Brisbane: FAIRA, 1993), 55.

11. The freehold standard requires native title to be treated in the same way as freehold title.

12. Moreton-Robinson, "Witnessing Whiteness in the Wake of Wik."

13. This is based on the author's knowledge of and involvment with the native title claim made by her mob, the Quandamooka people.

14. Harris, "Whiteness as Property," 111.

15. M. Taylor, *Bludgers in Grass Castles: Native Title and the Unpaid Debts of the Pastoral Industry* (Sydney: Resistance Books, 1998), 24 (emphasis in original).

16. Lipsitz, "The Possessive Investment in Whiteness," viii.

17. *7.30 Report*, ABC TV, September 4, 1997.

18. John Howard, quoted in the *Weekend Australian*, November 22–23, 1997, 23.

19. Professor John Holmes, emeritus professor of geography at the University of Queensland, was horrified by the prime minister's crude lesson in geography, because he estimates that only 40 percent of land now under pastoral lease is claimable.

20. John Howard, press release, May 8, 1997.

21. ANTaR, Submission to the Committee on the Elimination of All Forms of Racial Discrimination, 1999, 33, transcript available at http://www.faira.org.au.

22. Harris, "Whiteness as Property," 110.

23. P. Burke, "The Native Title Bill: What Happened in the Senate," *Indigenous Law Bulletin* 4, no. 9 (1998): 7.

24. John Howard, quoted in the *Weekend Australian*, November 22–23, 1997, 23.

25. Harris, "Whiteness as Property," 108.

26. Extracts from the report of the Country Rapporteur, March 1999, 3–12.

27. Ibid.

28. Lipsitz, "The Possessive Investment in Whiteness," vii.

29. Extracts from the Decision of CERD, 54th Session, March 1–19, 1999.

30. *Land Rights Queensland* (July 1999): 1.

31. Australia's comments on Decision 2 (54) of 18 March pursuant to Article 9 (2) of the Convention 1999, 1.

32. *Land Rights Queensland* (August 1999): 9.

33. Australian Human Rights Commission, *Social Justice Report 2000: Appendix 2—Concluding Observations on Australia of the Committee on the Elimination of Racial Discrimination*. CERD/C/304/Add.101, 56th session, March 6–24,

2000, 2, https://www.humanrights.gov.au/publications/social-justice-report-2000
-appendix-2-concluding-observations-australia-committee.

34. *Land Rights Queensland*, 1.

35. Harris, "Whiteness as Property," 110.

6. The High Court and the *Yorta Yorta* Decision

1. Wayne Atkinson, "Vital Statistics of the Yorta Yorta Land Claim, 1994–2002," in *Not One Iota: The Yorta Yorta Struggle for Land Justice* (PhD diss., La Trobe University, 2000), appendixes 1–8.

2. *Members of the Yorta Yorta Community v. Victoria & Ors* [1998] FCA 1606 (December 18, 1998).

3. *Members of the Yorta Yorta Community v. Victoria* [2002] HCA 58 (Gleeson, Gummow, and Hayne JJ), par. 96.

4. Noel Pearson, "The High Court's Abandonment of 'The Time-Honoured Methodology of the Common Law' in Its Interpretation of Native Title in *Mirriuwung Gajerrong* and *Yorta Yorta*," Sir Ninian Stephen Annual Lecture, Law School, University of Newcastle, March 17, 2003; Bruce Buchan, "Withstanding the Tide of History: The Yorta Yorta Case and Indigenous Sovereignty," *borderlands e-journal* 1, no. 2 (2002): 1–13, http://www.borderlandsejournal.adelaide.edu.au/vol1no2_2002/Buchan_laws.html; Mandy Paul and Gary Gray, *Through a Smokey Mirror: History and Native Title* (Canberra: Aboriginal Studies Press, 2002); Peter Seidel, "Native Title: The Struggle for Justice for the Yorta Yorta Nation," *Alternative Law Journal* 29, no. 2 (2004): 70–74.

5. Allan David Freeman, "Legitimizing Racial Discrimination through Antidiscrimination law: A Critical Review of Supreme Court Doctrine," in *Critical Race Theory: The Key Writings That Formed the Movement*, ed. Kimberlé Crenshaw, Neil Gotanda, Gary Peller, and Kendall Thomas (New York: New Press, 1995), 29–32.

6. Aboriginal and Torres Strait Islander Social Justice Commissioner, *Native Title Report* (Sydney: Human Rights and Equal Opportunity Commission, 2002), 79.

7. Carol Pateman, *The Sexual Contract* (Cambridge: Polity Press, 1988).

8. Richard Dyer, *White* (New York: Routledge, 1997), 9–10.

9. Margaret Thornton, "Revisiting Race," in *Racial Discrimination Act 1975: A Review* (Sydney: Race Discrimination Commissioner, 1995), 88.

10. Cheryl Harris, "Whiteness as Property," in *Critical Race Theory*, ed. Crenshaw et al., 278.

11. *Members of the Yorta Yorta Community v. Victoria* [2002] HCA 58 (Gleeson, Gummow, and Hayne JJ), par. 28.

12. Ibid., par. 10.

13. Ibid., par. 28.

14. Ibid., par. 49.

15. Ibid., par. 63.

16. Ibid., par. 69.

17. Ibid., par. 66.

18. Buchan, "Withstanding the Tide of History."

19. *Members of the Yorta Yorta Community v. Victoria*, par. 129.

20. Ibid., par. 133.

21. Ibid., par. 134.

22. Ibid., par. 174.

23. Ibid., par. 143.

24. Ibid., par. 174.

25. Ibid., par. 181.

26. Ibid., par. 184.

27. Ibid., par. 185.

28. Ibid., par. 186.

29. Ibid., par. 187.

30. *Yanner v. Eaton* (1999) HCA 53, [105].

31. *Members of the Yorta Yorta Community v. Victoria*, par. 190.

32. Ibid., par. 191.

33. Ibid., par. 103.

34. Ibid., par. 104.

35. Ibid., par. 109.

36. Ibid., par. 117.

37. Ibid., par. 114.

38. Ibid., par. 122.

39. Pearson, "The High Court's Abandonment of 'The Time-honoured Methodology of the Common Law' in its Interpretation of Native Title in *Mirriuwung Gajerrong* and *Yorta Yorta*," 19.

40. Ibid., 22.

41. Ibid., 25.

42. Ibid., 27–29.

43. Ibid., 7.

44. Harris, "Whiteness as Property," 277–78.

45. Gerald Torres and Kathryn Milun, "Translating 'Yonnodio' by Precedent and Evidence: The Mashpee Indian Case," in *Critical Race Theory*, ed. Crenshaw et al., 186.

46. Harris, "Whiteness as Property," 287.

47. Torres and Milun, "Translating 'Yonnodio' by Precedent and Evidence," 188.

7. Leesa's Story

1. T. H. Marshall, *Class, Citizenship, and Social Development* (Chicago: University of Chicago Press, 1964), 78.

2. J. Woolmington, *Aborigines in Colonial Society: 1788–1850* (Armidale: University of New England Press, 1988), 145.

3. Toula Nicolacopoulos and George Vassilacopoulos, "Racism, Foreigner Communities, and the Onto-Pathology of White Australian Subjectivity," in *Whitening Race: Essays in Social and Cultural Criticism*, ed. Aileen Moreton Robinson (Canberra: Aboriginal Studies Press, 2004), 33.

4. Cheryl Harris, "Whiteness as Property," *Harvard Law Review* 106, no. 8 (1993): 1710–91; 1721.

5. Jon Stratton, *Race Daze: Australia in Identity Crisis* (Annandale: Pluto Press, 1998), 9.

6. Aileen Moreton-Robinson, "'I Still Call Australia Home': Indigenous Belonging and Place in a White Postcolonizing Society," in *Uprootings/Regroundings: Questions of Home and Migration*, ed. Sara Ahmed, Claudia Castañeda, Anne-Marie Fortier, and Mimi Sheller (Oxford: Berg, 2003), 37.

7. Susanne Schech and Jane Haggis, "Postcolonialism, Identity, and Location: Being White Australian in Asia?," *Environment and Planning D: Society and Space* 16, no. 5 (1998): 615–29; 626.

8. Aileen Moreton-Robinson, "Writing Off Indigenous Sovereignty: The Discourse of Security and Patriarchal White Sovereignty," in *Sovereign Subjects: Indigenous Sovereignty Matters*, ed. Moreton-Robinson (Annandale: Allen and Unwin, 2008), 90.

9. On December 11, 2006, conflict broke out at Cronulla Beach between predominantly white youths and Lebanese youths. It was reported in the press as being in response to an attack on a lifesaver by a group of young Lebanese men the previous week.

10. John Howard, ABC News, December 12, 2005.

11. It is interesting to note the number of books and articles that have been published around the idea of Australian identity since the 1990s and how few consider that they are discussing white racialized groups. For example: T. Brabason, *Tracking the Jack: A Retracing of the Antipodes* (Sydney: University of New South Wales Press, 2000); Miriam Dixson, *The Imaginary Australian: Anglo Celts and Identity—1788 to the Present* (Sydney: University of New South Wales Press, 1999); David Malouf, "Made in England: Australia's British Inheritance," *Quarterly Essay* 12, no. 1 (2003).

12. For further discussion, see Aileen Moreton-Robinson and Fiona Nicoll, "We Shall Fight Them on the Beaches: Protesting Cultures of White Possession," *Journal of Australian Studies* 89 (December 2007): 151–62.

13. Ruth Frankenberg, *White Woman, Race Matters: The Social Construction of Whiteness* (London: Routledge, 1993).

14. Aileen Moreton-Robinson, "*Terra Nullius* and the Possessive Logic of Patriarchal Whiteness: Race and Law Matters," in *Changing Law*, ed. Austin Sarat (Hampshire: Ashgate, 2005).

15. D. T. Wellman, *Portraits of White Racism*, 2nd ed. (New York: Cambridge University Press, 1993), xi.

16. Ghassan Hage, *White Nation: Fantasies of White Supremacy in a Multicultural Society* (Annandale: Pluto Press, 1998).

17. For key writings in the area of critical race theory, see legal scholars such as Barbara J. Flagg, whose book *White Race Consciousness and the Law* (1998) explores how the transparency of white legal decision making contributes to the maintenance of white supremacy. Ian F. Haney Lopez's book *White by Law: The Legal Construction of Race* (1996) illustrates how law has shaped the characteristics of whiteness. Although the collection *Critical Race Theory*, edited by Kimberlé Crenshaw, Neil Gotanda, Gary Peller, and Kendall Thomas, is concerned with exploring the role of the law in social domination and subordination, Cheryl Harris's seminal article, "Whiteness as Property," in the *Harvard Law Journal*, addresses its constitutive properties.

18. Cheryl Harris, "Whiteness as Property."

19. Aborigines Protection and Preservation Act 1939–46.

20. David Theo Goldberg, *Racist Culture: Philosophy and the Politics of Meaning* (Oxford: Blackwell, 1993), 99.

21. Beth Gaze, "Has the Racial Discrimination Act Contributed to Eliminating Racial Discrimination? Analysing the Litigation Track Record 2000–04," *Australian Journal of Human Rights* 6 (2007): 4, http://www.search.austlii.edu.au/au/journals/AJHR/2005/6.html.

22. Ibid.

8. The Legacy of Cook's Choice

1. Chris Healy, *From the Ruins of Colonialism: History as Social Memory* (New York: Cambridge University Press, 1997), 2.

2. Michael Sahlins, *How "Natives" Think: About Captain Cook, for Example* (Chicago: University of Chicago Press, 1995).

3. Gananath Obeyesekere, *The Apotheosis of Captain Cook: European Mythmaking in the Pacific* (Princeton: Princeton University Press, 1997).

4. Robert Borofsky, "Cook, Lono, Obeyesekere, and Sahlins," *Current Anthropology* 38, no. 2 (April 1997): 255–65.

5. Herb Kawainui Kane, "Comments," *Current Anthropology* 38, no. 2 (April 1997): 265.

6. Theodore Allen, *The Invention of the White Race: Racial Oppression and Social Control*, vol. 1 (London: Verso, 1994), 54.

7. Winthrop D. Jordan, *White over Black: American Attitudes Toward the Negro, 1550–1812* (Chapel Hill: University of North Carolina Press, 1968), 6.

8. Ibid., 7.

9. J. C. Beaglehole, "On the Character of Captain James Cook," *Geographical Journal* 122, pt. 4 (December 1956): 417–29; 420.

10. Ibid., 420.

11. Brian W. Richardson, *Longitude and Empire: How Captain Cook's Voyages Changed the World* (Vancouver: University of British Columbia Press, 2005).

12. Beaglehole, "On the Character of Captain James Cook," 424.

13. Ibid., 421.

14. Stuart Banner, "Why Terra Nullius? Anthropology and Property Law in Early Australia" (2005), par. 5, http://www.histrycooperative.org/cgi-bin/printpage.cgi.

15. Ibid., par. 6.

16. Ibid., par. 20.

17. Margaret Davies and Ngaire Naffine, *Are Persons Property? Legal Debates about Property and Personality* (Aldershot: Ashgate Dartmouth, 2001), 32–33.

18. Joel Kovel, *White Racism: A Psychohistory* (New York: Columbia University Press, 1984), 18.

19. Toula Nicolacopoulos and George Vassilacopoulos, "Racism, Foreigner Communities, and the Onto-Pathology of White Australian Subjectivity," in *Whitening Race: Essays in Social and Cultural Criticism*, ed. Aileen Moreton-Robinson (Canberra: Aboriginal Studies Press, 2004), 35.

20. Ibid., 38.

21. James Cook, *Cook's Journals: Daily Entries* (July 19, 1770), http://southseas.nla.gov.au/journals/cook/17700719.html.

22. Peter Botsman, "The Lamb Enters the Dreaming" (2007), par. 3, http://www.workingpapers.com.au/publishedpapers/2517.html.

23. Deborah Bird Rose, "A Distant Constellation" (1990), 4, http://wwwmcc.murdoch.edu.au/ReadingRoom/3.2/Rose.html.

24. Hobbles, quoted in ibid., 4.

25. Hobbles, cited in Deborah Bird Rose, *Dingo Makes Us Human* (Cambridge: Cambridge University Press, 2000), 191.

26. Bird Rose, *Dingo Makes Us Human*, 190.

27. Garth Neittheim, "Justice or Handouts? Aboriginal Law and Policy," in *Ivory Scales: Black Australia and the Law*, ed. K. Hazlehurst (Sydney: University of New South Wales Press, 1987); Lorna Lippmann, *Generations of Resistance: The Aboriginal Struggle for Justice* (Sydney: Longman Cheshire, 1981); Marc Gumbert, *Neither Justice nor Reason: A Legal and Anthropological Analysis of Aboriginal Land Rights* (St. Lucia: University of Queensland Press, 1984).

28. Jean Woolmington, *Aborigines in Colonial Society: 1788–1850* (Armidale: University of New England Press, 1988), 145.

29. Barry Morris, *Domesticating Resistance: The Dhan-Gadi Aborigines and the Australian State* (Oxford: Berg, 1989), 8.

30. M. Dunn, "Early Australia: Wage Labour or Slave Labour," in *Essays in the Political Economy of Australian Capitalism*, vol. 1, ed. E. L. Wheelwright and K. Buckley, 33–46; 42 (Brookvale: Australian and New Zealand Book Company, 1975).

31. Laksiri Jayasuriya, David Walker, and Jan Gothard, *Legacies of White Australia: Race, Culture, and Nation* (Crawley: University of Western Australia, 2003); Jon Stratton, *Race Daze: Australia in Identity Crisis* (Sydney: Pluto Press, 1998).

32. John Altman, "The Political Economy of a Treaty: Opportunities and Challenges for Enhancing Economic Development for Indigenous Australians," *The Drawing Board: An Australian Review of Public Affairs* 3, no. 2 (2002): 65–81.

33. Aileen Moreton-Robinson, "A Possessive Investment in Patriarchal Whiteness: Nullifying Native Title," in *Left Directions: The Third Way*, ed. Carol Bacchi and Paul Nursey-Bray (Perth: University of Western Australia Press, 2001), 162–77.

34. George Lipsitz, *The Possessive Investment in Whiteness: How White People Profit from Identity Politics* (Philadelphia: Temple University Press, 1998), vii.

9. Toward a New Research Agenda

1. Michel Foucault, *Society Must Be Defended* (London: Penguin Books, 2004).

2. Irene Watson, "Aboriginal and the Sovereignty of Terra Nullius," *Borderlands* 1, no. 2 (2002): par. 4, http://www.borderlandsejournal.adelaide.edu.au. Taiaiake Alfred, "From Sovereignty to Freedom: Toward an Indigenous Political Discourse," http//www.taiaiake.com/words/articles/index.html.

3. Raymond Williams, *The American Indian in Western Legal Thought* (New York: Oxford University Press, 1990). Patricia Monture-Angus, *Journeying Forward: Dreaming Aboriginal People's Independence* (London: Pluto Press, 2000).

4. Aileen Moreton-Robinson, "The Possessive Logic of Patriarchal White Sovereignty: The High Court and the Yorta Yorta Decision," *Borderlands* 3, no. 2 (2004), http://www.borderlandsejournal.adelaide.edu.au.

5. Duncan Ivison, Paul Patton, and Will Sanders, eds., *Political Theory and the Rights of Indigenous Peoples* (Cambridge: Cambridge University Press, 2000).

6. Marcia Langton, Maureen Tehan, Lisa Palmer, and Kathryn Shain, eds., *Honour Among Nations? Treaties and Agreements with Indigenous People* (Carlton: Melbourne University Press, 2004); Paul Keal, *European Conquest and the Rights of Indigenous Peoples* (Cambridge: Cambridge University Press, 2003); P. Havemann, *Indigenous Peoples' Rights in Australia, Canada, and New Zealand* (Auckland: Oxford University Press, 1999).

7. Sarah Pritchard, ed., *Indigenous People, the United Nations, and Human Rights* (Annandale: The Federation Press, 1998); S. James Anaya, *Indigenous People in International Law* (New York: Oxford University Press, 1996).

8. Henry Reynolds, *Aboriginal Sovereignty* (St. Leonards: Allen and Unwin, 1996).

9. Bain Attwood, *Rights for Aborigines* (St. Leonards: Allen and Unwin, 2003).

10. Larissa Behrendt, "It's Broke So Fix It: Arguments for a Bill of Rights," *Australian Journal of Human Rights* 9, no. 1 (2003): 135–50.

11. Foucault, *Society Must Be Defended*, 57.

12. Ibid., 81.

13. Ibid., 60.

14. For example, Robert C. Young, *Colonial Desire: Hybridity in Theory, Culture, and Race* (London: Routledge, 1995); Homi Bhabha, *The Location of Culture* (London: Routledge, 1994).

15. Aileen Moreton-Robinson, "'I Still Call Australia Home': Indigenous Belonging and Place in a White Postcolonising Society," in *Uprootings/Regroundings: Questions of Home and Migration*, ed. Sara Ahmed, Claudia Casteñeda, Anne-Marie Fortie, and Mimi Sheller (Oxford: Berg, 2003).

16. Ann Laura Stoler, *Race and the Education of Desire* (Durham: Duke University Press, 1995).

17. Brad Elliott Stone, "Defending Society from the Abnormal: The Archaeology of Bio-Power," *Foucault Studies* 1 (2004): 77–91.

18. John Marks, "Foucault, Franks, Gauls," *Theory, Culture & Society* 17, no. 5 (2000): 127–47.

19. Eduardo Mendieta, "To Make Live and to Let Die—Foucault on Racism" (2002), http://www.sunysb.edu/philosophy/research/mendieta_3.pdf.

20. See, for example, *Meanjin* 51, no. 3 (1992); *Arena*, no. 2 (1993–94).

21. Richard Dyer, *White* (London: Routledge, 1997); Barbara Flagg, *Was Blind Now I See: White Race Consciousness and the Law* (New York: New York University Press, 1998); Ian F. Haney Lopez, *White by Law: The Legal Construction of Race* (New York: New York University Press, 1996); Kimberlé Crenshaw, Neil Gotanda, Gary Peller, and Kendall Thomas, *Key Writings That Formed the Movement* (New York: New Press, 1995); Richard Delgado and Jean Stefancic, *Critical Whiteness Studies: Looking Behind the Mirror* (Philadelphia: Temple University Press, 1997); Birgit Brander Rasmussen, Irene J. Nexica, Eric Klinenberg, and Matt Wray, *The Making and Unmaking of Whiteness* (Durham: Duke University Press, 2001); Toni Morrison, *Playing in the Dark: Whiteness and Literary Imagination* (Cambridge: Harvard University Press, 1992); Mike Hill, *Whiteness: A Critical Reader* (New York: New York University Press, 1997); Cynthia Levine-Rasky, *Working through Whiteness: International Perspectives* (Albany: State University of New York Press, 2002); Karen Brodkin, *How Jews Became White Folk* (New Brunswick, N.J.: Rutgers University Press, 1999); C. Cuomo and K. Hall, *Whiteness: Feminist Philosophical Reflections* (Lanham, Md.: Rowman and Littlefield, 1999); Cheryl Harris, "Whiteness as Property," in *Critical Race Theory;* Ruth Frankenberg, *White Woman Race Matters: The Social Construction of Whiteness* (London: Routledge, 1993).

22. Warren Montag, "The Universalization of Whiteness: Racism and Enlightenment," in *Whiteness: A Critical Reader*, ed. Mike Hill (New York: New York University Press, 1997), 285.

23. Ghassan Hage, *Against Paranoid Nationalism* (Annandale: Pluto Press, 2003); Warwick Anderson, *The Cultivation of Whiteness: Science, Health, and Racial Identity in Australia* (Melbourne: Melbourne University Press, 2001); Belinda McKay, ed., *Unmasking Whiteness: Race and Reconciliation* (St. Lucia: University of Queensland Press, 1999); Aileen Moreton-Robinson, "'I Still Call Australia Home,'" in *Whitening Race: Essays in Social and Cultural Criticism* (Canberra: Aboriginal Studies Press, 2004); Fiona Nicoll, *From Diggers to Drag Queens: Configurations of Australian National Identity* (Annandale: Pluto Press, 2001); "Reconciliation in and out of Perspective: White Knowing, Seeing, Curating, and Being at Home in and against Indigenous Sovereignty," in *Whitening Race*, ed. Moreton-Robinson.

24. Alison Ravenscroft, "Anxieties of Dispossession: Whiteness, History, and Australia's War in Viet Nam," in *Whitening Race*, ed. Moreton-Robinson. Nicoll,

"Reconciliation in and out of Perspective: White Knowing, Seeing, Curating and Being at Home in and Against Indigenous Sovereignty"; Toula Nicolacopoulos and George Vassilacopoulos, "Racism, Foreigner Communities, and the Onto-Pathology of White Australian Subjectivity," in *Whitening Race*, ed. Moreton-Robinson. Kate Foord, "Frontier Theory: Displacement and Disavowal in the Writing of White Nations," in *Whitening Race*, ed. Moreton-Robinson.

25. David Theo Goldberg, *Racist Culture: Philosophy and the Politics of Meaning* (Oxford: Blackwell, 1993), 149.

26. Foucault, *Society Must Be Defended*, 27.

27. Stoler, *Race and the Education of Desire*, 16.

28. Foucault, *Society Must Be Defended*, 171.

29. Aileen Moreton-Robinson, *Talkin' Up to the White Woman: Indigenous Women and Feminism* (St. Lucia: University of Queensland Press, 2000).

30. Laksiri Jayasuriya, David Walker, and Jan Gothard, *Legacies of White Australia: Race, Culture, and Nation* (Crawley: University of Western Australia, 2003); Jon Stratton, *Race Daze: Australia in Identity Crisis* (Sydney: Pluto Press, 1998).

10. Writing Off Sovereignty

1. Judith Brett, *Australian Liberals and the Moral Middle Class* (Cambridge: Cambridge University Press, 2003).

2. Ibid., 194.

3. Ibid.

4. Andrew Markus, *Race: John Howard and the Remaking of Australia* (Sydney: Allen and Unwin, 2001), xv.

5. Ibid., xiv.

6. Ghassan Hage, *Against Paranoid Nationalism: Searching for Hope in a Shrinking Society* (Sydney: Pluto Press, 2003).

7. Ibid., 74–78.

8. Ibid., 47.

9. Alison Ravenscroft, "Anxieties of Dispossession: Whiteness, History, and Australia's War in Viet Nam," in *Whitening Race: Essays in Social and Cultural Criticism*, ed. Aileen Moreton-Robinson (Canberra: Aboriginal Studies Press, 2004).

10. Michel Foucault, *Society Must Be Defended* (London: Penguin, 2003).

11. Carol Pateman, *The Sexual Contract* (Stanford: Stanford University Press, 1988).

12. Charles W. Mills, *The Racial Contract* (Ithaca: Cornell University Press, 1997).

13. Carol Johnson, "The Politics of Signs: Gay and Lesbian Issues in Comparative Perspective," paper presented at the Australasian Political Studies Association Conference, University of Adelaide, September 29–October 1, 2004, 10.

14. John Howard, "Australia and Britain: The Contemporary Partnership in a New International Environment," Sir Robert Menzies Memorial Lecture, Canberra, June 23, 1997, 7, http://www.pm.gov.au/news/speeches.html.

15. Ibid.

16. John Howard, Address to the Dinner Hosted by the Foreign Policy Association, New York, June 30, 1997, 1–6, http://www.pm.gov.au/news/speeches/1997/speeches.html.

17. Ibid.

18. Ibid., 3–4.

19. Fiona Nicoll, "Indigenous Sovereignty and the Violence of Perspective: A White Woman's Coming Out Story," *Australian Feminist Studies* 15, no. 33 (2000): 369–86.

20. John Howard, "Australia's International Relations—Ready for the Future," Address to the Menzies Research Centre, Canberra, August 22, 2001, 8, http://www.pm.gov.au/news/speeches/2001/speeches.html.

21. Ibid., 1–3.

22. Ibid., 3.

23. John Howard, "Australia's Engagement with Asia: A New Paradigm," Address to ASIALINK-ANU National Forum, August 13, 2004, http://www.pm.gov.au/news/speeches/index.cfm?speechYear=2004.

24. John Howard, Address at Asia Society Luncheon, Peninsula Hotel, Manila, July 15, 2003, 1, http://www.pm.gov.au/news/speeches/index.cfm?speechYear=2003.

25. Paulette Goudge, *The Whiteness of Power: Racism in Third World Development and Aid* (London: Lawrence and Wishart, 2003), 24.

26. John Howard, Address at the Federal Liberal Party Campaign Launch, Sydney, October 28, 2001, 7, http://www.pm.gov.au/news/speeches/2001/speeches.html.

27. Ravenscroft, "Anxieties of Dispossession," 7.

28. Johnson, "The Politics of Signs," 5.

29. John Howard, The Inaugural Prime Minister on Prime Ministers Lecture, Old Parliament House, September 3, 1997, 7, http://www.pm.gov.au/news/speeches/1997/speeches.html.

30. Jon Stratton, *Race Daze: Australia in Identity Crisis* (Sydney: Pluto Press, 1998), 79.

31. Brett, *Australian Liberals and the Moral Middle Class*, 212.

32. John Howard, Sir Donald Bradman Oration, Melbourne, August 17, 2000, http://www.pm.gov.au/news/speeches/2000/speeches.html; Commemorative Address on the Occasion of Remembrance Day, Australian War Memorial, November 11, 1997, http://www.pm.gov.au/news/speeches/1997/speeches.html.

33. Howard, Commemorative Address on the Occasion of Remembrance Day.

34. John Howard, Launch of the "Distinctively Australian" Policy, Chowder Bay Heritage Area, Mosman, December 18, 2003, 2, http://www.pm.gov.au/news/speeches/index.cfm?speechYear=2003.

35. John Howard, Address at the Economics Luncheon in Association with the AAA, BCIU, and Downtown Economists Association Asia Society, New York, July 15, 1999, http://www.pm.gov.au/news/speeches/1999/speeches.html.

36. John Howard, Official Opening of New Mandir Society of Australia Inc., Canberra, June 1, 1997, http://www.pm.gov.au/news/speeches/1997/speeches.html; address at the Traditional Candle Lighting Ceremony for the Jewish Festival of

Chanukah, Sydney, December 23, 1997, http://www.pm.gov.au/news/speeches/1997/speeches.html.

37. John Howard, "Australian Multiculturalism for a New Century: Towards Inclusiveness," Address at the Launch of the National Multicultural Advisory Council Report, Mural Hall, Parliament House, May 5, 1999, 1–3, http://www.pm.gov.au/news/speeches/1999/speeches.html.

38. Toula Nicolacopoulos and George Vassilacopoulos, "Racism, Foreigner Communities, and the Onto-Pathology of White Australian Subjectivity," in *Whitening Race*, ed. Aileen Moreton-Robinson (Canberra: Aboriginal Studies Press, 2004), 45.

39. In August 2001, the *MV Tampa*, a Norwegian cargo ship, had taken on board 460 people of mainly Afghan heritage who had become stranded 140 miles off the coast of Christmas Island on their way to seek asylum in Australia. Captain Rinn of the *Tampa* responded to a distress call from the *Palanga* and contacted Australian authorities requesting that he be allowed to dock at Christmas Island, as there were a number of sick people now on board his vessel and he was not equipped to service them. Under international law, it is a requirement that if emergency help is needed by a vessel, they must be allowed to dock at the nearest port, which was Christmas Island. At first the government agreed but then reneged on the decision, and when the *Tampa* captain decided to enter Australian waters to disembark the asylum seekers, John Howard sent in the Navy to prevent that happening.

40. John Howard, Address at the Federal Liberal Party Campaign Launch, Sydney, October 28, 2001, 7.

41. Aileen Moreton-Robinson, "A Possessive Investment in Patriarchal Whiteness: Nullifying Native Title," in *Left Directions: Beyond the Third Way*, ed. Paul Nursey-Bray and Carol Bacchi (Perth: Western Australia University Press, 2001), 162–77; 169.

42. John Howard, "Wik Statement—Address to the Nation," ABC TV, November 30, 1997, http://www.pm.gov.au/news/speeches/1997/speeches.html.

43. John Howard, Opening Address to the National Farmers Federation Conference, 20th Anniversary, Civic Centre, Longreach, Questions and Answers, May 18, 1999, 1–2, http://www.pm.gov.au/news/speeches/1999/speeches.html.

44. Aileen Moreton-Robinson, "The Possessive Logic of Patriarchal White Sovereignty: The High Court and the Yorta Yorta Decision," *Borderlands* 3, no. 2 (2004), www.borderlandsejournal.adelaide.edu.au/issues/vol3no2.html.

45. Corroborree 2000 was a series of events held during reconciliation week between May 27 and June 3, sponsored by the Council for Aboriginal Reconciliation to celebrate and commit to reconciliation. Part of the week's activities was a gathering of two thousand people at the Sydney Opera House, where the prime minister gave his address.

46. John Howard, "Towards Reconciliation," Address to Corroboree 2000, May 27, 2000, 1, http://www.pm.gov.au/news/speeches/2000/speeches.html.

47. Ibid., 2.

48. John Howard, "Perspectives on Aboriginal and Torres Strait Islander Issues," Menzies Lecture Series, December 13, 2000, 4, http://www.pm.gov.au/news/speeches/2000/speeches.html.

49. Nicolacopoulos and Vassilacopoulos, "Racism, Foreigner Communities, and the Onto-Pathology of White Australian Subjectivity."

50. In the past decade, neoliberal politics has nourished a "debate" played out within the media and the academy, which has become popularly known as the "history wars." The leading personality in this debate is Keith Windschuttle and his book *The Fabrication of Aboriginal History* (2000). Several responses to Windschuttle were mounted within the academy and public forums by Henry Reynolds, Robert Manne, Pat Grimshaw, Lyndall Ryan, and Stuart Macintyre. The publication of several books followed, such as Robert Manne's *Whitewash: On Keith Windschuttle's Fabrication of Aboriginal History* (2003), Bain Attwoods's *Telling the Truth about Aboriginal History* (2004), and Stuart MacIntyre and Anna Clark's *The History Wars* (2005).

51. J. Taylor and B. Hunter, "The Job Still Ahead: Economic Costs of Continuing Indigenous Employment Disparity," Aboriginal and Torres Strait Islander Commission, Canberra, 1998, 18, http://www.anu.edu/caepr/Publications/WP/jobahead.pdf.

52. Hage, *Against Paranoid Nationalism*, 47.

11. Imagining the Good Indigenous Citizen

1. Ulrich Raulff, "Interview with Giorgio Agamben—Life, A Work of Art without an Author: The State of Exception, the Administration of Disorder and Private Life," *German Law Journal* 5, no. 5 (2004): par. 2, http://www.germanlawjournal.com/print.php?id=437%23_ednref9.

2. Andrew W. Neal, "Foucault in Guantánamo: Towards an Archaeology of the Exception," *Security Dialogue* 37, no. 1 (2006): 31–46.

3. Michel Foucault, *The History of Sexuality: An Introduction* (New York: Vintage Books, 1990), 4.

4. Bain Attwood and Andrew Markus, *The 1967 Referendum; or, When Aborigines Didn't Get the Vote* (Canberra: Aboriginal Studies Press, 1997).

5. John Chesterman and Brian Galligan, *Citizens without Rights: Aborigines and Australian Citizenship* (Melbourne: Cambridge University Press, 1997).

6. Tom Calma, Aboriginal and Torres Strait Islander Social Justice Commissioner, "Achieving Aboriginal and Torres Strait Islander Health Equality within a Generation—A Human Rights Based Approach," The Right to Health of Indigenous Australians' Seminar, University of Melbourne Law School, March 16, 2006, http://www.hreoc.gov.au/about/media/speeches/social_justice/achieving_health_equality20060316.htm.

7. Australia was acquired in the name of the king of England. As such, patriarchal white sovereignty is a regime of power that derives from the illegal act of

possession and is most acutely manifested in the form of the Crown and the judiciary. The Crown holds exclusive possession of its territory, which is the very foundation of the nation-state. The nation-state, in turn, confers patriarchal white sovereignty on its citizens through what Carole Pateman (1988) argues is the "sexual contract." However, not all citizens benefit from or exercise patriarchal white sovereignty equally. Race, class, gender, sexuality, and ableness are markers that circumscribe the performance of patriarchal white sovereignty by citizens within Australian society.

8. Charles W. Mills, *The Racial Contract* (New York: Cornell University Press, 1997), 3.

9. Carole Pateman, *The Sexual Contract* (Stanford: Stanford University Press, 1988).

10. Michel Foucault, *Society Must Be Defended* (London: Penguin Books, 2003).

11. Ibid., 57.

12. Bart van Steenbergen, ed., *The Condition of Citizenship* (London: Sage, 1994).

13. Foucault, *Society Must Be Defended*, 81.

14. Achille Mbembe, "Necropolitics," *Public Culture* 15, no. 1 (2003): 25–26.

15. Aileen Moreton-Robinson, "The Possessive Logic of Patriarchal White Sovereignty: The High Court and the Yorta Yorta Decision," *Borderlands* 3, no. 2 (2004), http//:www.borderlandsejournal.adelaide.edu.au.

16. Foucault, *Society Must Be Defended*, 27.

17. Laksiri Jayasuriya, David Walker, and Jan Gothard, eds., *Legacies of White Australia: Race, Culture, and Nation* (Crawley: University of Western Australia Press, 2003). See also Jon Stratton, *Race Daze: Australia in Identity Crisis* (Sydney: Pluto Press, 1998).

18. House of Representatives Standing Committee on Aboriginal Affairs, "Our Future, Our Selves: Aboriginal and Torres Strait Islander Community Control, Management and Resources," August 1990, http://www.aph.gov.au/house/commit tee/atsia/ourfutureourselves.pdf.

19. Michael Dodson, "Indigenous Australians," in Robert Manne, ed., *The Howard Years* (Melbourne: Black Inc., 2004), 135.

20. *Ampe Akelyernemane Meke Mekarle* ("Little Children are Sacred"), Report of the Northern Territory Board of Inquiry into the Protection of Aboriginal Children from Sexual Abuse, Rex Wild and Patricia Anderson, Inquiry Co-chairs (Northern Territory Government, 2007), 22–27.

21. Noel Pearson, "The Light on the Hill," Ben Chifley Memorial Lecture, Bathurst Panthers Leagues Club, August 12, 2000, http://www.capeyorkpartner ships.com/team/noelpearson/lightonhill-12–8-00.htm (my emphasis).

22. Copies of Noel Pearson's papers are available at http://www.capeyorkpart nerships.com/team/noelpearson/papers.htm.

23. William Julius Wilson, "Citizenship and the Inner-City Ghetto Poor," in *The Condition of Citizenship*, ed. Bart van Steenbergen (London: Sage, 1994), 53.

24. Noel Pearson, "Hunt for the Radical Centre," *Australian*, April 21, 2007, http://www.theaustralian.news.com.au/story/0,20867,21591955–7583,00.html.

25. Michael Meadows, *Voices in the Wilderness: Images of Aboriginal People in the Australian Media* (Westport, Conn.: Greenwood Press, 2001).

26. Human Rights and Equal Opportunity Commission, *Racist Violence: Report of the National Inquiry into Racist Violence in Australia* (Canberra: Australian Government Publishing Service, 1991), 3.

27. Tony Jones, interview with Nanette Rogers, "Crown Prosecutor Speaks out about Abuse in Central Australia," *Lateline*, ABC TV, May 15, 2006, transcript available at http://www.abc.net.au/lateline/content/2006/s1639127.htm.

28. Aileen Moreton-Robinson, "Talkin' Up to the White Woman: Indigenous Women and Feminism" (PhD diss., Griffith University, 1998), 272–75.

29. *Ampe Akelyernemane Meke Mekarle* ("Little Children Are Sacred"), 8.

30. Human Rights and Equal Opportunity Commission, "Social Justice Report," 1993 to 2007.

31. Gary Banks, "Indigenous Disadvantage: Are We Making Progress?" (2005), 5, http://www.pc.gov.au/_data/assets/pdf_file/0005/7655/cs20050921.pdf.

32. Nick Bolkus, "Reconciliation: Off Track," Senate Legal and Constitutional References Committee, Canberra, October 2003, http://www.aph.gov.au/senate/committee/legcon_ctte/reconciliation/report/report.pdf.

33. Joel Gibson and Debra Jopson, "Black Dollars Go Everywhere but to Blacks," *Sydney Morning Herald*, August 21, 2007, http://www.smh.com.au/news/national/black-dollars-go-everywhere-but-to-blacks/2007/08/118746.

34. Natasha Robinson, "Northern Territory 'Short-Changing' Indigenous Aid," *Australian*, July 16, 2008, http://www.theaustralian.news.com.au/story/0,25197,24027311–601,00.html.

35. The Hon. Mal Brough MP, Minister for Families, Community Services, and Indigenous Affairs, "Commonwealth's Intervention into Aboriginal Communities in the Northern Territory," National Press Club, ABC TV, August 15, 2007, http://www.facsia.gov.au/internet/minister3.nsf/print/speech_nter_15aug07.htm.

36. Ibid., 2.

37. Ibid., 4.

38. The Hon. Mal Brough MP, Minister for Families, Community Services, and Indigenous Affairs, "Howard Government Getting on with the Job of Protecting Children in the Northern Territory," Media Release, August 6, 2007, http://www.facs.gov.au/internet/minister3.nsf/content/nter_6aug07.htm.

39. Human Rights and Equal Opportunity Commission, "A Human Rights Based Approach Is Vital to Address the Challenges in Indigenous Communities," Media Release, June 26, 2007, http://www.eniar.org/news/hreoc19.html.

40. Australian Council of Social Services, "Open Letter to The Hon. Mal Brough MP," June 26, 2007, http://www.acoss.org.au/News.aspx?displayID=99&articleID=2683.

41. Jon Altman, "The 'National Emergency' and Land Rights Reform: Separating Fact from Fiction: An Assessment of the Proposed Amendments to the

Aboriginal Land Rights (Northern Territory) Act 1979," Briefing Paper for Oxfam Australia, Centre for Aboriginal Economic Policy Research, Australian National University, Canberra, August 7, 2007, 2, http://www.anu.edu/caepr/Publications/topical/Altman_Oxfam.pdf.

42. Central Land Council, "From the Grassroots: Feedback from Traditional Landowners and Community Members on the Australian Government Intervention: An Initial Briefing Paper," Alice Springs, December 19, 2007, 2, http://www.clc.org.au/media/From_the_Grassroots_Briefing.pdf.

43. Aboriginal Rights Coalition, "Data Shows Intervention Is a Disaster: National Rallies Planned," June 5, 2008, 1, http://www.eniar.org/news/NTintervention29.html.

44. Paul Toohey, "Putting Paid to Perk for the Dole," *Australian*, July 12, 2008, 2, http://www.theaustralian.news.com.au/story/0,25197,24004457-5013172,00.html.

45. Margaret Wenham, "Indigenous Child Abuse in New Light," *Courier Mail*, May 25, 2008, http://www.news.com.au/couriermail/story/0,,23746618-5003416,00.html.

12. Virtuous Racial States

1. Katherine Dahlsgaard, Christopher Peterson, and Martin E. P. Seligman, "Shared Virtue: The Convergence of Valued Human Strengths across Culture and History," *Review of General Psychology* 9, no. 3 (2005): 203–13.

2. Carl Brickman, *Aboriginal Populations in the Mind: Race and Primitivity in Psychoanalysis* (New York: Columbia University Press, 2003), 22.

3. Grace Li Xiu Woo, "Canada's Forgotten Founders: The Modern Significance of the Haudenosaunee (Iroquois) Application for Membership in the League of Nations," *Law, Social Justice & Global Development Journal* 1 (2003), http://elj.warwick.ac.uk/global/03-1/woo.html.

4. Jeff Corntassel, "Toward Sustainable Self-Determination: Rethinking the Contemporary Indigenous-Rights Discourse," *Alternatives* 33 (2008): 105–32; UN Permanent Forum on Indigenous Issues, http://www.un.org/esa/socdev/unpfii/en/history.html.

5. Robert Jackson, *Sovereignty: Evolution of an Idea* (London: Polity Press, 2007), 8.

6. Jeff Corntassel, "Partnership in Action? Indigenous Political Mobilization and Co-optation during the First UN Indigenous Decade (1995–2004)," *Human Rights Quarterly* 29 (2007): 137–66; Megan Davis, "Indigenous Struggles in Standard-Setting: The United Nations Declaration on the Rights of Indigenous Peoples," *Melbourne Journal of International Law* 9 (2008).

7. Davis, "Indigenous Struggles in Standard-Setting," 9.

8. S. James Anaya and Siegfried Wiessner, "The UN Declaration on the Rights of Indigenous Peoples: Towards Re-empowerment," *Jurist Legal News and Research* (October 2007), 1, http://jurist.law.pitt.edu/forumy/2007/10/un-declaration-on-rights-of-indigenous.php.

9. Christopher J. Fromherz, "Indigenous Peoples Courts: Egalitarian Juridical Pluralism, Self-Determination, and the United Nations Declaration on the Rights of Indigenous Peoples," *University of Pennsylvania Law Review* 156 (2008): 1341–81; Davis, "Indigenous Struggles in Standard-Setting"; Ronald Kakungulu, "The United Nations Declaration on the Rights of Indigenous Peoples: A New Dawn for Indigenous Peoples Rights?" *Cornell Law School Inter-University Graduate Student Conference Papers*, Paper 18 (2009), http://scholarship.law.cornell.edu/lps_clacp/18; Siegfried Wiessner, "Indigenous Sovereignty: A Reassessment in Light of the UN Declaration on the Rights of Indigenous Peoples," *Vanderbilt Journal of Transnational Law* 41 (2008): 1141–76; Jeremie Gilbert, "Indigenous Rights in the Making: The United Nations Declaration on the Rights of Indigenous Peoples," *International Journal on Minority and Group Rights* 14 (2007): 207–30.

10. Fromherz, "Indigenous Peoples Courts," 1343.

11. Ibid.

12. United Nations Declaration on the Rights of Indigenous Peoples, General Assembly A/RES/61/295, adopted on December 13, 2007, 12, http://daccess-dds-ny.un.org/doc/UNDOC/GEN/NO6/512/07/PDF/NO651207.pdf?OpenElement.

13. Fiona Nicoll, "Indigenous Sovereignty and the Violence of Perspective: A White Woman's Coming Out Story," *Australian Feminist Studies* 15, no. 33 (2000): 369–86; 382.

14. Michel Foucault, *Society Must Be Defended* (London: Penguin Books, 2004), 57.

15. Ibid.

16. David Theo Goldberg, *The Racial State* (Oxford: Blackwell, 2002), 154.

17. Ibid., 99.

18. Andrew W. Neal, "Cutting Off the King's Head: Foucault's *Society Must Be Defended* and the Problem of Sovereignty," *Alternatives* 29 (2004): 373–98; Aileen Moreton-Robinson, "Towards a New Research Agenda? Foucault, Whiteness, and Indigenous Sovereignty," *Journal of Sociology* 42, no. 4 (2006): 383–95.

19. Jacques Derrida, *Rogues: Two Essays on Reason* (Stanford: Stanford University Press, 2005), 11.

20. Paul. W. Kahn, "The Question of Sovereignty," *Stanford Journal of International Law* 40 (2004): 259–82; 260.

21. Robert J. Miller, *Native America, Discovered and Conquered: Thomas Jefferson, Lewis and Clark, and Manifest Destiny* (Lincoln: University of Nebraska Press, 2008), 5.

22. Toula Nicolacopoulos and George Vassilacopoulos, "Racism, Foreigner Communities, and the Onto-Pathology of White Australian Subjectivity," in *Whitening Race: Essays in Cultural and Social Criticism*, ed. Aileen Moreton-Robinson (Canberra: Aboriginal Studies Press, 2004), 38.

23. Cheryl Harris, "Whiteness as Property," *Harvard Law Review* 106, no. 8 (June 1993): 1707–69; 1716.

24. United Nations Declaration on the Rights of Indigenous Peoples, 11.

25. Aboriginal Affairs and Northern Development, "Canada's Response to Haudenosaunee Six Nations Counteroffer," October 28, 2008, http://www.ainc-inac.gc.ca/ai/mr/is/crc-eng.asp.

26. United Nations Declaration on the Rights of Indigenous Peoples, 11.

27. Ibid., 12.

28. Observations of the United States with respect to the Rights of Indigenous Peoples, USUN Press Release, htpp://www.shunpiking.com/o10406/0406-IP-positionofUS.htm.

29. Jenny Macklin, Minister for Indigenous Affairs, "Statement on the United Nations Declaration on the Rights of Indigenous Peoples, Australia" (2009), http://www.jennymacklin.fahcsia.gov.au/statements/Pages/un_declaration_03apr09.

30. John Duncan, Indian Affairs Minister, "Canada's Statement of Support on the United Nations Declaration on the Rights of Indigenous Peoples," November 12, 2010, 2–4, http://www.ainc-inac.gc.ca/ap/ia/dcl/stmt-eng.asp.

31. Pita Sharples, Minister for Māori Affairs, "Supporting UN Declaration Restores NZ's Mana," Address to the UN Permanent Forum on Indigenous Issues in New York, 2010, 2, http://www.beehive.govt.nz/release/supporting+un+declaration+restores+nz039s+mana.

32. Remarks by the President at the White House Tribal Nations Conference, http://www.whitehouse.gov/thepress-office/2010/12/16/remarks-president-white-house, December 16, 2010.

33. Macklin, "Statement on the United Nations Declaration on the Rights of Indigenous Peoples."

34. Duncan, "Canada's Statement of Support on the United Nations Declaration on the Rights of Indigenous Peoples," 2–4.

35. Aboriginal Affairs and Northern Development Canada, "Canada Endorses The United Nations Declaration on the Rights of Indigenous Peoples," December 14, 2010, http://www.aadnc-aandc.gc.ca/eng/1292354321165/1292354361417.

36. Sharples, "Supporting UN Declaration Restores NZ's Mana," 2.

37. Remarks by the President at the White House Tribal Nations Conference, Washington, D.C., December 16, 2010, 2.

38. Macklin, "Statement on the United Nations Declaration on the Rights of Indigenous Peoples."

39. Duncan, "Canada's Statement of Support on the United Nations Declaration on the Rights of Indigenous Peoples," 2–4.

40. Ibid.

41. Sharples, "Supporting UN Declaration Restores NZ's Mana," 3.

42. Announcement of U.S. Support for the United Nations Declaration on the Rights of Indigenous Peoples: Initiatives to Promote the Government-to-Government Relationship & Improve the Lives of Indigenous Peoples, http://usun.state.gov/documents/organization/153239.pdf.

43. Ibid., 3.

44. Foucault, *Society Must Be Defended.*

Afterword

1. Sara Ahmed, *Queer Phenomenology: Orientations, Objects, Others* (Durham: Duke University Press, 2006), 111.

2. Linda Tuhwai-Smith, *Decolonising Methodologies: Research and Indigenous People* (New York: Zed Books, 2012).

3. Robert A. Williams Jr., *Savage Anxieties: The Invention of Western Civilization* (New York: Palgrave Macmillan, 2012).

PUBLICATION HISTORY

Chapter 1 was previously published as "I Still Call Australia Home: Indigenous Belonging and Place in a White Postcolonising Society," in *Uprootings/Regroundings: Questions of Home and Migration,* ed. Sara Ahmed, Claudia Castañeda, Anne-Marie Fortier, and Mimi Sheller, 23–40 (Oxford: Berg, 2003).

Chapter 2 was previously published as "The House That Jack Built: Britishness and White Possession," *Australian Critical Race and Whiteness Studies Association Journal* 1, no. 1 (2005): 21–29.

Chapter 3 was previously published as "Bodies That Matter: Performing White Possession on the Beach," *American Indian Culture and Research Journal* 35, no. 4 (2013): 57–72. Permission granted by the American Indian Studies Center, UCLA; copyright 2013 Regents of the University of California.

Chapter 4 was previously published as "Writing Off Treaties: White Possession in the United States Critical Whiteness Studies Literature," in *Transnational Whiteness Matters,* ed. Aileen M. Moreton-Robinson, Maryrose Casey, and Fiona Nicoll, 81–96 (New York: Lexington Books, 2008).

Chapter 5 was previously published as "A Possessive Investment in Patriarchal Whiteness: Nullifying Native Title," in *Left Directions: Is There a Third Way?,* ed. Paul Nursey-Bray and Carol Lee Bacchi, 162–77 (Crawley: University of Western Australia Press, 2001). The publisher and author are grateful for permission to reproduce the following chapter.

Chapter 6 was previously published as "The Possessive Logic of Patriarchal White Sovereignty: The High Court and the *Yorta Yorta* Decision," *Borderlands* 3, no. 2 (2004), http://www.borderlands.net.au/.

Chapter 7 was previously published as "Witnessing the Workings of White Possession in the Workplace: Leesa's Testimony," *Australian Feminist Law Journal* 26 (2007): 81–94.

Chapter 8 was previously published as "White Possession: The Legacy of Cook's Choice," in *Imagined Australia: Reflections around the Reciprocal Constructions of Identity between Australia and Europe,* ed. Renata Summo-O'Connell, 27–42 (Bern: Peter Lang, 2009).

Chapter 9 was previously published as "Towards a New Research Agenda? Foucault, Whiteness, and Indigenous Sovereignty," *Journal of Sociology* 42, no. 4 (2006): 383–95.

Chapter 10 was previously published as "Writing Off Indigenous Sovereignty: The Discourse of Security and Patriarchal White Sovereignty," in *Sovereign Subjects: Indigenous Sovereignty Matters,* ed. Aileen M. Moreton-Robinson, 86–102 (Crows Nest: Allen and Unwin, 2007).

Chapter 11 was previously published as "Imagining the Good Indigenous Citizen: Race War and the Pathology of Patriarchal White Sovereignty," *Cultural Studies Review* 15, no. 2 (September 2009): 61–79.

Chapter 12 was previously published as "Virtuous Racial States: The Possessive Logic of Patriarchal White Sovereignty and the United Nations Declaration on the Rights of Indigenous Peoples," *Griffith Law Review* 20, no. 3 (2011): 641–58.

INDEX

AILEEN MORETON-ROBINSON (Goenpul, Quandamooka First Nation) is professor of Indigenous studies and director of the National Indigenous Research and Knowledges Network at Queensland University of Technology. She is author of *Talkin' Up to the White Woman: Indigenous Women and Feminism* and editor of several books, including *Sovereign Subjects: Indigenous Sovereignty Matters.*